REPRODUCIBLE SKITS · FOR USE WITH AGES 10 TO ADULT

MORE BIBLE SKITS

52 SERIOUSLY FUNNY BIBLE TEACHING SKITS

BY TOM BOAL

YOU MAY MAKE COPIES OF THE SKITS IN THIS BOOK IF:

▲ you (or someone in your organization) are the original purchaser;

▲ you are using the copies you make for a noncommercial purpose (such as teaching or promoting a ministry) within your church or organization;

▲ you follow the instruction provided in this book.

HOWEVER, IT IS ILLEGAL FOR YOU TO MAKE COPIES IF:

▲ you are using the material to promote, advertise or sell a product or service other than for ministry fund-raising;

▲ you are using the material in or on a product for sale;

▲ you or your organization are not the original purchaser of this book.

By following these guidelines you help us keep our products affordable.

Thank you.

Gospel Light

Gospel Light

©1994 Gospel Light, Ventura, CA 93006. All rights reserved. Printed in U.S.A.

CONTENTS

ABOUT THE AUTHOR

Tom Boal lives in Leduc, Alberta with his wife, Marilyn, and their two teenage children, Christian and Kelly. Tom writes skits for his fifth and sixth grade Sunday School class as a diversion from his profession of accounting.

EDITORIAL STAFF

Publisher, Billie Baptiste • **Senior Consulting Publisher,** Dr. Elmer L. Towns •
Senior Editor, Gary S. Greig, Ph.D. • **Senior Consulting Editor,** Wes Haystead, M.S.Ed. •
Managing Editor, Lynnette Pennings • **Contributing Editors,** Mary Gross, Sheryl Haystead,
Linda Mattia, A. Michele Sveiven • **Designer,** Curtis Dawson

Using This Book

BRING BIBLE STORIES TO LIFE!

Drama activities in a classroom are valuable learning opportunities because of the process group members experience, not because of the quality of the final performance. Bible stories come alive when acted out, and Bible truth is seen to be relevant when applied to contemporary situations. In addition:

▲ Acting out a situation will push group members to think about the application of Bible truth to a real-life circumstance.

▲ Dramatic activities provide a unique opportunity to briefly step into another person's shoes and experience some of his or her attitudes and feelings.

COPIES OF THE SKITS

Purchase of this book includes the right to make copies of the skits for those who will be involved in putting on the skits.

SKIT FEATURES

The skits contain the following features to help you prepare: **Scripture, suggested topics, Bible background, performance tips, discussion questions, characters list** and a **pronunciation guide** for those tough biblical names. Optional props are often suggested, but any real prop can be replaced by an imaginary one simply by miming accordingly.

CHOOSING A SKIT

The skits may be used in a variety of ways:

▲ to **summarize** a Bible story;

▲ to **illustrate** a concept or topic;

▲ to **introduce** a Bible character;

▲ to **reinforce** a Bible story or life application.

The skits will be enjoyed in a variety of settings by students from **ages eleven through adult**:

▲ Sunday School, churchtime or midweek programs;

▲ large or small groups;

▲ special events.

To help you find a skit that matches a topic or Bible story you will be studying, indexes list:

▲ **Scripture references** (p. 227);

▲ **Topics** (p. 229);

▲ **Bible characters** (p. 224);

▲ **Gospel Light Junior Curriculum, Year B** (p. 222).

GETTING READY

After you've chosen and reproduced copies of the skit for the participants, here are some tips for preparing to lead the group:

▲ Read the Scripture passage. Familiarize yourself with the corresponding Bible story, if applicable.

▲ Read the skit, noting any vocabulary or pronunciation help you will need to give your group.

▲ Adapt the script if needed by reducing or increasing the number of characters, adding a scene, etc.

▲ Take note of the discussion questions. Decide which questions will be most appropriate for your group.

▲ Collect props.

PRACTICAL TIPS

One of the nicest things about skits is that they are easy to prepare. Skits are not big Broadway-type productions. They can be informal and spontaneous. They can be primped and polished to the hilt when the mood strikes. A lot or a little—it all depends on how you want to do it. Here are the basics to go on:

▲ Good acting is a plus, but it's not essential in order to have a positive experience. What is essential is that the lines are heard by the audience. The performers need to speak slowly and clearly—with their mouths directed at the audience.

▲ It is not necessary for performers to memorize the script. Reading works just as well. Provide several highlighter pens for performers to mark their parts. You may give out the script ahead of time for the performer to practice. However, if you hand out the scripts ahead of time, bring extra copies on performance day, because someone will undoubtedly forget his or her copy.

▲ Practicing the skits ahead of time will be most important for younger groups and groups for whom English is a second language.

USING THE SKITS WITH GOSPEL LIGHT JUNIOR CURRICULUM

Each skit in this book corresponds with a lesson in Gospel Light Junior Curriculum, Year B, and can be used to enhance understanding and interest. Vary the way in which the skits are used:

▲ to replace a **Bible Readiness** choice;

▲ to present the **Bible story**;

▲ to expand the **Life Application**;

▲ to provide an additional **Bible Learning Activity**;

▲ to supplement **Bible Sharing** activities.

The information given in the Bible Background section and the Discussion Questions in each skit will help you expand the curriculum.

USING SKITS WITH POOR READERS

If your group includes students with poor reading skills or learning disabilities, or those for whom English is a second language, don't lose heart! With a little planning and some TLC, you can help poor readers gain badly needed confidence and self-esteem and liven up your classroom with Bible skits.

The following list of ideas can be adapted for use in any setting. Choose the techniques that best suit your group and resources.

FOR INFORMAL PRESENTATIONS AND READ-THROUGHS:

▲ Highlight each character's lines on a separate copy of the script and add pronunciation pointers as needed.

▲ Have the entire group read through the skit in pairs or small groups before presenting the skit to the whole group.

▲ Give everyone in the group a script to follow as selected readers read aloud. Receiving information through more than one sense makes the drama more accessible. This technique also assists students who are better visual than aural learners. It can also ease performers' nerves a bit by providing something other than the readers on which to focus.

▲ Use lots of visual aids and props.

▲ If a skit is particularly long or has long speeches, the teacher or leader can summarize a portion of the skit. Never feel obligated to perform a skit in its entirety; use only as much as your group can handle.

Use a "jump-in" technique that gives readers control over how much they want to read: When a volunteer has read as much as he or she wants, another volunteer jumps in and continues reading. Or let each reader choose a helper to consult whenever necessary.

On an overhead projector or chalkboard, post a word bank or key with pronunciations and/or definitions to words the group might have trouble with. Before the group reading, review the words and locate them in the script with the group.

FOR MORE FORMAL PRESENTATIONS AND PERFORMANCES:

▲ Assign a "drama coach" to each reader to provide one-on-one help in interpreting and learning lines. Coaches may be other students or an adult.

▲ The leader may read aloud all character parts before they're assigned. The leader should also discuss the tone of the skit, pronunciation and meaning of difficult words, and make suggestions for changes and word substitutions.

▲ Students practice reading their parts into a cassette recorder. To provide extra help, the leader may record each character part on a separate cassette to distribute to readers. Record each part twice, the first time speaking slowly and distinctly with no dramatic flair, the second time with dramatic flair so students hear how the lines should be delivered.

▲ For struggling readers, write out each sentence on a separate index card; this technique makes the job look smaller, and each line is an accomplishment.

▲ Hand out the script well in advance of the performance date; call and have the student read his or her part to you over the phone to practice.

▲ Give permission to improvise. Students who understand the sense of a speech, and whose verbal skills exceed their reading skills, may communicate better if allowed to paraphrase.

You Were Saying?

SCRIPTURE: 1 Samuel 3

SUGGESTED TOPICS: Listening to God; respect for elders; obeying God

BIBLE BACKGROUND

An Israelite man, Elkanah, had two wives: Peninnah and Hannah. The first bore Elkanah children, but Hannah was barren. In ancient societies, the inability to bear children was a deplorable situation for a woman. At best, she was scorned as being an unworthy wife; at worst, she was seen as being punished by God. In spite of Hannah's situation, Elkanah apparently loved her deeply (see 1 Samuel 1:5-8). However, Elkanah's affection for her was not sufficient to overcome Hannah's unhappiness. Hannah deeply wanted a child, specifically a son. In her anguish, she cried out to the Lord and promised that if He would grant her a son, the boy would be dedicated to the Lord to serve Him all of his days.

Hannah was living when the leadership of the judges in Israel was nearing an end. Eli was high priest and his two sons, Hophni and Phinehas, were judges over Israel. However, in spite of Eli's goodness, his sons were corrupt. But God, in His infinite wisdom and mercy, did not desert Eli. Instead, while answering the prayer of Hannah, God gave Eli a third child to raise up and instruct in His ways, a child who would listen.

PERFORMANCE TIPS

1. Suggested props: a scroll, a table, a cot for Eli (if a cot is not available, improvise by placing three or four chairs together).

2. Samuel is young and energetic; Eli is old. Their movements should reflect their ages.

3. Prior to the skit, explain Samuel's presence in the Tabernacle by summarizing the story of Hannah's prayer and Eli's response. Or start with the skit, then backtrack. Say, "Let's see why Samuel was living in the Tabernacle."

4. After the skit, continue Samuel's story to show how he listened to God. Have someone read 1 Samuel 7:3,4.

DISCUSSION QUESTIONS

1. What things can interfere with listening?

2. Do you need to be an adult to serve God? Why or why not?

3. Samuel heard God's voice call him. What other ways does God speak to His people?

4. Many people who do terrible things claim that God talks to them and that they are following God. How can you be sure God is speaking to you? How can you judge if someone else is listening to God?

5. What can you do to obey God this week? Think of one specific way you can obey God.

YOU WERE SAYING?

CHARACTERS
SAMUEL
ELI

ELI: Samuel!

SAMUEL: Here I am, sir. What do you want?

ELI: The scroll I had with me—where is it? I laid it down right here, and now I can't find it.

SAMUEL: It's right over there, sir. On the table.

ELI: On the table? That's right. I remember. That's where I put it.

SAMUEL: Shall I get it for you, sir?

ELI: No. I won't need it until morning. My eyes are no longer strong enough to read by candlelight. Finish your chores and then go to bed.

SAMUEL: Very good, sir. I'm almost finished.

ELI: Good boy. *(Pats SAMUEL affectionately.)*

(SAMUEL exits.)

ELI: *(Yawns.)* There's nothing for me to do until the sun comes up. I guess I'll go to sleep. *(Snores for several seconds.)*

SAMUEL: *(Enters.)* Here I am, sir!

ELI: Huh? What? Who?

SAMUEL: It's me, sir. I was just drifting off to sleep when I heard you call.

ELI: I didn't call. I was sleeping.

SAMUEL: But you must have called, sir. There's no one else in the Tabernacle.

ELI: I tell you, I was sleeping! It was probably just the wind making noise. Go back to your room and get some sleep.

SAMUEL: Yes, sir. *(Exits.)*

ELI: Young people! Can't tell the voice of the wind from the voice of a man. Now, then. Back to sleep. Ba-ack to slee-eep. *(Snores.)*

SAMUEL: *(Enters.)* Here I am, sir!

ELI: Huh? What? Who?

SAMUEL: It's me, sir. I was sleeping, but I heard you call.

ELI: Why do you disturb my slumbers? I am an old man. I need my rest.

SAMUEL: Yes, sir. You do, sir. But you DID call. I heard you.

ELI: I did nothing of the sort. You must have been dreaming. What did you have for supper tonight?

SAMUEL: Nothing unusual. Vegetables, meat, a little goat's milk.

ELI: Hmm. You used pepper, didn't you?

SAMUEL: Yes, sir. I like pepper.

ELI: That'll do it. Spicy food before bed. You were having a dream.

More Bible Skits ©1994 Gospel Light. Permission granted to photocopy

SAMUEL: But I didn't use very MUCH pepper, sir.

ELI: It doesn't take much. Now go to bed and let me get some sleep!

SAMUEL: Yes, sir. *(Exits.)*

ELI: These foolish young people. Always putting things on their food. Mixing things together. If this keeps up, soon they'll be putting tomato sauce and cheese on bread and baking it. Terrible thought. Ah, sleep. *(Snores.)*

SAMUEL: *(Enters.)* Here I am, sir!

ELI: Huh? What? Who?

SAMUEL: It's me, sir. I know you called me. I heard you very distinctly.

ELI: How many times must I tell you...

SAMUEL: But you called. I heard my name called. "Samuel!" Just like that. It wasn't a dream and it wasn't the wind.

ELI: Have pity on a tired old man. How could I call you when I was asleep?

SAMUEL: Perhaps you called me in your sleep, sir?

ELI: I don't talk in my sleep. You are hearing things. Hallucinations.

SAMUEL: What?

ELI: You're hearing things that aren't real. Hallucinations.

SAMUEL: Hallucinations?

ELI: Yes. Something like visions. Now go to bed.

SAMUEL: Yes, sir. *(Starts to leave.)*

ELI: Hallucinations. Visions. Wait! Come back!

SAMUEL: Yes, sir?

ELI: What did this vision say to you?

SAMUEL: Nothing, sir. I only heard my name being called.

ELI: What you are hearing is not a hallucination. It is a vision.

SAMUEL: A vision?

ELI: Yes. The Lord is speaking to you.

SAMUEL: But, how can that be? I've never had visions. Besides, surely the Lord would speak to you, His high priest!

ELI: The Lord speaks to whom He chooses. Now, listen closely.

SAMUEL: Yes, sir?

ELI: If the voice should call again, you must answer, "Speak, Lord; for your servant hears." Repeat it.

SAMUEL: Speak, Lord; for your servant hears.

ELI: That's right. *(Pats SAMUEL.)* And when He speaks, LISTEN. For He must have chosen you for some important purpose. Go back to bed now. And remember, when the Lord speaks, listen.

SAMUEL: *(Exiting.)* Speak, Lord; for your servant hears. Speak, Lord; for your servant hears.

ELI: Aah! *(Smiles and rubs chin.)* The Lord is speaking to Samuel! He is still with His people. Now I know I can really rest. *(Snores.)*

JUDGE, NOT!

SCRIPTURE: 1 Samuel 8

SUGGESTED TOPICS: Obedience to God; importance of Bible reading; ignoring God's instructions; effects of sin

BIBLE BACKGROUND

Upon the death of Eli and his sons (see 1 Samuel 4:14-18), Samuel was quickly recognized as the undisputed leader of Israel. He ruled wisely and, under his leadership, Israel prospered. After many years of faithful service, old age overtook Samuel. The job of judging Israel was too much for him and he passed the mantle of responsibility on to his sons, Joel and Abijah. Having seen the problems that could happen from having judges that did not listen to God (Phinehas and Hophni), one would expect that Samuel would have ensured that his two sons were well versed in the law and were honorable men who would take their responsibility seriously. However, this was not to be. For whatever reason, Samuel allowed two bribe-takers to assume the role of judge, and the people of Israel rebelled against their injustice. Then, against all warnings from Samuel (see 1 Samuel 8:11-18), the people demanded a king to rule over them.

PERFORMANCE TIPS

1. Suggested props: chairs for Joel and Abijah, a table to sit behind, a gavel.
2. If there has been a scandal reported in the news recently involving abuse of power, use it as an example of how greed and injustice continue as they did in Samuel's time.
3. Joel and Abijah are portrayed as being lazy. Have the students playing those parts act as if they are unwilling to give any effort to their jobs.
4. Mammon should be self-assured. He is rich and knows that money can buy anything.
5. Hadad should be very humble. He has come to plead his case.
6. The entire class can participate as the people. Have a few scripts available to distribute throughout the class.
7. After the skit, finish telling the story of the choosing of a king in Israel.

DISCUSSION QUESTIONS

1. Have you ever been treated unfairly? How did it make you feel?
2. What can a kid your age do to keep from being unfair?
3. What do people mean when they say, "Treat others as you want to be treated"? Do you agree? Why or why not?
4. What are some ways we can show God's love to people around us?

JUDGE, NOT!

CHARACTERS

SAMUEL
JOEL
ABIJAH (ah-BUY-jah)
CLERK
MAMMON (MAM-on)
HADAD (HAY-dad)
BENJAMIN
PEOPLE

SCENE ONE

SAMUEL: *(Beckons with a stiff hand.)* Come here, my sons.

JOEL: Yeah, Dad?

ABIJAH: What is it, Dad?

SAMUEL: My sons, I am growing very old. Too old to be Israel's judge any longer. I want you to be the judges of Israel now.

JOEL: You mean both of us?

ABIJAH: Why not just one of us?

SAMUEL: It's a big job. There will be plenty for both of you to do.

JOEL: OK. We'll be the best judges...

ABIJAH: ...that money can buy.

SCENE TWO

JOEL: OK, what's the first case?

CLERK: Hadad versus Mammon.

JOEL: So what's the problem that needs to be settled?

MAMMON: This whining pimple borrowed money from me. Three shekels.

JOEL: And you claim that you did not borrow money from him?

HADAD: Oh, no! I did indeed borrow three shekels from him.

JOEL: Then what could possibly be the problem?

MAMMON: When I asked for my money back, he only gave me three shekels. He refused to pay me any interest.

HADAD: That's because the Law of Moses says you're not supposed to charge interest to a brother.

MAMMON: Well, there's no problem because you're not my brother. Now give me my money. All of it. Three shekels plus interest.

HADAD: Please, Joel. Give us a ruling that is fair. Mammon has much money and land

and does not need more. But if I am forced to pay interest, then I will be poor again and forced to borrow once more.

JOEL: This is a tough problem. Let me consult my brother for a minute.

ABIJAH: This is tough, Joel. I think what father would do is to read the Law and do what it says, but that sounds like a lot of work. Maybe we can think of something easier.

JOEL: I'm all for something that takes less work. But if we have to think, that sounds even harder than reading.

ABIJAH: Well, we have to do something.

MAMMON: If it will help you to decide, settle in my favor and half the interest is yours.

JOEL and ABIJAH: Are you trying to bribe us?

MAMMON: Well...uh...yes.

HADAD: You have made a big mistake. No son of Samuel would take a bribe. Now you have lost for certain.

JOEL and ABIJAH: We find in favor of Mammon.

HADAD: What?

JOEL: He made an excellent point. You are not his brother.

ABIJAH: And even if you were, I'm not certain that the old Law would apply anyway. It's probably outdated. Next case.

JOEL: This job is going to be easier than I thought.

ABIJAH: And better paying.

SCENE THREE

BENJAMIN: Samuel, we have a couple of problems.

SAMUEL: So take them to Joel and Abijah. They are your judges.

BENJAMIN: They are also our problems.

SAMUEL: What do you mean?

BENJAMIN: There is no longer justice in Israel. Only people who have enough money to bribe your sons can get judgments in their favor.

SAMUEL: This is terrible! I will dismiss them and appoint a new judge—one who will be fair.

PEOPLE: No! No more judges! We want a king!

SAMUEL: But if you have a king, he will rule over you with an iron fist. He will take your sons and daughters to be his servants. He will take the best of your crops for his use. You will be forced to plow his fields. You DON'T want a KING.

PEOPLE: We want a king! We want a king! We want a king!

SAMUEL: But if you have a king, he will make you miserable.

PEOPLE: We want a king! We want a king! We want a king!

SAMUEL: I will ask God. If He will permit it, I will appoint a king to reign over you. But when things go wrong because you have a king, don't go crying to God about it. I am old and I will soon be gone. But you will have to live with your choice.

PEOPLE: We want a king!

(SAMUEL shakes head slowly.)

WHEN I SAY JUMP

SCRIPTURE: 1 Samuel 13

SUGGESTED TOPICS: Obeying God; respecting authority

BIBLE BACKGROUND

Against Samuel's strong objections, the people of Israel demanded a king to rule over them so they could be like their neighbors. Samuel warned the people of the disasters that would befall them, but they refused to listen. So Samuel called the people together (see 1 Samuel 10:17) and had them pass before the Lord in their individual tribes, thousand by thousand. First, the tribe of Benjamin was chosen. Then, the family of Matri. Finally, Saul himself was selected to be king of Israel.

From a human standpoint, Saul was an excellent choice. Standing a full head higher than the other Israelites, he cut an impressive figure. In the beginning, he recognized his own inability to rule. Surely, he would be a man who would seek the Lord's guidance to reign over God's people. However, the reign that began so well ended in dismal failure when the Lord had to wrest the kingdom from Saul and give it to a man "after his own heart" (1 Samuel 13:14).

PERFORMANCE TIPS

1. Suggested props: army fatigues, binoculars for the captain, a radio (walkie-talkies), maps.
2. The characters in the skit are soldiers. They should speak crisply and clearly.
3. The captain should speak slowly and distinctly whenever he explains something; the sergeant should salute each time he says "Yes, sir."

DISCUSSION QUESTIONS

1. What are some times a person might be disobedient? What do you think causes someone your age to disobey?
2. What other things might cause people to disobey? What are some excuses people might give for disobeying?
3. Why is it important for soldiers to obey orders? What was wrong with the captain's leadership?
4. Have you ever thought of yourself as one of God's soldiers? (See 2 Timothy 2:3.)
5. What are some of God's orders to His soldiers? What can you do to remember these orders and to obey them?

WHEN I SAY JUMP

CHARACTERS

CAPTAIN
GUNNERY SERGEANT
RADIO OPERATOR

CAPTAIN: Sergeant, come here!

SERGEANT: Yeah?

CAPTAIN: What did you say?

SERGEANT: I said, "Yeah?"

CAPTAIN: That's no way to address a superior. Let's try it again. Sergeant!

SERGEANT: *(Salutes.)* Yes, sir!

CAPTAIN: Bring the terrain maps here and let's go over them.

SERGEANT: *(Salutes.)* Yes, sir! I have them here, sir!

CAPTAIN: *(Looks at map.)* What is this?

SERGEANT: It's the train map, sir! It shows where all the trains go. And here's the schedule that gives all their departure and arrival times.

CAPTAIN: Not the TRAIN map. *(Speaks slowly.)* The TERRAIN map. The map that shows the ground we have to go over and where the mountains and valleys and rivers are.

SERGEANT: Oh. The contour map. I have that here.

CAPTAIN: "I have that here" what?

SERGEANT *(puzzled)*: I have that here contour map?

CAPTAIN: No! *(Speaks slowly.)* How do you address me?

SERGEANT: I have that here, sir! *(Hands map to CAPTAIN.)*

CAPTAIN: That's better. Never forget; you're in the army.

SERGEANT: *(Salutes.)* Yes, sir!

CAPTAIN: Are the men ready?

SERGEANT: Awaiting your orders, sir!

CAPTAIN: Good. Have them continue to stand by.

SERGEANT: Permission to speak, sir?

CAPTAIN: Go ahead.

SERGEANT: Thank you, sir. The men have been on alert for three days now. They're beginning to tire. Wouldn't it be better to wait until the battle is about to begin to have the troops on alert at their battle stations?

CAPTAIN: Are you questioning my orders, Sergeant?

SERGEANT: No, sir. I was just pointing out...

CAPTAIN: Well, don't! This is the army! You obey your superior officers. When I say jump, you say...

SERGEANT: How high, sir?

CAPTAIN: And don't you forget it. Dismissed!

SERGEANT: *(Salutes.)* Yes, sir. *(Exits.)*

CAPTAIN: *(Studies map.)* Now, let's see. The enemy's ammo dump is over here in the northeast. Prevailing winds from the west. Allow two degrees for drift and we should...

RADIO OPERATOR: Excuse me.

CAPTAIN: Excuse me, what?

RADIO OPERATOR: *(Salutes.)* Excuse me, sir!

CAPTAIN: That's better. What is it, soldier?

RADIO OPERATOR: New orders from HQ, sir! *(Hands CAPTAIN a piece of paper.)*

CAPTAIN: *(Mutters as he reads, then crumples paper and throws it away.)* Nonsense! What are those fools at HQ thinking anyway? Dismissed!

RADIO OPERATOR: *(Salutes.)* Yes, sir! *(Exits.)*

CAPTAIN: Sergeant!

SERGEANT: *(Salutes.)* Yes, sir!

CAPTAIN: The battle is about to start. *(Point to map.)* Now our primary target is this ammo dump. How quickly can your men take it out?

SERGEANT: As soon as you give the order, sir!

CAPTAIN: Good. Tell the men to stand by for the order to fire.

SERGEANT: *(Salutes.)* Yes, sir! *(Notices paper on ground. Picks it up and reads it.)* Permission to speak, sir?

CAPTAIN: What is it? I thought I gave you an order.

SERGEANT: *(Salutes.)* Yes, sir. But THESE orders, sir. HQ says our primary target has been changed. We're supposed to give artillery support along the southern front.

CAPTAIN: I can read, Sergeant. Those desk jockeys at HQ don't know the situation firsthand like we do. We have to take out the ammo dump so the enemy doesn't have so much fire power. Now go and obey my orders.

SERGEANT: *(Salutes.)* Yes, sir! *(Exits.)*

RADIO OPERATOR: Message from HQ, sir.

CAPTAIN *(studying map)*: I'm busy. Read it to me.

RADIO OPERATOR: It says, "Fire when ready."

CAPTAIN: Aha! The battle begins. We'll show those skunks a thing or two. Give me that radio. Sergeant! Can you hear me? Good. Fire! *(Looks through binoculars.)* Beautiful!

SERGEANT: A direct hit, sir! The ammo dump has been destroyed.

CAPTAIN: Good work, Sergeant. Commend the men on their swift obedience to orders.

SERGEANT: *(Salutes.)* Yes, sir!

RADIO OPERATOR: Message from HQ, sir.

CAPTAIN *(looking through binoculars)*: What is it? Read it to me. I'm busy.

RADIO OPERATOR: "Our commandos killed in explosion at ammo dump. Enemy breaking through on southern perimeter. Retreat from position and join with B Company at specified coordinates..."

CAPTAIN: Nonsense! We have the best defensive position we could hope for right here. Sergeant! Turn those guns around to the south.

SERGEANT: But, sir. The orders...

CAPTAIN: I'M giving the orders! We have to do everything ourselves. Those idiots at HQ have no idea what's really happening. Now go and obey my orders!

SERGEANT: *(Salutes.)* Yes, sir!

GRUDGE MATCH

SCRIPTURE: 1 Samuel 15:1-24

SUGGESTED TOPICS: Obeying God's Word completely; ignoring God's instructions; making excuses

BIBLE BACKGROUND

Saul had been chosen king of Israel by God Himself (see 1 Samuel 9:15,16). Surely, if any man would obey God, a king chosen by God would be the man. Unfortunately, Saul quickly forgot who had given him power in Israel, and began to rely on his own understanding (see Proverbs 3:5). First, he offered sacrifices in direct contradiction to Samuel's instructions to him. Then, in his battle against the Amalekites, he again refused to listen to God's instructions and saved King Agag and the best of the spoils of the battle. When Samuel called him to task for his disobedience, Saul went so far as to blame the other Israelites (see 1 Samuel 15:21) instead of accepting responsibility for his own actions.

PERFORMANCE TIPS

1. Suggested props: microphones for the announcers.
2. Joram should start his commentary quietly, but become more and more excited as the "game" continues.
3. After the skit, finish the story of Saul's disobedience. Emphasize verse 22.

DISCUSSION QUESTIONS

1. How was Saul obedient to God? How did he disobey God?
2. What were the consequences of Saul's disobedience? (Also read 1 Samuel 16:1.)
3. When have you ever been disobedient? What are some excuses you have tried to give to explain your disobedience? Did anyone really believe your excuses?
4. What are some different ways you can learn what God wants you to do?
5. If you disobey God, what should you do? Why?

GRUDGE MATCH

CHARACTERS
JORAM (JO-ram)
PEKAH (PEE-kah)
SAMUEL

PRONUNCIATION GUIDE
Agag (AY-gag)
Amalekites (uh-MAL-uh-kites)
Kenites (KEY-nites)

JORAM: Hello, sports fans. It's a beautiful day for today's game. The temperature's in the low seventies, there's just a sight breeze and the sun's shining brightly. Joining me on today's telecast is our color commentator, Pekah. Pekah, tell us about today's matchup and who we should expect to be the leaders on each side for today's game.

PEKAH: Well, Joram, I don't think there's any doubt about who the leaders will be today. The Israelites have been unstoppable this season, and it has to be because of their new captain, Saul. Sure, they had some minor victories over the past few seasons, but this year, they've been THE dominant power on the field. Nobody except the Philistines have come close in any game this season. So for the Israelites to do well today, they will need a strong performance from their captain.

JORAM: What about Jonathan, the son of Saul? Some have suggested that his play has made Saul look better than he really is.

PEKAH: Well, there's no doubt that Jonathan is the player of the future. But right now, Saul is it. Saul is the hope of Israel.

JORAM: OK. So much for Israel. Now, how about your thoughts on the Amalekites? What should we look for from them?

PEKAH: The Amalekites are, and always have been, an also-ran team. Oh sure, they've had some success in the past, but they've never won the cup. And don't look for them to go very far in the playoffs this year. But any team can come up with a win on any given day and this could be their day.

JORAM: Who should we be watching for the Amalekites?

PEKAH: First and foremost, their captain, Agag. Like Saul, he is the heart and soul of his team. He's a guy who always gives a hundred percent on the field. Also, the Amalekites have bolstered their team with some new faces from the Kenites. These fellows are unknowns and may make their presence felt in a big way today.

JORAM: Thank you for your analysis of today's game. We're almost ready for the start. But first, let's get a few words with the Israelite's coach, Samuel. Samuel, welcome to today's telecast.

SAMUEL: Thank you, Joram.

JORAM: Coach, could you tell us a little bit about your game plan for today? How are you going to beat these fellows?

SAMUEL: Well, to tell you the truth, I haven't developed a game plan.

JORAM: Are you trying to tell us that you just send the team in without telling them how to defeat their opponents? How can you justify your salary if you aren't going to instruct your team?

SAMUEL: I have given them instructions on what to do when the game is won. But I do not have to give any special instructions on how to win, because it will be won in the ordinary manner—by the superior team.

JORAM: That sounds a little overconfident, but I guess Pekah said much the same thing in his commentary. Could you tell us about the special instructions you have given your team?

SAMUEL: They have been instructed to completely destroy the Amalekites and all that the Amalekites have.

JORAM: Wow, that's putting it right on the line. Thank you for taking some time to be with us today, Samuel. Pekah, could I get your reaction to Samuel's comments?

PEKAH: Well, Samuel is not really a very organized coach. He seems to prefer doing things on the spur of the moment. He calls it "being led by the Lord." If we look at his record in all fairness, the Israelites have never lost a game when they followed his game plan.

JORAM: But what about his special instructions? Don't you find them a bit surprising?

PEKAH: Yes and no. You must remember, this is a grudge match. Everyone remembers, of course, how bitterly the Amalekites tried to prevent the Israelites from moving into Canaan. You might almost say that Israel is now trying to return the favor.

JORAM: That would, of course, explain why Samuel wants the team wiped out. But to destroy all of the Amalekites' possessions as well? Why would he want to do that?

PEKAH: That part of his plan makes no sense to anyone. If I were Saul, I would ignore that part of Samuel's instructions.

JORAM: We're almost ready for the start of the game. And look at the size of Israel's team! I've never seen such a large team! How many men would you say they have, Pekah?

PEKAH: Saul has easily got two hundred thousand, maybe even two hundred and ten thousand men with him today. No wonder Samuel seemed so confident.

JORAM: The game has started. But Saul isn't swooping onto the Amalekites as quickly as we would have expected. What is he doing? Why is he waiting?

PEKAH: Saul has approached one of the problems we discussed in the pregame show. Didn't we say the Kenites would be an unknown factor in the game, that the Kenites could make the difference? As you can see, Saul has convinced them to leave the Amalekites. Right at the beginning of the game, Saul has made a brilliant play to weaken the Amalekite team.

JORAM: It doesn't take a genius to see that this game will be very short lived. All that remains to be seen is, will Saul obey Samuel's instructions?

PEKAH: I don't see Samuel on the sidelines. This has always been another knock against him as a coach. He seems to think that he has more important things to do than to stay and watch the game.

JORAM: Well, that should actually make Saul's job easier. I wouldn't want to be the captain of a team of two hundred thousand and tell them that after the game, they won't be receiving any more than their regular paycheck.

PEKAH: This is very true. Everybody knows that most of a player's salary comes from his share of the booty that is taken at the end of a game. However, Saul seems to be following Samuel's plan to a tee. Everyone and everything is being utterly destroyed.

JORAM: Wait! Look! Saul is doing what we thought would be best. Look behind that chariot. One of the best sheep has been saved by Saul. Yes! A superb play. He is saving the best of the animals. No doubt his teammates will appreciate this and will play even better for him next game, knowing that he is a player's captain.

PEKAH: Not only that—he has executed another major coup. Although he SEEMED to be following Samuel's instructions, he has spared the life of Agag!

JORAM: I don't understand. How was that a smart play?

PEKAH: Saul knows that the Amalekites do have friends. If he had killed all of the Amalekites, then their friends might form an alliance and try to destroy Israel. But by saving the captain, Saul is telling Amalek's allies, "Look. We can get along." If anything unusual does happen this season and the Israelites should be defeated, Saul may be counting on the victors remembering what Saul has done and sparing his life, also.

JORAM: Well, it's all over now except for the shouting. Israel has won another stunning victory. We have to go now. But remember: Follow Saul's example and always watch out for yourself!

LAST BUT NOT LEAST

SCRIPTURE: 1 Samuel 16:1-13

SUGGESTED TOPICS: Trustworthiness; using abilities given by God;
inner character versus outer qualities

BIBLE BACKGROUND

Saul's reign as king was coming to an end. He had repeatedly ignored the law and instructions of God and so had proven unworthy to be king over God's people. God had searched the hearts of the Israelites and found a replacement, a young man after God's own heart: David.

Outwardly, David did not appear to be the man for the job. At the time of his anointing, he was little more than a boy. But God does not look at outward appearances. David had all the inner qualities God required for the king of His people: most importantly, a love and reverence for God.

PERFORMANCE TIPS

1. Suggested props: Bible-times costumes and an animal horn. If an animal horn is not available, roll a piece of construction paper in the shape of a cone.
2. If a cow costume is available, consider having someone play the cow.
3. If cast members are few, Jesse's other sons and the town elders could be played by two or three people alternating parts. Change headgear to indicate a different person.
4. Town elders can speak in unison or alternate lines individually.
5. David should be considerably shorter than other cast members. If no one is that short, consider strapping sandals to David's knees and have him "walk" in on his knees.

DISCUSSION QUESTIONS

1. What do you think are the two most important qualities a person can have?
2. Many people think that money, looks and intelligence are what make people important. Do you agree? Why or why not? Does God agree?
3. Jesus told His disciples they were not servants, but friends (see John 15:15). What can you do to show that you are Jesus' friend?

LAST BUT NOT LEAST

CHARACTERS

SAMUEL

JESSE

TOWN ELDERS

ELIAB (ee-LYE-ab)

ABINADAB (a-BIN-a-dab)

DAVID

JESSE'S OTHER SONS

SCENE ONE

SAMUEL *(straining on rope)*: Come on, Bossy. Move those legs. I thought you were a cow, not a mule.

TOWN ELDERS: Samuel?

SAMUEL: Excellent! Help! Would some of you get behind this beast and push?

TOWN ELDERS: You are Samuel?

SAMUEL: Of course I am. Now, are you planning to stand around or help me?

TOWN ELDERS: That depends.

SAMUEL: On what?

TOWN ELDERS: On whether you come in peace.

SAMUEL: Of course I come in peace. I am the Lord's servant.

TOWN ELDERS: True. But Saul sometimes gets upset with you. You didn't come to do something that will anger Saul, did you?

SAMUEL: I came to Bethlehem to make a sacrifice to the Lord. How could that make Saul angry? Sanctify yourselves and come to the sacrifice. Oh—and bring Jesse and his sons with you. But first, help me move this beast.

SCENE TWO

JESSE: It was good of you to invite my family to the sacrifice. It is a great honor to be here with God's servant.

SAMUEL: But you are alone. Where are your sons?

JESSE: They're coming. Here they are. *(SONS other than DAVID enter.)*

SAMUEL: What fine-looking young men! You must be very proud of them.

JESSE: I am indeed! *(SONS strike different bodybuilder poses.)*

SAMUEL: Introduce me to them.

JESSE: This is the eldest, Eliab.

SAMUEL: Look at him. So tall and handsome. Truly I must be looking at Israel's next king. Good thing I brought my horn of anointing oil. *(Takes horn from belt, stops and* cups his hand to his ear. Looks upward.) Not him, Lord? But look at him. No? (Pats ELIAB on back.) I'm sure you're a fine young man.

JESSE: Then, of course, my next eldest, Abinadab.

SAMUEL: The very model of manhood. (Takes horn from belt, stops and cups his hand to his ear. Looks upward.) Not him, either? (Pats ABINADAB on back.)

JESSE: Then, Shammah.

SAMUEL: Oh, yes! (Takes horn from belt, stops and cups his hand to his ear. Looks upward.) No? (Pats SHAMMAH on back.) (In pantomime, JESSE continues to introduce his other four SONS. Same actions as before.)

SAMUEL: None of them. Could I have been mistaken? Maybe the Lord said go to Bethel, not Bethlehem. No, I'm sure He said Bethlehem. Jesse?

JESSE: Yes, Samuel?

SAMUEL: Have you any other sons?

JESSE: Only the youngest, the baby of the family. He's out tending the sheep.

SAMUEL: We cannot continue with the sacrifice until he comes. Please send for him.

JESSE: (To SONS.) Go and bring your brother.

ALL SONS: Yes, Father. (Exit.)

SAMUEL: Tell me about this boy, David.

JESSE: Well, there's not much to tell. He's the youngest.

SAMUEL: What does he look like?

JESSE: He's not very big. A little sunburned, from being out with the sheep all day. But, on the whole, he's reasonably handsome.

SAMUEL: Does he have any hobbies?

JESSE: Now that you mention it, he's a fine musician. He plays his harp so beautifully, you would think he was an angel.

SAMUEL: How about his work habits?

JESSE: Funny you should ask. Most conscientious. A more trustworthy lad you'd never find if you searched through all Israel. Keeps his eyes open and makes sure the sheep find good grazing land and quiet waters.

SAMUEL: But you must be worried; him alone with the sheep. So many dangers.

JESSE: I never thought about it before, but never has he lost so much as a single lamb. Even when the bear and the lion tried to snatch one away, did he run for help? Not David. Took the lion by the beard and slew it. Killed the bear, too, come to think of it.

SAMUEL: I think I truly want to meet this boy.

JESSE: Your wish is granted. Here they come now. (SONS enter, with DAVID bringing up the rear.)

SAMUEL: I must have been mistaken. The Lord must have said Bethel. (Cups hand to ear and looks upward.) Are you sure, Lord? But he's so young and so small. How could one such as this be a king? Very well. (Takes horn from belt.) David, come forth. The Lord has told me to anoint you king of Israel. May His Spirit be upon you all your days and His wisdom and power be with you.

DRAGNET FOR DAVID

SCRIPTURE: 1 Samuel 18

SUGGESTED TOPICS: Friendship and loyalty; sin of jealousy

BIBLE BACKGROUND

Saul was still king, but David had been anointed by Samuel to be king instead of Saul. David remained loyal to Saul, who should have felt honored to have a friend and subject such as David. However, David's popularity aroused such jealousy in Saul, it was as though a green mist passed over the king's eyes every time he saw the young warrior. Instead of seeing a soldier who won great victories on his king's behalf, Saul saw a usurper of whom the women sang, "Saul has slain his thousands, and David his tens of thousands" (1 Samuel 18:7).

Later events show that Saul had nothing to fear from David. Even when given the opportunity, David chose not to destroy Saul out of his reverence for God (see 1 Samuel 24:6).

The man who had cause to be jealous of David was Saul's son Jonathan. Jonathan would have been next in line to be king, but David had been anointed in his place. Even though Jonathan knew that David would become king (see 1 Samuel 23:17), friendship with David was more important to Jonathan than worldly acclaim and power.

PERFORMANCE TIPS

1. Suggested props: a palace wall with two holes in it, a notebook for Pete, a crown and purple robe for King Saul.
2. Joe should speak matter-of-factly, almost monotone. (Joe is a takeoff on the "Joe Friday" character from the "Dragnet" TV series.)
3. King Saul should be inconsistent, sometimes speaking rationally, sometimes ranting and raving.
4. If your class is not familiar with the story of David and Jonathan, explain what Jonathan was doing when he went out for archery practice.

DISCUSSION QUESTIONS

1. Do you agree with Joe concerning David's whereabouts? Why or why not?
2. Why do you think Saul was so intent on finding David?
3. What caused the two holes in the wall? What made Saul behave this way?
4. What does "jealousy" mean? Have you ever been jealous of someone?
5. If you are jealous of someone, what can you do about it?

DRAGNET FOR DAVID

CHARACTERS
JOE
PETE
SAUL

PRONUNCIATION GUIDE
Michal (MY-kul)

JOE: This is the city. It's the place where I work. I love it. In the city are a thousand stories. This is one of them.

PETE: Is it my turn yet?

JOE: Not yet. I'm still in the middle of my dramatic introduction. Now, where was I? Oh, yes. My name is Sabbath. Joe Sabbath. I'm a cop. Sgt. Jacobs and I had been called to the palace on a missing persons case.

PETE: Boy, this is sure exciting. Being on an important case for the king.

JOE: They're all exciting, Pete.

PETE: Yeah. But the king! How many people ever get a chance to talk to the king?

JOE: Probably more than you think. Let's go inside.

PETE: Shouldn't we ring the doorbell first?

JOE: No.

PETE: Why not?

JOE: Because we're here on authority. And doorbells haven't been invented yet.

PETE: Look! That's Jonathan, the king's son. What do you think he's doing?

JOE: I suspect that he's going hunting.

PETE: Why do you think that?

JOE: He has a BOW. And a quiver full of ARROWS. And a small boy to FETCH the arrows.

PETE: Maybe he's going to fight a mighty battle against the Philistines.

JOE: I doubt it.

PETE: Why not?

JOE: Because if he was going to battle, he would take soldiers with him. Not just a little boy.

PETE: Oh, yeah. Good thinking. So who do you think is missing?

JOE: I don't waste time in idle speculation when somebody can give me the facts. That's all I want. Just the facts.

PETE: But who is going to give us the facts?

JOE: The king.

PETE: But how are you going to find the king?

SAUL *(from behind)*: You could try turning around.

PETE: Oh!

JOE: Your Majesty! We came as soon as we got your message. Now, please give us the facts. Who is missing?

SAUL *(yelling)*: Servant!

PETE: We need a better description than that. Which servant?

SAUL: Which servant what?

JOE: Which servant is missing?

SAUL: None of my servants are missing.

PETE: Then why did you say that one was?

SAUL: Oh, no. I was calling for a servant to bring us some wine.

JOE: No, thank you. We're on duty. So who exactly is missing?

SAUL: David!

PETE: Can we get a description of this David?

JOE: We won't need one. Everybody in the city knows David.

SAUL *(bitterly)*: They certainly do.

PETE: Are we talking about the David that killed Goliath?

SAUL: That's the one.

JOE: And now he's missing?

PETE: I've got a theory. Maybe he's afraid of being brought to trial for the murder of Goliath, and he ran away to hide.

SAUL: I hardly think that's likely.

PETE: Begging your pardon, Your Royalness. But you don't know how the criminal mind operates. Being trained policemen, we do.

SAUL: Why should he be afraid of being brought to trial for killing Goliath when he has already been promoted for that deed?

JOE: You're forgetting, Pete. Goliath was a Philistine.

PETE: Oh, yeah. Now I remember. I keep getting the two sides mixed up.

SAUL: Can we get on with this? I really need to find David.

JOE: Certainly, Your Majesty. I imagine that the loss of a hero is distressing to you.

PETE: A HERO? Do you mean that we're looking for the hero, David? The one that the women are always singing about? You've heard that song *(Sings.)*, "Saul has slain his thousands and David his tens of thousands," that the women are always singing in the streets. Is something wrong, Your Highnessest?

SAUL: What? Ah, no. No. Nothing. Why do you ask?

JOE: You had turned a little green there for a minute. Pete doesn't realize the effect that his singing has on most people. Now, Your Majesty, what can you tell us about David and his habits?

SAUL: Very little. His closest friend is my son, Jonathan. He could tell you things about David, but he's out taking a little target practice.

JOE: Maybe you could tell us all that you do know. Just the facts, sir.

SAUL: Well, he's my son-in-law. He's married to my daughter, Michal.

PETE: Joe.

SAUL: What?

PETE: Joe.

SAUL: What about Joe?

PETE: You just called him Michael.

SAUL: No, I didn't.

PETE: Yes, you did. I have it written down. When Mr. Sabbath asked you to tell us all you knew, you said that David was married to your daughter, and you called him Michael.

SAUL: No, I didn't. I called HER Michal.

PETE: Begging your pardon, Your Kingliness, but when you're talking about a man, you don't use the word "her."

JOE: Allow me, Your Majesty. Pete, the king's daughter's name is Michal.

PETE: Oh. There should be a law against giving a girl a boy's name. It gets very confusing.

JOE: You were saying that David is married to Michal. Has it been a happy marriage? Perhaps David just wanted to get away from the little woman for a while.

SAUL: I hardly think so. They've only been married a short time. And to get her, well, you should have seen the dowry that he gave.

JOE: I understand David was a shepherd before he became a soldier. Where would a shepherd get a large dowry?

SAUL: Oh, he didn't give me money. He killed two hundred Philistines to have her hand in marriage.

PETE: *(Sings softly.)* Saul has slain his thousands and David his tens of thousands.

SAUL: *(Yells and pulls hair.)* Arrghhh! *(Throws imaginary spear.)*

PETE: Wowee! Where did that spear come from? Whoowee! That nearly pinned me to the wall, just like a butterfly in a display case.

SAUL: Sorry. It's that wretched song—when I get upset, I throw things. Don't you do that sometimes?

JOE: Sometimes. But I always make sure that they don't have sharp-pointed ends and that nobody is in the way. However, Pete doesn't realize what his singing does to people. Any judge would have ruled it justifiable homicide.

PETE: Look at that! That spear went all the way through the wall!

SAUL: Can we please get back to the investigation?

JOE: Certainly, Your Majesty. What else can you tell us about David?

SAUL: Well, he's an excellent musician. Sometimes when I feel a little down, he sits over there and plays the harp for me. *(Points to wall.)*

JOE: Beside the wall with the two holes in it?

SAUL: That's right.

JOE: Hmmm. Thank you, Your Majesty. I think we have enough to begin our preliminary investigation. Come on, Pete. It's time to go.

PETE: Right through the wall! Boy! Is he strong. Wow!

JOE: It's time to go, Pete. Let's move it.

PETE: Do you think we've got enough to solve the case, Joe?

JOE: Sure. It's easy to figure out. A former shepherd, a musician, just married. Obviously, he's gone off into the hills to write a love song for his new bride. He'll be back in a few days. Nothing LIFE threatening. Well, Pete, another case wrapped up.

THE FUGITIVE

SCRIPTURE: 1 Samuel 21:1-9; 22:6-19; 24

SUGGESTED TOPICS: Compassion; respect for God's leaders; God's timing

BIBLE BACKGROUND

Saul's jealousy of David flared into a raging fire. No longer was David safe when he was anywhere near Saul. In spite of David's valor in battle against Saul's enemies, his marriage to Saul's daughter, his friendship with Saul's son, and his unswerving loyalty to Saul as king, David became a hunted criminal. His "crime" was two-fold: he was more popular than Saul (see 1 Samuel 18:8) and he had been annointed to be the next king of Israel.

David's actions during this conflict show why David was called a man after God's own heart (see 1 Samuel 13:14). With his popularity, he could have raised up an army to lead a rebellion against Saul. Instead, he fled and offered no opposition to Saul, trusting God to bring about His purpose in His own way. Even when given the opportunity to destroy Saul, David refused, not because Saul was king and David was afraid of the consequences of killing the secular head of the kingdom, but because Saul was "the Lord's anointed" (1 Samuel 24:6). David never lost sight of Saul's position in God's order, even when Saul proved himself unworthy of that position.

PERFORMANCE TIPS

1. Suggested props: a butter knife, a large sword for David, weapons for soldiers, a crown for Saul.

2. Soldiers and servants can double as David's men if actors are in short supply.

3. Saul's moods change rapidly. He should be played with large movements, sweeping gestures, etc.

DISCUSSION QUESTIONS

1. Why did Saul hate David? What had David done to Saul?

2. How do you think David felt when he was treated so unfairly? (Read Psalm 57. It is believed that David wrote this Psalm when Saul was chasing him.)

3. Often we let our feelings guide our actions. Did David do this? How did David control his feelings and act in a different manner?

4. Do you think Saul deserved David's friendship? Why or why not?

5. Why should you show friendship like David's?

6. As Christians, we are called to be like Christ. How did Jesus show His friendship to us? How can we show this kind of friendship to others?

THE FUGITIVE

CHARACTERS

NARRATOR

DAVID

AHIMELECH (ah-HIM-eh-lek)

SAUL

DOEG (DOH-egg)

SERVANTS and SOLDIERS

FIRST MAN

SECOND MAN

SCENE ONE

NARRATOR: Unjustly accused of treason, David has had to flee for his life. Aided by Saul's son, Jonathan, David escaped from the palace. For now, the sentence of death has been delayed. David is free. Free to jump at every shadow, free to hide from the king's men, free to roam from place to place hoping to find a haven to rest his weary head. Free to be...THE FUGITIVE.

(Sound of knocking on door.)

AHIMELECH: Who's knocking on my door so late at night? Go away! I'm trying to prepare my sermon.

DAVID *(whispering)***:** Ahimelech. It's David. Please, open your door.

AHIMELECH: David? Captain of the king's army? Trusted servant of Saul?

DAVID *(whispering)***:** Yeah. Open up, will you?

AHIMELECH: The king's favorite is always welcome here. But should you be out on a cool night when you have a touch of laryngitis?

DAVID *(whispering)***:** I don't have laryngitis. I'm just being careful.

AHIMELECH: Well, come in. Come in. It's safe to speak here. Why all the secrecy?

DAVID: *(Looks right and left and motions AHIMELECH closer.)* I'm on a secret mission for the king.

AHIMELECH: Say no more.

DAVID: I can say no more. But I need some provisions.

AHIMELECH: But would the king not have provided you with food?

DAVID: There was no time. This secret mission is of the greatest importance and I had to leave immediately. I had no time to stop for food.

AHIMELECH: Say no more.

DAVID: I can say no more. Can you spare five loaves of bread? Or anything you might have.

AHIMELECH: I have some communion bread. Yes, you may have it.

DAVID: What was that noise?

AHIMELECH: Doeg.

DAVID: I didn't know you had a dog.

AHIMELECH: Not dog. Doeg. Saul's chief herdsman.

DAVID: Did he see me?

AHIMELECH: Perhaps. But you're both the king's servants. What difference can it make whether he saw you or not?

DAVID: Maybe none. But my mission is top secret...

AHIMELECH: Say no more.

DAVID: I can say no more. Do you have any weapons I could take with me?

AHIMELECH: I am a man of God. Why would I have weapons? You're the soldier.

DAVID: Yes, but the king's business required haste. I had no time to stop for my own armament. You must have some weapon.

AHIMELECH: A butter knife? No, hardly satisfactory. Wait! I do have this museum piece. A GOLIATH sword. *(Produces a large sword.)*

DAVID: Excellent! There is none other like it in the land. Farewell, my friend. May you be rewarded for your friendship. Farewell! *(Exits.)*

AHIMELECH *(thoughtfully)***:** A strange young man. But a good and faithful servant.

SCENE TWO

(SAUL enters court filled with SERVANTS and SOLDIERS.)

SAUL *(screaming with rage)***:** You call yourselves servants?

SERVANTS and SOLDIERS *(mumbling)***:** Yes, m'lord.

SAUL: Are you all conspiring with David against me?

SERVANTS and SOLDIERS: No, m'lord.

SAUL: *(To SERVANTS.)* Can David give you vineyards and fields?

SERVANTS: No, m'lord.

SAUL: *(To SOLDIERS.)* Can David give you promotions?

SOLDIERS: No, m'lord.

SAUL: Then why do you all conspire with him? *(Voice changes to whining.)* Doesn't anybody care? You all knew Jonathan, my own son, was helping him. And now he has four hundred men helping him. Everybody hates me. You're all no good. Isn't anybody sorry for me? Won't anybody help me? *(Buries face in hands and sobs.)*

DOEG: Yes, m'lord!

SAUL: *(Looks up.)* Who are you?

DOEG: Doeg.

SAUL: How dare you insult me! Call me a dog, will you?

DOEG: No, m'lord. My NAME is Do-eg.

SAUL: Oh, yes. Your name. Quite. Well, what do you want?

DOEG: I have important information for you.

SAUL: Nothing's important anymore. Nobody loves me. Everybody conceals things from me. Nobody will tell me where to find David so I can kill him.

DOEG: I will.

SAUL: You know where David is?

DOEG: No. But I know where he was. He was visiting Ahimelech. And Ahimelech helped David. He gave him food and a sword.

SAUL: Bring Ahimelech here!

(SERVANTS hurry out and return with AHIMELECH.)

SAUL: So, you're the traitor. And you call yourself a priest.

AHIMELECH: I'm not a traitor, O King. How can you say such a thing?

SAUL: You aren't a traitor? Didn't you give David food and weapons?

AHIMELECH: Of course.

SAUL: Ha! You admit you're a traitor!

AHIMELECH: I'm not a traitor. Why shouldn't I give things to David? He is your son-in-law. He is the most faithful of all your men. He sits in an honored place in your home. How was I supposed to know you hated him?

SAUL: I won't have traitors in my country! Soldiers! Kill him!

SOLDIERS *(muttering among themselves)*: But he's a priest! We can't kill him.

DOEG: *(Jumps up and down.)* Me! Me! Let me! I'll kill him for you. And all the other priests who were with him and all his family and his cat and his dog and his sheep and...

SAUL: Why can't ALL my servants be as faithful as Doeg?

SCENE THREE

(Stage area is inside of cave. DAVID and MEN are in cave.)

SAUL: *(From offstage.)* We've been searching all over these rocks for David. It's time to sleep. Hmm. Kind of looks like rain. Guards, you wait here and I'll sleep in this cave. *(Enters.)* It's kind of dark in here. But it's dry. Oh, chasing fugitives is so tiring. *(Lays down and covers himself.)*

More Bible Skits ©1994 Gospel Light. Permission granted to photocopy.

FIRST MAN: *(Punches DAVID's shoulder.)* Look! The day spoken of by the Lord has come to pass.

SECOND MAN: Yes. The Lord has delivered Saul into your hands!

FIRST MAN: You can do whatever you want to him.

SECOND MAN: You could kill him!

DAVID: Wait here. *(Creeps down to where SAUL sleeps and cuts off piece of cloak.)*

FIRST MAN: That's IT?

SECOND MAN: Why not cut off his whole coat, right about throat level?

DAVID: God forbid that I should hurt or kill His anointed. Let him rest and go in peace.

(DAVID and MEN crouch, watching SAUL. SAUL wakes and stretches.)

SAUL: Oh, that's better. Nothing like a good night's sleep to restore the body. Now I can resume chasing that no-good, cowardly, lily-livered, traitorous David. *(Exits.)*

(DAVID rushes to mouth of cave.)

DAVID: My lord, the king!

SAUL: Who's there?

DAVID: *(Bows down.)* Why do you listen to men who say, "David wants to hurt you"? I could have cut your throat as you lay sleeping in this cave. I have never sought to hurt you, and I never will. Look! This piece of your cloak I cut off could easily have been your THROAT!

SAUL: Is this the voice of my son, David?

DAVID: It is.

SAUL: Oh, how could I be so cruel and stupid? You have shown me how good you are. Now I KNOW the kingdom will be yours. Show your mercy to me, my son, and promise me one thing.

DAVID: You have but to ask.

SAUL: When the Lord gives you the kingdom, do not destroy all my family. Do not blot out my name from the earth.

DAVID: As surely as the Lord reigns, this I promise you.

NARRATOR: And so Saul went home. But David remained on the run, for he knew that Saul would soon forget his remorse and seek David's life again. This is the life of one on the run. Never to rest in complete peace, always vigilant against the threat of renewed efforts to kill him. Such is the life of...THE FUGITIVE.

WRONG!

SCRIPTURE: 1 Samuel 28

SUGGESTED TOPICS: Listening to God; friendship; astrology

BIBLE BACKGROUND

After David spared Saul's life, Saul wept with guilt and admitted that David had no evil intent towards him. But Saul's change of heart concerning David did not last long. Soon he was chasing David again, seeking to destroy him. In spite of everything David had done, Saul still feared him as a threat. Perhaps because Saul knew the evil within himself, he was unable to trust the goodness in his most loyal ally.

Saul and David show the contrast between a person who seeks God and one who would rather do things his own way. As Saul moved further away from God, he did not repent and ask for God to forgive him. Instead, he sought out a witch, something forbidden in the Law as an abomination to God. David was not perfect, either. But when he saw his sin, he cried out to his heavenly Father for forgiveness and guidance.

PERFORMANCE TIPS

1. Suggested props: newspaper, table, Yellow Pages, Bible.
2. When April quotes the Bible, have her look up the passages. Consider having her actually read Deuteronomy 18:10-12.

DISCUSSION QUESTIONS

1. Why do people consult horoscopes, witches, fortunetellers, etc.?
2. Read Deuteronomy 18:20. What is God's penalty for false prophets? Why do you think God would make the penalty so harsh?
3. Do friends always agree with each other? What makes a person a true friend?
4. What ways did April show her friendship to June?
5. What are some other ways friends can help you?

WRONG!

CHARACTERS
APRIL

JUNE

PRONUNCIATION GUIDE
diviners (dih-VINE-urs)

necromancers (NEK-row-man-sers)

APRIL: Hi, June. What are you doing?

JUNE: *(Looks up from newspaper.)* Hi, April. I'm trying to make a decision.

APRIL: What kind of decision?

JUNE: I'm trying to decide what to do with my life.

APRIL: Wow! Have you talked to people who could help you decide? Parents, teachers, counselors, your pastor? Not friends, I guess, because this is the first I've heard about it.

JUNE: No. I thought of something easier to help me.

APRIL: You're checking the want ads to see what's available?

JUNE: No. I'm reading my horoscope to see what the stars hold for me.

APRIL: You're not serious!

JUNE: Well, of course I'm serious. My life is serious stuff. I need the best advice I can get.

APRIL: Well, you won't find it there.

JUNE: *(Folds newspaper.)* I guess you're right.

(JUNE goes to table, picks up Yellow Pages and thumbs through them.)

APRIL: NOW what are you doing?

JUNE: Following your advice. You're right about newspaper horoscopes. I need an astrologer to make me a personal horoscope, just like you said.

APRIL: I didn't say that!

JUNE: Here's one, Mr. Armand. He sounds reliable.

APRIL: June, don't be crazy!

JUNE: You're right. I need a woman astrologer. She'll understand me better.

APRIL: What do you mean, "I'm right"? You're not listening to me! Don't consult astrologers and the stars. None of them can help you.

JUNE: There. Just like you said. Here's a better one. Madame Shasta. Sounds mystical. She'll be able to see my future.

APRIL: June! Look at me! Read my lips! DO...NOT...GO...TO...AN...ASTROLOGER! None of them can help you.

JUNE: Why not? Astrology is really catching on.

APRIL: Astrology may be popular, but it's not right.

JUNE: Sure it is. Even the Bible says so.

APRIL: Wrong! The Bible never says that.

JUNE: Sure it does. The wise men followed the star and it led them right to Jesus in Bethlehem.

APRIL: Are you sure about that?

JUNE: Sure. I see it every Christmas.

APRIL: If you read the Bible, you'll see that ONE star led the wise men to JERUSALEM. King Herod had the REAL wise men, the scribes and chief priests, consult the Scriptures to find where the Messiah was to be born. The wise men found Jesus in Bethlehem because they followed the Scriptures.

JUNE: Oh. Well. *(Thinks.)* I've got it. *(Looks into Yellow Pages again.)*

APRIL: Now what?

JUNE: Where do you think I should look for witches? I can't find any listing for them under *W.*

APRIL: Look under *E,* for evil.

JUNE: Evil? Oh, don't worry. I'd only consult a good witch.

APRIL: Don't you understand? There are no good witches.

JUNE: Oh, sure there are. They're called "white witches."

APRIL: Not according to God.

JUNE: What do you mean?

APRIL: In Deuteronomy 18:10-12, God calls ALL diviners, enchanters, witches, charmers, consulters of familiar spirits, wizards and necromancers DETESTABLE. Today, we call those people witches, astrologers, psychics, fortune-tellers.

JUNE: What does "detestable" mean?

APRIL: That's a word God uses to describe something He hates absolutely.

JUNE: Got it. I'll consult a prophet.

APRIL: No, no, no!

JUNE: But prophets are good! People always consulted them in the Bible.

APRIL: But how will you know you're consulting one of GOD'S prophets? Many times in the Bible, people consulted FALSE prophets—with awful consequences!

JUNE: I'll just find one with a good record.

APRIL: Will you find one with a perfect record?

JUNE: Of course not. Nobody's perfect.

APRIL: Then you'll be consulting a false prophet! If a prophet makes even ONE mistake, it means his information didn't come from God and that prophet is a phony!

JUNE: Then what can I do? How can I decide?

APRIL: Pray. Ask God to guide you. You don't need anyone to do that for you.

JUNE: But I don't know how to pray. I've never really done it before.

APRIL: I'll pray with you, if you'd like. We can ask God to show you what would be best for you and help you meet people who can help you make wise decisions.

JUNE: He's already doing that. Thanks, April. Friend.

ISRAELI HOME SHOPPING CLUB

SCRIPTURE: 2 Samuel 2—3:1

SUGGESTED TOPICS: Loyalty to God, not men; making wise choices

BIBLE BACKGROUND

"The king is dead; long live the king!" This is a familiar phrase to any who live in a monarchy. When the old king dies, the country expresses its allegiance to the new king. Saul had committed suicide and three of his sons had been killed in battle against the Philistines (see 1 Samuel 31:2-4). Who then would be Israel's king?

Abner, the commander of Saul's army, threw his allegiance behind Ishbosheth. This was a logical choice, as Ishbosheth was a son of Saul. Tradition dictates that the new king be a son of the previous king, but God does not follow the traditions of men. He had already chosen David to be the new king of Israel. Because of Saul's sin, the kingdom was taken from his family by God (see 1 Samuel 15:28). Abner, a brave and skilled warrior, ignored God's clear intention, and the result of this unwise choice was destruction.

PERFORMANCE TIPS

1. Suggested props: purple robe (or piece of cloth), cardboard or wooden scepter.
2. Announcer is trying to sell cheap merchandise, passing it off as top quality. He should speak fairly quickly and excitedly.
3. After the skit, continue the story to show the wise choices David made.

DISCUSSION QUESTIONS

1. Did Abner make wise choices? What might have influenced him to make the choices he did?
2. What were some choices David made? Were they wise choices? Why or why not?
3. What kinds of decisions do you have to make? How can you help ensure wise choices?

ISRAELI HOME SHOPPING CLUB

CHARACTERS
ANNOUNCER

ABNER

PRONUNCIATION GUIDE
Ishbosheth (ISH-bow-sheth)

ANNOUNCER: It's great to be back on the air with you again at the Israeli Home Shopping Club! And do we have some bargains for you today! Let's not waste any more time. Look at the first item. *(Pause, allowing viewers to see the item.)* Look at that robe! All in royal purple with a hem sewn in genuine gold stitching! You would expect to pay up to a talent of gold for this item anywhere else but not if you're a member! Certainly not! Look at this low members' price. Seven shekels. That's right! No, we haven't gone totally crazy here at the Club, but we wanted to start off today's show with a real bargain. The phones have been ringing off the hooks on this one already. Let's talk to one of the shoppers. Hi, who am I talking to?

ABNER: This is Abner.

ANNOUNCER: Abner. Terrific name. Are you related to the Abner who was the captain of Saul's guard?

ABNER: That's me. I'm the same Abner.

ANNOUNCER: Well, that's great. Because having been around King Saul for so long, you would certainly know the value of a wonderful garment like the one we're offering!

ABNER: Well, yes. I have seen many beautiful robes in my time at the king's palace. And this one does look beautiful.

ANNOUNCER: It more than LOOKS beautiful. It IS beautiful! I mentioned the color before and the gold stitching, but this has almost too many features to mention!

ABNER: Go ahead. Mention some.

ANNOUNCER: Did I talk about the beautiful, royal, purple color?

ABNER: Yes.

ANNOUNCER: What about the gold stitching?

ABNER: Yes.

ANNOUNCER: What about this? ONE SIZE FITS ALL! That's right! It doesn't matter if you're as tall as Goliath or as short as David, this robe will fit you!

ABNER: Why did you mention David? Has HE ordered a robe, too?

ANNOUNCER: I was merely using a well-known metaphor here in Israel. Everybody knows that Goliath was huge and that David is short. But back to the robe. What sort of money would Saul have paid for a robe like this?

ABNER: Well, he was sometimes a bit extravagant when it came to clothes. Not unusually so, you understand. After all, he WAS the king. But I would never reveal any of the king's secrets.

ANNOUNCER: Abner. What are you afraid of? Saul is dead. He can't do anything to you for revealing an innocent secret. Come on. Tell us a little palace gossip. What sort of money would Saul have paid for a robe like this one?

ABNER: No. I can't betray the secrets of a king, even if he is no longer with us. But I CAN tell you that he would certainly have paid more than seven shekels for one.

ANNOUNCER: OK! Great! There you have it folks, a testimonial direct from the palace! This is one GREAT bargain! There's only a few seconds left to order your very own "kingly" robe. That's it! Time's up on this item. But we still have more terrific buys coming up on the Israeli Home Shopping Club. Here comes the next item now. There it is! *(Pause to allow time for audience to see.)* An ABSOLUTELY GORGEOUS, SOLID GOLD-PLATED scepter! You can see the beauty and craftsmanship built into this item. Fully three feet long and encrusted with ten genuine cubic zirconias. No king would dream of purchasing a scepter for less than two full talents of gold. But this one can be picked up for a psalm. Look at that members' price—TEN SHEKELS! I can't believe that one myself. I wish that you could be here in the studio with me to see this in person. Just think! For a mere ten shekels you will not only be king of your house, but you will have the scepter to prove it. If you want one of these beauties, you'd better call in quickly, or you'll miss out. Let's talk to one of our buyers. Hi! You're on the Israeli Home Shopping Club! So what do you think of this item that we're offering now?

ABNER: I think that it looks like a very good buy. That's why I'm buying it.

ANNOUNCER: You know, you sound a lot like a previous caller. Who is this?

ABNER: It's Abner.

ANNOUNCER: Well, you are doing a lot of shopping tonight, Abner. What's the big occasion? Are you planning to dress up and show the little woman that you're king of the home?

ABNER: Actually, I'm buying them for a friend. Ishbosheth.

ANNOUNCER: Bless you. That's a nasty sneeze you have there.

ABNER: I didn't sneeze. That's my friend's name. Ishbosheth.

ANNOUNCER: Well, I'm certainly glad that he didn't call in himself. I'd never have been able to pronounce his name. I'd probably have ended up calling him Sneezy.

ABNER: I wouldn't joke about his name too much. And I would learn how to pronounce it if I were you. Because he's going to be the next king of Israel.

ANNOUNCER: Politics really isn't my thing, but I thought that David was going to be the next king of Israel. That's what all MY neighbors are saying, anyway.

ABNER: Well, they're all wrong. Ishbosheth will be the next king.

ANNOUNCER: It's been nice chatting with you, Abner. But we're just about out of time on our portion of the show today. Stay tuned for Deborah. Deb's going to have some terrific buys for all you ladies out there. I'll be back tomorrow with some more "kingly" purchases for you men. Until then, so long and see you again.

ONE RIGHT ROAD

SCRIPTURE: 2 Samuel 6:1-8

SUGGESTED TOPICS: Making wise choices; ignoring God's instructions; courage

BIBLE BACKGROUND

Throughout human history, God has given people the ability and the responsibility to make choices. Eve had to choose between obedience to God or following the advice of the serpent; Adam, between God and Eve. The Israelites, after arriving at the Promised Land, had to choose between accepting the advice of Joshua and Caleb or the other ten spies. Joshua, in his final exhortation to the people of Israel, told them to choose between the gods they left behind in Egypt, the gods of the Amorites or the Lord. Ruth had to choose between going with Naomi or returning to her own country. The disciples had to choose between obeying Jesus' command to preach the good news or the command of the Jewish religious leaders to keep silent.

We do not always choose the best path. Even a man after God's own heart could make mistakes and follow his own understanding instead of God's. David knew the rules for the movement of the Ark of the Covenant. We will never know why he chose to move it by cart instead of having it carried by the priests as God had commanded. The consequences of his wrong choice were disastrous. But God, in His mercy, is quick to forgive anyone who humbly turns back to Him.

PERFORMANCE TIPS

1. Suggested props: pith helmets and safari jackets for the explorers, a map, a ruler, newspapers and chairs for the club.
2. The explorers should speak with a thick British accent and walk with a military bearing. They mistake posture for ability.
3. After the skit, tell the story of David moving the Ark of the Covenant to Jerusalem. Tell the class to listen for good and bad choices David made.

DISCUSSION QUESTIONS

1. What are some of the choices the explorers tried to make? What might have been the consequences of those choices?
2. How valuable is a map if you do not read it correctly? What can happen if you don't believe what the map tells you?
3. Why do you think the explorers wouldn't listen to their guide?
4. The Bible is a map for our lives. What are some of the ways it tells us to go?
5. Who are some of the guides in your life who can show you the correct path to follow?

ONE RIGHT ROAD

CHARACTERS
EXPLORER ONE
EXPLORER TWO
GUIDE

SCENE ONE

EXPLORER ONE *(consulting map)*: Here we are, right here.

EXPLORER TWO *(pointing on map)*: And the lost city of Beluba should be over there.

EXPLORER ONE: So we must go from here to there.

EXPLORER TWO *(measuring with a ruler)*: Shouldn't take long. It's only a few inches.

EXPLORER ONE: Now then, what would be the best way to get from here to there?

EXPLORER TWO *(tracing on map)*: We could go south, over this river. *(Scans the horizon.)* The south looks like an easy route.

EXPLORER ONE: But we might get our feet wet. I promised Mother not to get my feet wet. *(Traces on map.)* What about this northern route? Absolutely no rivers or lakes of any kind. No chance of getting my feet wet.

EXPLORER TWO: Capital! *(Scans horizon in other direction.)* It also appears to be easy going.

EXPLORER ONE: Good! Then it's decided. Where's that guide chappie?

GUIDE: *(Steps from behind explorers.)* Here.

EXPLORER TWO: Capital. We've decided upon our route.

EXPLORER ONE: *(Shows map to guide.)* We've decided to follow this northern route.

EXPLORER TWO: Why bother showing the map to him?

EXPLORER ONE: Quite. It's not as if he would know how to read it.

GUIDE: *(Studies map and turns map one-quarter turn.)* Eastern route not good.

EXPLORER TWO: I say! Were we looking at the map incorrectly?

EXPLORER ONE: By jove! So we were.

GUIDE *(pointing to map)*: Beluba city here.

EXPLORER TWO: It is NOT here. We're here. The city is THERE. *(To EXPLORER ONE.)* Chap doesn't even speak the Queen's English properly.

EXPLORER ONE: Quite! Good help is so hard to come by.

GUIDE: Go now. Toward setting sun.

EXPLORER TWO: Go west? I hardly think so, young man.

EXPLORER ONE: Quite. There are mountains to the west.

EXPLORER TWO: Don't relish the idea of crossing mountains.

GUIDE: Best route.

EXPLORER ONE: Nonsense! Look here! If we go a little to the north, we miss the mountains completely.

EXPLORER TWO: Capital!

GUIDE: Route no good. No water.

EXPLORER ONE: Excellent! Then I shan't get my feet wet. Mummy will be pleased.

EXPLORER TWO (*pointing*)**:** Onward!

GUIDE: Route no good. No water.

EXPLORER ONE: You've said that before.

GUIDE: Route no good. No water.

EXPLORER TWO: What is the matter with you, chap? We don't wish to go where our feet might get wet.

EXPLORER ONE: We could catch a cold. Be the death of us.

EXPLORER TWO: And our boots could get muddy.

EXPLORER ONE: And the tent could get all mildewy in the damp.

EXPLORER TWO: Best to go the dry route.

GUIDE: Need water to drink.

EXPLORER ONE: Oh. Yes. Hadn't thought of that.

EXPLORER TWO: Should be a consideration, I suppose.

EXPLORER ONE: See here, chap. Other routes would have water without mountains.

EXPLORER TWO: Yes. What about a bit to the south? No mountains there.

GUIDE: Go toward setting sun. Best route.

EXPLORER ONE: There's no reasoning with these people.

GUIDE: Go toward setting sun. Best route.

EXPLORER TWO: But if we go a bit to the south, we miss the mountains.

EXPLORER ONE: Saves all the hard work of climbing.

EXPLORER TWO: And the vegetation is lush. Should be plenty of water.

GUIDE: Too much water. Go toward setting sun.

EXPLORER ONE: There is just no pleasing this chap. First, no water. Now, too much.

EXPLORER TWO: Sounds just like a farmer.

EXPLORER ONE: Quite! Now then, guide chappie. We've decided. Southwest.

EXPLORER TWO: So lead on.

GUIDE: Swamps. Quicksand. Mosquitos.

EXPLORERS ONE and TWO: Mosquitos? Eeeww!

GUIDE: Go toward setting sun. Best route.

EXPLORER ONE: I hadn't realized this exploring would be so difficult. Wait!

EXPLORER TWO: What? Have you an idea?

EXPLORER ONE: Yes. Let's go back the way we came.

EXPLORER TWO: Capital! That was a very pleasant route.

GUIDE: But, Beluba city other direction.

EXPLORER ONE: But the club is this way.

EXPLORER TWO: Capital! I could use a soda right now.

EXPLORER ONE: Onward.

EXPLORER TWO: We'll find the lost city next year.

(ALL exit.)

SCENE TWO

(EXPLORERS enter club, sit in chairs and open newspapers.)

EXPLORER ONE: Good to be back in civilization.

EXPLORER TWO: Indeed it is.

EXPLORER ONE: I say! Did you read this bit about Hadley?

EXPLORER TWO: Saw his name, stopped reading. Insufferable chap, Hadley.

EXPLORER ONE: Made a bit of a splash, though.

EXPLORER TWO: Fell into the Thames, did he?

EXPLORER ONE: No. Listen. "Ronald Hadley, noted explorer..."

EXPLORER TWO: Noted? Hadley? Hardly. Nothing more than an amateur.

EXPLORER ONE: "...announced major archaeological find."

EXPLORER TWO: Chap couldn't find archaeology if he looked in a dictionary.

EXPLORER ONE: "...discovered lost city of Beluba."

EXPLORER TWO: He did what?

EXPLORER ONE: "...discovered lost city of Beluba. Donating treasures to British Museum in London."

EXPLORER TWO: Horned in on our expedition. Told you the chap was insufferable.

EXPLORER ONE: Quite.

THE ORPAH SHOW (DAVID'S DESIRE)

SCRIPTURE: 2 Samuel 11:1—12:23

SUGGESTED TOPICS: Obeying God; consequences of sin; making wise choices

BIBLE BACKGROUND

King David was a man after God's own heart. But in spite of his efforts to please God in all ways, being human, David still sinned. The difference between David and Saul was their attitude towards their sin. Whereas Saul sought an alibi for his sin, David admitted and repented (although sometimes only after a prompting from God), begging God's forgiveness. David's desire to please God led to God's greatest promise: the Messiah would come from the seed of David (see 2 Samuel 7:5-16).

Naturally, in Bible times, there were no afternoon television talk shows. But if there had been, and David were a guest on the show, what topic would hold the most interest for the hostess and her viewers? Would it be the good life David had led, his wise leadership, his conquering the land and establishing a peaceful kingdom? Or would the focus of the program be on the darker side of his life, exploring the times he failed?

PERFORMANCE TIPS

1. Suggested props: a microphone for Orpah, a crown for David.
2. When the audience asks questions, Orpah should go over to the person, holding the microphone for him or her to speak into.
3. David should not be portrayed as angry with Orpah. Rather, he is disappointed with himself and ashamed of his former conduct.
4. Orpah should encourage the audience members who want to discuss Bathsheba by smiling, nodding her head, etc., while appearing bored by questions about David's good conduct and leadership.

DISCUSSION QUESTIONS

1. Have you ever watched a TV talk show? What topics were discussed on the show?
2. Which do you think would be more important to a talk show host and producer, a sensational topic or a nonsensational topic? Why?
3. How did Orpah lead the conversation to topics of her choosing?
4. If David was a God-centered king, why would he commit sins like adultery and murder?
5. How might David have prevented himself from sinning?
6. Do you always make the right decisions in your life? What things can cause you to make wrong choices?
7. What can you do to help yourself make wise choices?
8. When you do make a wrong choice (sin), what should you do?

THE ORPAH SHOW (DAVID'S DESIRE)

CHARACTERS
ORPAH
DAVID
ANNOUNCER
MEMBER ONE
MEMBER TWO
MEMBER THREE
AUDIENCE

ORPAH: *(Looks at watch.)* OK, King David. It's almost air time. Do you have any last-minute questions?

DAVID: I just want to be sure that I understand what we'll be talking about. We will be talking about my reign and how I've helped Israel to become a strong and mighty nation under God, right?

ORPAH: *(Big smile.)* Sure. That's it exactly. Look out! It's show time!

ANNOUNCER: And now, live from our studios in Shiloh, it's "The Orpah Show!" Orpah's guest today is the king of Israel, David!

AUDIENCE: *(Loud cheers.)*

ORPAH: Yes, we are pleased to have David as our guest today. David, it's no surprise to anybody who knows you that you have led Israel into being the great and mighty nation that it has become. But has it ever surprised you?

DAVID: No, it hasn't really, Orpah...

ORPAH: That sounds a little conceited. What do you think, audience?

AUDIENCE: *(General murmurs of agreement.)*

DAVID: Please, let me explain. When I was younger, God anointed me to be king of Israel. I knew if I obeyed Him, He would prosper Israel under my leadership.

ORPAH: And you always try to obey God.

DAVID: Yes, that's true.

ORPAH: *(Leans toward DAVID.)* Maybe you could explain how this little incident with Bathsheba was obeying God.

DAVID: *(Leans away.)* Well, that was an incident I would rather not talk about. I did an evil thing and people suffered because of it. However, that subject is now closed.

ORPAH: It sounds to me as though you're trying to cover something up. What do you think, audience? Don't we want to hear the details of this?

AUDIENCE: *(Cheers and applause.)*

DAVID: *(Wipes brow.)* I assure you, I am not trying to cover anything up. All Israel knows about it. It's just that it's a rather sordid affair that I would rather forget.

ORPAH: Well, not everybody here is from Israel, so why don't you just tell us the basic story and be done with it?

DAVID: There's really not much to tell. I saw a beautiful woman having her evening bath, I coveted her, we conceived a child together, and I had her husband killed so he wouldn't learn about it. Then, I married her myself. As I said, it's an ugly story. I'm not proud of it, and I would rather forget it.

ORPAH: We have to take a short break, but we'll be right back with King David.

DAVID: Are we off the air?

ORPAH: Yes. This show is going to be a great one!

DAVID: I thought you said that we would be talking about how Israel was becoming a strong and mighty nation. I do not intend to sit here and have you try to embarrass me and my family for the entertainment of your audience. I'm leaving. *(Gets up to leave.)*

ORPAH: *(Holds up hand.)* But you swore an oath that you would come on the show. Is your word nothing but empty sounds?

DAVID: But this is not the kind of show that I agreed to come on.

ORPAH: You didn't swear an oath to come on a special kind of show. You swore an oath to come on the Orpah Show. But, if you would rather leave and have all Israel say that their king's word is worthless....Besides, we're going to have audience questions now. I'm sure that many of them will want to know about the restoration of Israel's greatness.

DAVID: All right. I'll stay. But only because I swore an oath.

ANNOUNCER: And now, once again, here's Orpah!

ORPAH: Hi. We're back, talking with King David about how Israel has become a mighty nation once again, in spite of David's indiscretion with Bathsheba. Does our audience have any questions for King David?

MEMBER ONE: I'm not from Israel. But I understand that Israelites are not known for traveling around much. How did you manage to see Bathsheba without her husband learning about it?

DAVID: Please, I beseech you. This is something I'd rather not discuss.

ORPAH: *(Shoves mike in DAVID's face.)* Come on, King David, what are you trying to hide?

DAVID: I am NOT trying to hide anything! Very well. Her husband was one of my soldiers and they were out fighting Ammon at the time.

MEMBER ONE: But I thought that YOU always led your army into battle.

DAVID: Usually I did. But this once, I tarried in Jerusalem. *(Looks at ceiling.)* If only I had gone instead!

ORPAH: Let's take another question.

MEMBER TWO: How do you feel that God is leading Israel at this time?

DAVID: I believe that God is using me to subdue the surrounding countries so that Israel will have many years of rest and prosperity under her next king...

ORPAH: There's another question here?

MEMBER ONE: I don't understand this country and its customs. I thought that the women were modest. How did you see this Bathsheba woman bathing? Do you have public baths in Jerusalem?

DAVID: Must you continue this prying?

ORPAH: What are you trying to cover up, David?

DAVID: There is nothing to cover up! This is all public knowledge! I just hate talking about it. Very well. It is customary to bathe on the roof of one's house in the evening. It's usually quite private, but her house was next to mine and mine had a higher roof.

ORPAH: Another question?

MEMBER TWO: I was wondering...

ORPAH: Sorry. You've had a question before. Does somebody else have a question?

MEMBER THREE: Could you please tell us why you had Bathsheba's husband killed? You're the king! Why didn't you just take her for your wife and tell her husband that he would have to get another? That's the way civilized countries would do it.

DAVID: (Sighs.) Obviously I must resign myself to talking about this painful subject. Israel has different laws from all the other countries, because we worship the one true God. His ways are different from all others. I could not take Bathsheba away from Uriah, because God considers the marriage covenant to be sacred. Under Mosaic law, she was Uriah's wife until death.

MEMBER THREE: But you're the king! Why not just tell Uriah that you had blessed his family and that the child was yours? He should have been thrilled.

DAVID: By this time I had grown to love Bathsheba. Under Mosaic law, if a woman is found to be unfaithful in her marriage covenant, the punishment is death. I did not want Bathsheba to die.

MEMBER THREE: But why kill her husband, what's-his-name?

DAVID: Uriah.

MEMBER THREE: Yeah, him. Why kill him? Surely an intelligent man like you could trick him into thinking that the baby was his.

DAVID: I tried. But everything failed.

ORPAH: As long as we're discussing this anyway, how were you found out? Who would tattle on the king?

DAVID: Nobody tattled. I forgot during that time that nothing is hidden from God. He sent a prophet to rebuke me for my sin. Oh, the agony that I went through for the next seven days. And the trouble that still follows me.

ORPAH: Yes, you have another question?

MEMBER ONE: I'm going to be in Israel for a few more days. I wonder if, when I'm in Jerusalem, it would be possible to stop and see the child. If the mother is as beautiful as you say, and you are indeed a handsome man, why the child must be gorgeous!

DAVID: No! It's impossible! The child is dead! (Buries face in hands.) Oh, how long must I suffer for this sin? How long, O Lord?

ORPAH: I wish we could continue this show forever, but our time's up. Be with us tomorrow when all of David's sons will be here. We'll hear from each one why HE should already be crowned king. Until tomorrow, this is Orpah!

THE ORPAH SHOW II (DREAMS OF GLORY)

SCRIPTURE: 2 Samuel 15—18

SUGGESTED TOPICS: Respect for parents; family problems; consequences of disobedience

BIBLE BACKGROUND

Although King David was a God-centered king, he did not always make wise choices. God makes it clear to us that, although He is merciful and ready to forgive, He is also righteous. God's righteousness cannot permit the presence of sin, since sin is a direct attack on God. God demonstrated this perfectly balanced nature with David. The child born through adultery with Bathsheba died; Solomon, born of Bathsheba in wedlock, became king of Israel and is honored as the wisest man who ever lived.

Not all consequences of sin are a direct punishment of God. God reminds us that making the wrong choices will naturally result in problems. For instance, gluttony leads to weight problems, which in turn lead to health problems. In David's case, his lack of guidance as a parent led to conflicts within his family as each son vied for the position of David's successor. Absalom even went so far as to lead a revolt while David was still alive.

If the mythical "Orpah Show" were on the air and David's sons were guests, how might each one act in public?

PERFORMANCE TIPS

1. Suggested props: a microphone for Orpah, Bible-times costumes.

2. Orpah should hold the microphone for audience members when they ask questions.

3. To achieve the right sound in the fight scene, Absalom could hit his palm with his fist to mimic the sound of hitting Amnon.

4. After the skit, finish the story of Absalom's revolt.

DISCUSSION QUESTIONS

1. From their appearance on the talk show, which of David's sons do you think would be the best candidate for king? Why?

2. How does Absalom try to win people to his side?

3. What can we learn about David as we watch and listen to his sons?

4. Read Exodus 20:12. What does it mean to honor your father and your mother?

5. Does the Bible say to honor your parents only if they are good parents? How can you honor them even if they do wrong things?

THE ORPAH SHOW II (DREAMS OF GLORY)

CHARACTERS
ORPAH
ADONIJAH (AD-ah-NYE-jah)
SOLOMON
AMNON
ABSALOM (AB-suh-lum)
MEMBER ONE
MEMBER TWO

PRONUNCIATION GUIDE
Tamar (TAY-mar)

ORPAH: We're here today with some of the sons of King David. Each one is going to explain to us why he should be the next king of Israel. Welcome to the show, Absalom, Amnon, Adonijah and Solomon.

SONS: Happy to be here.

ORPAH: Instead of my asking each of you different questions, I'm going to ask you all the same one. What is wrong with the monarchy today and how would you fix it if you were king? Adonijah?

ADONIJAH: The current king is too old and relies too strongly on the advice of old men, like Nathan. If I were king, I would change the administration so that younger, more forward-thinking men were in charge. Of course I would not throw out all of the older men—not those who recognize the importance of new thinking, like Joab and Abiathar.

SOLOMON: When you criticize the king, you are criticizing our father. That's not right.

ADONIJAH: Listen, mama's boy! The future belongs to the bold. And that's ME!
(Hits chest with fist.)

AMNON: I think you're on the right track, Adonijah, but you're looking at it from the wrong perspective. We need younger men, that's true, but we need a complete overhaul of the legal system. I mean, look at all the laws we have now. They all date from MOSES' time! We particularly need to look at the laws concerning relations between stepbrothers and stepsisters.

ABSALOM: You come anywhere near my sister, Tamar, and you're a dead man.

AMNON: See? Even Absalom is a living relic of the past.

ABSALOM: *(Begins to rise.)* You come anywhere near Tamar and you'll soon be a DEAD relic.

SOLOMON: Brothers, let's not fight in public this way. Can't we settle any differences we may have in a peaceful manner?

ADONIJAH: Keep out, mama's boy. Let them tear each other apart!

ORPAH: We still haven't heard from you, Absalom. What would you do to improve the government in Israel?

ABSALOM: Unlike my brothers, I think that the basic laws are OK. What we need is better enforcement of existing laws. Dad did a great job in the past, but he's too old to effectively control his judges. What we need is someone who is young and vital enough to handle the problems that are being ignored by our public officials!

SOLOMON: Maybe we could be good sons and HELP our father.

AMNON: How can you help someone who won't change? He still thinks that those laws thought up by Moses are worth keeping!

ADONIJAH: *(Stands.)* If we want things to improve, we have to be ready to seize each opportunity that presents itself! Dad spends too much time seeking the advice of men like Nathan to get anywhere.

ABSALOM: I think that Solomon has a good point. I'm all for doing whatever I can to help Israel and her leaders.

ORPAH: We have to take a short break, but we'll be back with more from the sons of David after this message.

SOLOMON: But I didn't get a chance to say what I think needs to be done.

ORPAH: Sonny, all you've said so far is that things aren't too bad. That doesn't get ratings. People want to watch conflict, not wisdom and goodness. So get off your high horse and give us some fights worth watching!

SOLOMON: *(Stands.)* But it's not RIGHT.

ORPAH: *(Pushes him into seat.)* But it SELLS! And that's all that interests me. OK, boys. Sit down. We're ready to roll again....Hi. We're back. I wish you could all have been here during the break because we had a beautiful knock-down-drag-'em-out fight. Fortunately, we have it on videotape. Let's get a replay of that.

ABSALOM: I thought I told you to leave Tamar alone!

AMNON: All I SAID was that she's a good-looking woman!

ADONIJAH: What's the big deal, Absalom? She's my sister, too, and you don't see ME getting all worked up.

ABSALOM: *(Stands.)* Maybe you're just too stupid to know better! I'm warning you, Amnon. Leave her alone. *(Shakes fist.)* Don't even mention her NAME again!

More Bible Skits ©1994 Gospel Light. Permission granted to photocopy.

AMNON: It's a relatively free country, stepbrother. And I'm a son of the king. I'll talk about and see whoever I want....Ow! *(ABSALOM exaggerates a right hook; AMNON staggers back, holding jaw.)*

ORPAH: Nice right hook, Absalom. OK, audience. Do you have any questions for our guests before they beat each other up?

MEMBER ONE: My brother is a bond servant to another Israelite and has been for over six years now. But his current master has not released him. What can you do about it?

AMNON: Well, that's too bad. But he shouldn't have got in debt in the first place.

ADONIJAH: Go and see your brother. Tell him that when the time is ripe, he should run away and free himself. After all, the future belongs to the quick and the brave.

ABSALOM: Where are you from, friend?

MEMBER ONE: Gibeon.

ABSALOM: This is a travesty. It's almost unbelievable that things like this could be happening in Gibeon. The law clearly states in Deuteronomy 15:12 that your brother should be freed. *(Looks up to heaven.)* Unfortunately, I can't help you because I'm not the king and do not have any real power. But if *I* were king, I would have heard your complaint and have already had your brother freed from bondage.

SOLOMON: I think...

ORPAH *(quickly)*: Is there another question?

MEMBER TWO: I had some financial trouble a short time ago and had to borrow some money from a rich neighbor. But when I went to pay him back what I had borrowed, he said it was not enough. He wants fifty percent interest! Can you help me?

ADONIJAH: *(Shakes fist.)* Stand up to him. Tell him that's all he gets. Punch him in the nose if you have to. Remember, the future belongs to the guys with guts!

AMNON: If he has a good-looking sister, get close to her. She could probably get him to drop the interest rate considerably.

ABSALOM: Where are you from, my friend?

MEMBER TWO: I'm from Bethel.

ABSALOM: Oh, the horror of it! Even BETHEL has forgotten the laws of our fathers. I would not have thought that such injustice could happen in Bethel. We all know that unfair loans are a crime. It's right there in Leviticus 25:36. You are perfectly right. He cannot charge you interest. If only I were the KING—then I could DO something for you. Oh, how my soul cries out for you. How long, O Lord, must your people suffer oppression?

SOLOMON: Perhaps if we went to see Father, he would...

ORPAH: *(Interrupts.)* We're out of time. Be sure to tune in tomorrow when we look at the problems of intergalactic marriage.

COUNT THE COST

SCRIPTURE: 2 Samuel 24; 1 Chronicles 21:1; 22; 28; 29:1-22

SUGGESTED TOPICS: Listening to God; ignoring God's instructions; repentance

BIBLE BACKGROUND

How often are we faced with decisions that seem simple, but are really complex? Often, a choice that seems so natural has deeper implications. What could possibly be wrong with a king conducting a census of his army? By and of itself, nothing; but underlying the action itself is the reason for the action. David was not just academically curious as to how many soldiers he had, nor was he trying to estimate how much he would need to pay his army and make a budget. He was estimating his chances of victory in upcoming conflicts based solely on the strength of his army.

God reminded David that his actions as the leader of Israel would affect all of Israel. Consequences of allowing himself to slip away from God's guidance would influence the well-being of every citizen. David's census was a clear act of turning away from trust in God. In spite of such repeated failings, David never turned against God, nor did he complain of the treatment he received. Instead, he gave God the honor and glory for his victories and, when he sinned, he always returned to the forgiveness God was ready to offer to the humbled heart.

PERFORMANCE TIPS

1. Suggested props: Bible-times costumes, blueprints and plans for the Temple.
2. Possibly end the skit by having David read 1 Chronicles 29:10-19 to show the class his prayer for Israel and Solomon.

DISCUSSION QUESTIONS

1. Why was David wrong to count the soldiers in his army? Why do you think the people of Israel had to suffer a plague for three days because of David's sin?

2. Everybody sins (see Romans 3:23). What kind of sin happens in the life of a kid your age? How does this sin affect you? How does it affect the people around you?

3. What good choices have you made? How did these choices affect you? How did they affect the people around you?

COUNT THE COST

CHARACTERS
DAVID
SOLOMON
GAD
GUARD

PRONUNCIATION GUIDE
Araunah (uh-RAW-nuh)
plague (playg)

SCENE ONE

GUARD: Someone to see you, Sire.

DAVID: Is Joab finished counting the troops? Good. Send him in.

GUARD: No, Sire.

DAVID: What do you mean, "No, Sire"? *(Points.)* I ORDER you to send Joab in.

GUARD: I can't do that, Sire. Joab isn't here.

DAVID: Then who is?

GUARD: Gad, Sire.

DAVID: Gad? Good! God's prophet. Send him in.

GUARD: Immediately, Sire. If not sooner. *(Exits and GAD enters.)*

DAVID: Gad, it's good to see you.

GAD: Perhaps so. Perhaps not.

DAVID: Hey! Why so downcast? You can't be worried about the Philistines attacking, can you? Don't worry. I'm having the troops counted now. I think we'll find we've got all the manpower we need to stop anyone.

GAD: You think so?

> *(GUARD enters.)*

GUARD: Excuse the interruption, Sire. But Joab has finished the count. We've got eight hundred thousand soldiers in Israel and five hundred thousand in Judah.

DAVID: Wonderful! You see, Gad. We can defeat ANYONE with this army.

GAD: Can you defeat the Lord God Almighty?

DAVID: Of course not. I'm not at war with HIM.

GAD: You are NOW. Have you forgotten that the Lord is your sword and buckler? He goes out before you and defeats your enemies.

DAVID: Well, perhaps I overlooked it...

GAD: Why do you need to count your soldiers, to rely on their strength?

DAVID: Well, it's only human to want to know...

GAD: Exactly! Because you have sinned, the Lord is giving you three choices: you may choose three years, three months or three days.

DAVID: Well, that's very generous of Him...

GAD: You are to choose which Israel will have. Will it have three years of famine, three months of defeat at the hands of your enemies or three days of plague?

DAVID: What a choice. Oh, Lord, how could I have sinned? I beg you, Lord, put away the wrongdoing of your servant. I have done a foolish and wicked thing.

GAD: The Lord awaits your answer. Famine, defeat or plagues?

DAVID: Must I choose? MUST this punishment happen?

GAD: It must.

DAVID: Then I choose three days of plague. For the Lord is merciful. Let me fall into the hands of God, but let me not fall into the hands of my human enemies.

GAD: So be it. The Lord has heard your answer.

SCENE TWO

GUARD: Sire, the latest figures are in. Seventy thousand have died in the last three days.

DAVID: Why, oh why was I such a fool? *(Falls to his knees.)* Lord, *I* am the man responsible for the census of Israel. The people did nothing wrong. Take away the plague from them. Let me and my house be the ones to suffer.

(GAD enters.)

GAD: The Lord has heard your plea. He commands you to go to the threshing floor of Araunah and make an offering there.

DAVID: I shall do so. At once. Guard, do you think six hundred shekels of gold will be enough to buy a threshing floor? I will need to take enough with me to pay Araunah.

GUARD: Sire, live forever! But you will not need to buy the threshing floor. When you explain to Araunah why you want it, I'm sure he'll GIVE it to you. He might even throw in the wood and the oxen for the sacrifice.

DAVID: No. I will not take something from someone else to offer a sacrifice for my own sin. I failed to count the cost previously. No more. From now on, I THINK first. No longer will others pay for my folly. *(Beckons.)* Come! We must go and make the sacrifice immediately.

SCENE THREE

DAVID: *(Puts arm around SOLOMON.)* Solomon, I'm glad you're here. I have much to discuss with you.

SOLOMON: Fire away, Dad.

DAVID: As you know, for years I have wanted to build a house of worship in Jerusalem.

SOLOMON: Yes. Are you ready to start?

DAVID: No. The Lord will not allow me to build His house. For I am a man of war and the house of the Lord must be built by a man of peace. You are that man.

SOLOMON: Dad! I'm just a kid. I don't know how to build temples.

DAVID: I've thought of that. You don't have to worry. The Lord has promised to be with you. As He has been with me, so He will be with you. Remember what He has done for me; remember what He did for Moses. Be strong and of good courage.

SOLOMON: Well, I guess I could give it a shot. But how will I start?

DAVID: I have counted the cost. Look, here are blueprints for everything. Here's a complete list of the materials you'll need. And here's a detailed breakdown of the number of man hours necessary for completion.

SOLOMON: You seem to have thought of everything. Except for the money.

DAVID: I have counted the cost. I may never see the Temple completed, but I wish to contribute to it. Here's a little something to get you started. *(Indicates imaginary coins.)*

SOLOMON: *(Surprised.)* That's a hundred thousand talents of gold! And a million talents of silver!

DAVID: Not only that. There's so much bronze and iron available that I didn't even bother to weigh it. And there's timber and stones and the workmen necessary to fit and cut the materials.

SOLOMON: Then I have all I'll need!

DAVID: Nonsense. This is only the beginning. You'll need much more to complete a house of worship for the Almighty God. But all Israel will be at your command. Do you think, when they see what I have contributed, they will not also be moved to give what they can?

SOLOMON: This is such a huge task. I don't know if I can do it.

DAVID: *(Hand on SOLOMON's shoulder.)* You can, my son. Listen to God before you make decisions and you will be the wisest king the world will ever know. Count the cost. Listen to God and He will help you.

CHRISTMAS QUIZ

SCRIPTURE: Isaiah 9:6; 53:3-6; Jeremiah 23:5,6; Micah 5:2; Matthew 2:1,2,11; Luke 1:30-32; 2:8,25-30,36-38

SUGGESTED TOPICS: Fulfillment of prophecy; coming of the Savior; God's love for His people

BIBLE BACKGROUND

From the moment of the Fall, God had a plan for our salvation. The Old Testament sets the scene for God's dealing with His people and people's inability to live up to God's standards. Throughout history, one fact stands out above all others. If people were ever to be rescued from sin and the vast damages it has caused, God would have to do it Himself. This is the good news, the gospel of our Lord Jesus Christ. God loved the world so much that He gave His one and only Son (see John 3:16). Without the willing sacrifice of the perfect Son of God (i.e., God Himself), all people would be condemned to eternal punishment. But in the fullness of time, the Savior came to all who would receive Him.

PERFORMANCE TIPS

1. Suggested props: loud sports jacket and tie for the Quiz Master; Bible, chair and table for the judge; question cards for the Quiz Master; bells or buzzers for the contestants.

2. Have the teacher play the part of the Quiz Master. If possible, have the judge played by the pastor, an elder, a deacon or some other prominent person in the church. Contestants may respond as a group, or you may designate teams or individuals to compete against each other. Be creative!

3. Much of the skit will have to be ad-libbed, as the knowledge levels of each class will be different. Don't be afraid to give clues if necessary.

4. Answers may be oral or written. You might want to make up answer cards to give students multiple-choice answers and have the students hold up what they believe is the correct answer.

5. The skit could be used in conjunction with a Christmas party.

6. To extend the quiz, supplement with extra questions found on page 59 or write your own.

DISCUSSION QUESTIONS

1. What special event do we celebrate at Christmas? Why?

2. Why did God need to send a Savior?

3. Why was it important for God to give Old Testament promises and prophecies about the Savior?

4. What is sin? Is there sin in your life? Do you know anyone who never sinned?

5. How can you show God you are glad for His great gift given to us on that first Christmas?

EXTRA QUESTIONS FOR CHRISTMAS QUIZ

1. Why was Jesus born in a stable? (No room in the inn. See Luke 2:7.)

2. To whom did the angel tell the meaning of the name "Jesus"? (Joseph. See Matthew 1:21.) And why did the angel tell Joseph to give Him this name? (He would save His people from their sins. See Matthew 1:21.)

3. Who was the king in Jerusalem around the time of Jesus' birth? (Herod. See Matthew 2:1,2.) And how did Herod say he felt about the new King? (He said he wanted to worship Him. See Matthew 2:8.)

4. What was the name of the angel who came to Zechariah to tell him about the birth of John? (Gabriel. See Luke 1:19.)

5. How long did Mary stay with her cousin Elizabeth when she went to visit? (Three months. See Luke 1:56.)

Christmas Quiz

CHARACTERS

QUIZ MASTER

JUDGE

CONTESTANTS (All audience members)

QUIZ MASTER: Welcome to everyone's favorite game show, Holiday Quiz! I'm your favorite game show host, *(give name)*. Our contestants today are *(name contestants)*. This week's special holiday is...

(Give CONTESTANTS time to answer.)

QUIZ MASTER: Correct! Everybody scores one point! Now the contest really begins. First question, who is the Messiah?

(Give CONTESTANTS time to answer.)

QUIZ MASTER: Excellent! We have some truly great contestants today. Now, a multiple answer. For one point each, what are the names given to the Messiah in Isaiah, chapter 9?

(Give CONTESTANTS time to answer.)

QUIZ MASTER: This one's too tough for me. Judge, may we have the official answer?

JUDGE: *(Reads Isaiah 9:6.)*

QUIZ MASTER: Wow! There are four names there. How many got all four? OK. Next question. God promised to send the Messiah as Savior. According to Isaiah, why was God going to send the Savior?

(Give CONTESTANTS time to answer.)

QUIZ MASTER: What about it, Judge?

JUDGE: *(Reads Isaiah 53:3-6.)*

QUIZ MASTER: Wow! That's God's love for you! Ready for the next question? Alright! Who would be the Savior's most famous earthly ancestor?

(Give CONTESTANTS time to answer.)

QUIZ MASTER: Well, judge, right or wrong?

JUDGE: *(Reads Jeremiah 23:5,6.)*

QUIZ MASTER: So it was David. Now, the topic is geography. According to the book of Micah, in what town would the Savior be born?

(Give CONTESTANTS time to answer.)

QUIZ MASTER: Everybody sounds sure. Judge?

JUDGE: *(Reads Micah 5:2.)*

QUIZ MASTER: Lots of points to be awarded on that one. Now, shortly before the Savior was born, people wondered WHEN He would be born. God revealed this secret to someone. Who was the first person God told?

(CONTESTANTS answer. If nobody has an answer, give clues.)

QUIZ MASTER: Would God give such important news to a young girl? Judge?

JUDGE: *(Reads Luke 1:30-32.)*

QUIZ MASTER: So God does tell things to ordinary people. Now for an easy question. True or false? Jesus was born in a manger.

(Give CONTESTANTS time to answer.)

QUIZ MASTER: Judge?

JUDGE: Jesus was BORN in a stable and LAID in a manger. False.

QUIZ MASTER: Oh, ho! A trick question. You have to listen closely in this game. On the night Jesus was born, some people were outside in the dark. Who were they and what were they doing?

(Give CONTESTANTS time to answer.)

QUIZ MASTER: They sound pretty sure of themselves. How about it, Judge?

JUDGE: *(Reads Luke 2:8.)*

QUIZ MASTER: These contestants are too smart. We need a hard question. Aha! Here's one. When Jesus was forty days old, Mary and Joseph took him to the Temple to dedicate him. They also took an offering. What was their offering?

(Give CONTESTANTS time to answer.)

QUIZ MASTER: I thought that might stump you. Judge, what's the answer?

JUDGE: *(Reads Luke 2:24.)*

QUIZ MASTER: There, now we all know. Another tough question. Two people saw Jesus in the Temple: an elderly man and an elderly woman. What were their names?

(Give CONTESTANTS time to answer.)

QUIZ MASTER: Was anybody right?

JUDGE: *(Reads Luke 2:25-30 and 2:36-38.)*

QUIZ MASTER: Now, for another easy question. How many wise men came to see Jesus in the stable?

(Give CONTESTANTS time to answer.)

QUIZ MASTER: Let's hear the correct answer, Judge.

JUDGE: *(Reads Matthew 2:1,2 and 11. Emphasizes the word "house.")* That means NONE of the wise men saw Jesus in the stable.

QUIZ MASTER: There you have it. The three wise men saw Jesus in a house.

JUDGE: You weren't listening. The Bible doesn't say THREE wise men. It just says "wise men." It never tells us how many.

QUIZ MASTER: Oh. So I guess I have things to learn about Christmas, too. Let's tally up the scores and hand out the prizes.

GREETING CARDS

SCRIPTURE: 1 Samuel 25:1-19

SUGGESTED TOPICS: Ingratitude; thankfulness; wise and foolish actions; sharing

BIBLE BACKGROUND

David was on the run from Saul. Although Saul had temporarily sworn a peace treaty with David, David had seen Saul change his mind before. Wisely, David and his men chose to remain in the hills, away from Saul's power.

While living in the hills, David and his men assisted the hired shepherds of a wealthy Israelite from the house of Caleb, a man named Nabal (meaning "fool"). Nabal, in spite of his great wealth, compares poorly with both his famous ancestor and his "intelligent and beautiful" wife. At a festive time of year when most farmers were celebrating God's goodness, Nabal could not see beyond his profits. Shortsightedly, he saw no profit in sharing with one whom the king of Israel had been chasing through the hills. Rarely has lack of gratitude so vividly been the cause of a man's downfall.

PERFORMANCE TIPS

1. Suggested props: greeting cards, swords for David and his men.

2. Letter verses on the cards for the actors to read.

3. If some in the class have an artistic bent, have them decorate the front of the cards in an appropriate manner.

4. Complete the story. Show the class what happened to Nabal and Abigail as a result of their thankfulness or lack thereof.

DISCUSSION QUESTIONS

1. Why did David assume Nabal would be willing to share?

2. What might be some reasons Nabal was so selfish?

3. What was David's reaction to Nabal's selfishness? (See 1 Samuel 25:34.)

4. What good things has God given you? How have you repaid God?

5. How can you show God that you are thankful for what He has done?

GREETING CARDS

CHARACTERS
DAVID
NABAL (NAY-bal)
ABIGAIL
FIRST MAN
SECOND MAN
SERVANT

SCENE ONE

DAVID: What's all the noise?

FIRST MAN: Sheep.

DAVID: I know it's sheep. But why so MUCH noise?

SECOND MAN: Because it's sheep shearing time.

DAVID: Sheep shearing time! I remember it well. A time of festivity, rejoicing. Let's have a party!

FIRST MAN: I wish we could.

DAVID: Why not? I hereby decree this to be a feast day!

SECOND MAN: But we have nothing to feast with.

DAVID: True. We've been on the run from Saul. What DO we have?

FIRST MAN: A few loaves of bread...

SECOND MAN: A bit of dried fruit...

FIRST MAN: A little beef jerky...

DAVID: Not exactly a feast.

SECOND MAN: No.

DAVID: Aha! An idea. All the time we've been camped here, we've protected the flocks and the shepherds of Nabal. If someone had done this for my dad, he would have already sent a gift over to them.

FIRST MAN: Then, why didn't Nabal send us anything?

DAVID: He probably doesn't know what we've done. His shepherds just haven't reported it to him. Here! *(Hands card to MEN.)* Take this card to Nabal with our warmest greetings.

SCENE TWO

FIRST MAN *(walking):* Do you think Nabal will share some of his flock with us?

SECOND MAN *(walking):* Well, of course he will. He's rich! He has three thousand sheep and a thousand goats.

FIRST MAN: But you KNOW how rich people can be.

SECOND MAN: Nonsense! Rich people are just like other people.

FIRST MAN: But why would he share with us?

SECOND MAN: Because, if we hadn't been out there, protecting his flocks and shepherds, he would probably have lost lots of sheep and goats—if not to the wild animals, then to the Philistines.

FIRST MAN: That's true.

SECOND MAN: And we're coming from David. You know how well respected David is.

FIRST MAN: True again. You're right. Nabal will be more than happy to share with us.

SECOND MAN: Look! There he is. Remember, David said to be respectful.

FIRST MAN: *(Holds out hand.)* Hello, neighbor.

NABAL *(snarling)*: What do you want?

SECOND MAN: *(Hands card to Nabal.)* We come bringing the warmest regards of our master, David.

NABAL *(snarling)*: What's this? Some cheap card? Let's see. *(Reads card.)*

> "Peace be to you and to your house,
>
> Your children and your loving spouse.
>
> May all you touch turn into gold
>
> And all you give return tenfold."

So, what does David want in return for this cheap sentiment?

FIRST MAN: We have lived on the hills, among your shepherds...

SECOND MAN: During that time, we helped protect your flocks from all dangers...

FIRST MAN: In fact, during this past year, you haven't lost so much as a single lamb.

SECOND MAN: Don't take our word for it. Ask your men. They'll tell you.

NABAL *(snarling)*: Cut the fancy talk and get down to it. What do you want?

FIRST MAN: David only asks that if we have found favor in your sight...

SECOND MAN: Perhaps, during this glad time of harvest, you would be willing to share a small amount of your good fortune.

NABAL *(snarling)*: I thought so. Looking for a handout. Here! *(Hands men a card.)* Take THIS to your precious David. And tell him that's all he gets!

SCENE THREE

(MAN gives card to DAVID.)

DAVID: Let's see. What does Nabal have to say? *(Reads card.)*

> "Who is this man you say you serve?
>
> I've never met him or his kin.
>
> Because he's David, he thinks he deserves

More Bible Skits ©1994 Gospel Light. Permission granted to photocopy.

Meat from my table or grain from my bin?

He's nothing more than a common thief

Who's run away from his master, Saul.

I'll give him nothing else but grief

And kick him out, should he come to call."

(Looks up.) Is this some kind of a joke?

FIRST MAN: I don't think so.

SECOND MAN: He seemed serious.

DAVID: Then he wants WAR. Everyone! Put on your swords! We've got work to do.

FIRST MAN: Swords?

SECOND MAN: Are we going into battle?

DAVID: We kept everything Nabal owns safe for the whole season. Is this our reward? I swear to you, by morning, he will be left with nothing!

SCENE FOUR

SERVANT: And that's what happened. Our master was most rude to David's men.

ABIGAIL: Did these men truly protect you and the flocks?

SERVANT: Truly, they did. They were like a strong, protective wall about us, night and day. We knew we were safe with them on guard.

ABIGAIL: I can't believe Nabal would treat David that way! But then again, knowing Nabal, I CAN believe it.

SERVANT: Madam, please think of something to do. Quickly! For David is a man of war. I don't think he will take this insult lightly.

ABIGAIL: You're right. Get me two hundred loaves of bread, two bottles of wine, the meat from five sheep, five measures of corn, one hundred clusters of raisins and, oh—two hundred cakes of figs. Load them onto donkeys and start toward David's camp. I'll follow, just as soon as I find the right card to give David.

SERVANT: Even as you speak, it is done, Madam. *(Exits.)*

ABIGAIL: Let's see. *(Pulls several cards from pocket and thumbs through them.)* Ah! Here's the perfect one. *(Reads card.)*

"David, my lord, long may you live;

Accept this humble gift I give.

Nabal's name translates as 'fool'

He lacks the sense God gave a mule!

Put Nabal's sin upon my soul

Then let our friendship be made whole."

I just hope this does the trick. *(Sighs.)* Men! Always ready to quarrel!

SHEPHERD'S PSALM

SCRIPTURE: 2 Samuel 23:8-17; Psalm 23

SUGGESTED TOPICS: Friendship; trusting in God; thankfulness

BIBLE BACKGROUND

David's life was not idyllic. Being the youngest of eight sons, he had often been regarded as the least important. When Samuel was sent to anoint the next king of Israel from among Jesse's sons, David was tending the flock and nobody thought to call him for the sacrifice. When Goliath scorned the Israelite army and David asked why no one would fight him, older brother Eliab suggested David only came down to get a thrill by watching a battle (see 1 Samuel 17:28). Faithfully serving Saul won David favor until he became more popular than the king. Then, Saul sought to kill him, forcing David into a life on the run as a fugitive.

Even when he became king, David's life had its valleys. The Lord was with him and helped him to overcome his enemies, but temptations beset him. In a moment of weakness, He coveted Bathsheba. The child born from their illicit union died at the hand of the Lord. David's sons continually fought among themselves and, eventually, Absalom attempted to overthrow his father.

Through his trials, David learned to depend upon the goodness of the Lord. When David sinned, he repented and asked for the Lord's forgiveness. And when David unintentionally sent three of his men on a fool's errand (to draw water from a well in enemy territory), he demonstrated his love and concern for his men by giving the water as an offering to the Lord, claiming the water represented the blood of the three soldiers who had risked their lives to obtain the water

The Bible does not tell us when David wrote Psalm 23. He might have written it as a young man tending the flocks. More likely, he wrote it later in life, remembering peaceful times on the hill with his father's flock, likening the Lord's care for him to the ways he had cared for his family's sheep.

PERFORMANCE TIPS

1. Suggested props: pen and pad for David, Bible-times costumes.

2. The entire psalm may be written out on the pad for David to read.

DISCUSSION QUESTIONS

1. Why would David write a psalm using a shepherd as a metaphor (word picture)? If you wanted to express similar feelings, what kind of metaphor might you choose?

2. How do you think David's three mighty men would have felt when they first brought back the water from Bethlehem and gave it to David? Why?

3. David had many hardships in his life. How did they affect his attitude toward God?

4. If you have a friend who would risk his or her life for you, how could you show your gratitude to that person for his or her friendship?

5. Jesus gave His life on the cross for you. How can you give thanks to Jesus for His gift?

SHEPHERD'S PSALM

CHARACTERS
DAVID
BENAIAH (beh-NYE-ah)

PRONUNCIATION GUIDE
Josheb-Basshebeth (JAH-sheb-bah-SHEB-eth)
Eleazar (el-ee-AY-zur)
Shammah (SHAM-ah)

DAVID *(speaking as he writes)*: "...dwell in the house of the Lord forever."

BENAIAH: Hey, chief! Whatcha doin'?

DAVID: Writing a psalm.

BENAIAH: You got a catchy tune for this one?

DAVID: Not yet. I've just finished the lyrics. I haven't started on the tune yet.

BENAIAH: Can I hear it?

DAVID: Well, I'd like to wait until I have the music...

BENAIAH: Please? Pretty please? With sugar on it?

DAVID: OK. For a man of war you make some strange pleadings.

BENAIAH: Yeah. But they work. Lay the psalm on me.

DAVID: *(Clears throat.)*

BENAIAH *(looking at paper)*: How do you spell that?

DAVID: That's not part of the psalm. I was just clearing my throat.

BENAIAH: Oh.

DAVID: *(Reads.)* "The Lord is my shepherd, I shall not want."

BENAIAH *(gasping)*: Ah!

DAVID: *(Looks up.)* What? Did you hear something? Is the enemy approaching?

BENAIAH: No. I was just surprised by your poem.

DAVID: Why?

BENAIAH: You just said you didn't want the Lord to be your shepherd.

DAVID: No, I didn't.

BENAIAH: Sure you did. You said, "The Lord's a shepherd I don't want."

DAVID: No. I said "The Lord is my shepherd, I shall not want." Didn't you hear the pause after the word shepherd?

BENAIAH: Sure, but the words are still the same.

DAVID: You don't understand. These are two thoughts. First, I affirm that the Lord IS my shepherd. Then, I continue to say that he gives me all I need: "I shall not want."

BENAIAH: I still don't get it. "Want" means you wish something was different.

DAVID: Here's another way to say it. See if you can understand it. "The Lord leads me and gives me everything I need, so I do not want for anything."

BENAIAH: That I understand. You should change your psalm.

DAVID: But the other way is better poetry. Besides, if you hear the whole poem, you'll understand the meaning.

BENAIAH: OK. I'll listen, but I still think you ought to change that.

DAVID: OK, try this on for size: "The Lord is my shepherd, I shall not BE IN want."

BENAIAH: Yeah, much better. Go on.

DAVID: "He makes me lie down in green pastures, He leads me beside quiet waters."

BENAIAH: I don't know. Shouldn't He give you a bed to sleep in? And maybe some wine instead of just water?

DAVID: No. You don't understand. The psalm is a metaphor.

BENAIAH: You met a what?

DAVID: A metaphor. The psalm talks about the Lord as being my shepherd. That means, I am a...*(Waits for BENAIAH to fill in.)*

BENAIAH: Sheep. I get it. You're a little, woolly, dumb, fuzzy...

DAVID: OK. So. The psalm tells us this shepherd finds good places for His sheep to eat and drink. Green pastures and still waters.

BENAIAH: I get it. Metaphor. I'll have to remember that word.

DAVID: *(Reads.)* "The Lord is my shepherd, I shall not be in want.

He makes me lie down in green pastures,

He leads me beside quiet waters, He restores my soul.

He guides me in paths of righteousness for His name's sake.

Even though I walk through the valley of the shadow of death, I will fear no evil,

For You are with me; Your rod and Your staff, they comfort me."

BENAIAH: Where's that valley? I've never heard of it.

DAVID: It's part of the metaphor. See if you can figure it out.

BENAIAH: *(Scratches head, thinks hard.)* Oh!

DAVID: You understand?

BENAIAH: I think so. If you're in a valley then there's lots of shadows. And these shadows are all death. So, it's like, even if you're in danger, you're not really afraid because you know God's there.

DAVID: That's the idea.

BENAIAH: So that's why you haven't been afraid, even while Saul's been chasing you.

DAVID: That's it.

BENAIAH: Then, your men aren't important to you? You don't need us?

DAVID: Of course I need you. All of you. You men are part of the Lord's "rod and staff" to me. You are one of the wonderful gifts God has given me.

BENAIAH: But when Josheb-Basshebeth, Eleazar and Shammah gave you a gift, you threw it away.

DAVID: No, I didn't. I made an offering to the Lord.

BENAIAH: It looked to me like you poured the water they gave you on the ground.

DAVID: Yes, I did. Don't you understand why I did it?

BENAIAH: No. I was surprised that the guys weren't angry.

DAVID: They weren't angry because they understood. Remember what happened?

BENAIAH: Sure. You were sitting around having a pity party...I mean...

DAVID: No, you're right. I was only foolishly feeling sorry for myself.

BENAIAH: Well, we were near Bethlehem, near where you were born. But you couldn't go to Bethlehem because the Philistines set up their camp there.

DAVID: That's right. And because I was feeling sorry for myself, I began to complain. I said, "If only I could drink from Bethlehem's well. Boy! That's the best water in the whole world."

BENAIAH: So Josheb-Basshebeth, Eleazar and Shammah, risking their lives, crept through the enemy lines and got some water for you. And then you threw it away.

DAVID: No. I offered it to the Lord! You see, when I saw how much my soldiers would risk for me, I realized how I shouldn't complain. They risked being killed just to bring me a drink of water.

BENAIAH: Which you threw away.

DAVID: I couldn't drink that water! By risking their lives, my soldiers had made that water as precious as their blood. If I drank it, I would be saying "Go ahead, risk your lives for a glass of water. Your lives aren't important."

BENAIAH: Oh.

DAVID: So, I made an offering to the Lord. By pouring the water on the ground, I was thanking Him for giving me such good and faithful friends. Friends I didn't deserve.

BENAIAH: So that's why they weren't angry. Oh—the poem.

DAVID: It's right here.

BENAIAH: Yeah. Read me some more.

DAVID: It's almost finished.

"You prepare a table before me in the presence of my enemies.

You anoint my head with oil; my cup overflows."

BENAIAH: That doesn't sound like sheep. Oh, I get it. The metaphor about sheep is finished.

DAVID: Right.

BENAIAH: So you're saying the Lord shows you honor when your enemies are watching. And He gives you so much, it runs out of your cup.

DAVID: Right. To continue,

"Surely goodness and love will follow me all the days of my life,

And I will dwell in the house of the Lord forever."

BENAIAH: That's a good poem. I'm glad you told me all this. Now I know for sure that you care about us just like we care about you. Good night, David.

DAVID: Good night, Benaiah.

PRAY, TELL ME

SCRIPTURE: Psalm 27:7,8

SUGGESTED TOPICS: Prayer; patience

BIBLE BACKGROUND

One of the evidences of David as "a man after God's own heart" is his readiness to pray. We see him dancing in praise, repenting of his sin, pleading with God for the life of his child, asking that his long-time advisor's counsel will not aid Absalom's rebellion against him. The glimpses we see of David's life and the many psalms he wrote provide a rich tapestry of communion with God in a wide variety of situations. For David, prayer was not an activity relegated to periodic visits to the Tabernacle, nor was it a device to fall back on when nothing else worked. Instead, prayer was woven into the fabric of his life, a life filled with awareness of God's constant presence.

PERFORMANCE TIPS

1. Suggested props: a Bible for Jenny.
2. Consider having others read portions of the applicable Scripture (e.g., 2 Samuel 12:16,17,22; Psalm 3; 51:1-4,9-13; 92:1-5) during or after the skit.
3. Read Matthew 6:5-13 with the class.

DISCUSSION QUESTIONS

1. Why do you think Jamie's prayer wasn't answered?
2. What other kinds of prayer are there? Give an example of that kind of prayer.
3. Does God promise to give us everything we want? Why might He not give us something?
4. If your prayer doesn't seem to be answered, does that mean you're doing something wrong? What else might it mean?
5. Why should we pray?

PRAY, TELL ME

CHARACTERS
JAMIE
JENNY

PRONUNCIATION GUIDE
Bathsheba (bath-SHEE-buh)
Uriah (yoo-REYE-uh)

(JENNY enters, JAMIE is seated on the floor in a contorted position.)

JENNY: Hi, Jamie. What are you doing? Some new kind of exercise?

JAMIE: Nope. I'm trying to figure out this prayer thing.

JENNY: What's to figure out?

JAMIE: Well, I didn't get what I asked for, so I figure I did something wrong. Maybe I was praying in the wrong position. So, I'm experimenting.

JENNY: That's just plain silly.

JAMIE: I'm not so sure. But this is uncomfortable. Just a minute. *(Changes to a normal position.)* Whew! That's better.

JENNY: Now, explain what that was all about.

JAMIE: I told you. I've been doing something wrong when I pray. So, I'm trying new positions.

JENNY: What makes you think you've been doing something wrong?

JAMIE: Well, three days ago, I was lying in bed and I prayed, "Lord, give me a new bicycle." Next day, nothing. So that night, I sat in a chair and prayed, "Lord, give me a new bicycle." The next day, nothing. So last night, I knelt and prayed, "Lord, give me a new bicycle." This morning, nothing. I've used up all the positions I know. I have to find some new ones.

JENNY: Do you really believe that your physical position when you pray makes a difference?

JAMIE: Well, it must. Those yoga guys have all kinds of special positions.

JENNY: But it doesn't mean they know God!

JAMIE: You're right. I'll bet it's the words! I need to use different words. Let's see. How about this? "O, Lord, granteth this Thy servant whateth he wisheth. Showeth Thine great giving power and giveth to me a new bicycle."

JENNY: Oh, brother.

JAMIE: You don't think it sounded spiritual enough?

JENNY: I think it sounded stupid. You can't impress God with the way you stand or the words you say.

JAMIE: Well, I've got to impress Him somehow. I really want a new bike.

JENNY: I think you need to learn a little something about prayer.

JAMIE: Yeah, like how to get God to give me the stuff I want.

JENNY: No. You need to learn what prayer IS.

JAMIE: That's easy. Prayer is asking God to give you stuff.

JENNY: No it isn't. It's talking with God. And it's not just asking for stuff.

JAMIE: It isn't? What else could it be?

JENNY: First, it's praise.

JAMIE: You mean, I should say, "Good job, God!" Like that?

JENNY: Not exactly. *(Opens Bible.)* Here, look at Psalm 92. That's one of David's prayers of praise to God.

JAMIE: I thought psalms were poems.

JENNY: They are, but poems can be prayers. See how David says to praise God? He says you can sing or play a musical instrument. And when David brought the Ark of the Covenant to Jerusalem, people praised by shouting and dancing. Praise is thanking God for who He is and the wonderful things He has done. *(Closes Bible.)*

JAMIE: But how is that going to get me a new bicycle?

JENNY: FORGET the bicycle for a minute! Prayer is important.

JAMIE: I don't see what this praise stuff does for me.

JENNY: It helps to remind you of who GOD is. And who YOU are.

JAMIE: If you say so. What else is prayer?

JENNY: Another kind of prayer is confession.

JAMIE: Con-fes-sion. Hmm. I don't like the sound of that.

JENNY: Why not? Confession is only telling God you've sinned.

JAMIE: Yeah. But if I tell Him, maybe He won't give me my new bicycle.

JENNY: The bike, again! Do you think God doesn't KNOW you've sinned?

JAMIE: Well, no. But if He already knows, why should I tell Him again?

JENNY: Confession isn't for GOD to know what's going on. It helps us to see how we need God's help. *(Opens Bible.)* Look at Psalm 51. Most people think David wrote this after he sinned with Bathsheba.

JAMIE: You mean after he stole that guy's wife away and killed the guy?

JENNY: Uriah.

JAMIE: I'm what?

JENNY: The dead guy's name was Uriah.

JAMIE: Oh.

JENNY: David's prayer here shows God's love. Confession helps us, because it reminds us that if we are sorry for our sins, God is willing to forgive. It also helps us to remember that we're not perfect but that God's strength is there to help us. *(Closes Bible.)*

JAMIE: And THEN God will give me my new bicycle.

JENNY: Bicycles! Aagh!

JAMIE: What's wrong with bicycles?

JENNY: Nothing. But you're supposed to be learning about prayer! Another type of prayer is intercession.

JAMIE: That's when you go to the snack bar and get a drink. Kind of a break between prayers.

JENNY: Not interMISSION. InterCESSION. Praying for someone ELSE besides yourself!

JAMIE: No way! If Joey wants a bike, let HIM pray for it. There's not enough to go around. I'm praying for my OWN bike.

JENNY: I'm not talking about bikes! I'm talking about people! Aren't people more important than bikes?

JAMIE: Not if you want to get to the park in a hurry.

JENNY: AAGH!

JAMIE: Well, I guess most of the time people are more important. But everyone can pray for themselves, can't they?

JENNY: What about in 2 Samuel 12? David prayed for his little baby. Could a baby pray for itself?

JAMIE: Well, I guess not.

JENNY: And what about people in comas? Can they pray for themselves?

JAMIE: Well, I guess not.

JENNY: And what about people who don't know God? Can they pray for themselves?

JAMIE: Well, maybe not. But God doesn't care about them.

JENNY: Of COURSE He does! He loves ALL people enough to die on a cross for them.

JAMIE: Oh. Yeah.

JENNY: And other Christians need prayer. Nobody can pray perfectly. So we help each other by praying for each other.

JAMIE: Great! *(Punches JENNY playfully.)* So you can help me pray for a new bike!

JENNY: Which leads us to another type of prayer. Petition.

JAMIE: What's that? Are we finally getting around to asking for stuff?

JENNY: That's one way to describe it.

JAMIE: Good! This is the one I need. How do I get my new bike?

JENNY: Maybe you don't.

JAMIE: Don't tell me God doesn't give stuff to people. I've heard people thanking God for giving them stuff. Right in church, I've heard it.

JENNY: I didn't say God doesn't give. But He gives what's best for us, and He gives it in His time. *(Opens Bible.)* Look in 2 Samuel 15:31. One of David's prayers was for God to have Absalom's counselor give him bad advice. And God answered David's petition. And in Psalm 3, David tells how he feels about God's answer.

JAMIE: I TOLD you God gives people stuff. So how come I don't get my bike?

JENNY: I didn't say you won't get a bike. I said, maybe you won't get it. Look at Matthew 26:39. Jesus didn't want to suffer pain on the cross. He asked His Father to be spared that pain. But Jesus also said, "You make the decision, Father. Do whatever is best."

JAMIE: But I don't WANT whatever is best. I want a BIKE. Maybe if I stand on my head and hold my breath...

O WORSHIP THE KING

SCRIPTURE: 2 Samuel 8:9—9:12; Psalm 96

SUGGESTED TOPICS: Keeping promises; friendship

BIBLE BACKGROUND

David's regard for the Lord caused his behavior to differ vastly from that of other kings of his time. Allowing the relatives, particularly sons and grandsons, of the former king to live was considered grave foolishness. As long as they lived, so did the possibility of a rebellion to restore the throne to the former dynasty. This fear sometimes grew to extreme paranoia, as evidenced by the actions of Athaliah (see 2 Kings 11:1-3). David, however, recognized that to worship God with words while being vindictive and unjust would be the worst form of hypocrisy. So David, being a man of his word, fulfilled his oath sworn to Jonathan years before (see 1 Samuel 20:42).

Joab was a man who swore his allegiance to David. However, he was not always sympathetic to what he saw as David's weaknesses (see 2 Samuel 3:23-27; 19:5-7). Although he is not mentioned as being present when David interviewed Ziba, the skit uses him as the one man in David's army who would not be afraid to question David's wisdom, and thereby prod David to explain the meaning of true worship.

PERFORMANCE TIPS

1. Suggested props: crown for David, chairs for David and Ziba, weapons for Joab (sword, spear, shield, etc.), Bible-times costumes.

2. Consider having readers read Psalm 96 when Joab refers to it.

3. Ziba should be suspicious of David and indicate this by his manner. He knows that new kings always killed off all the former king's sons and grandsons.

4. Joab is a man of war. He should act rough, with a loud voice and large gestures.

DISCUSSION QUESTIONS

1. Why do you think Ziba would be so afraid of David?

2. Why would Joab think David would want to kill Mephibosheth?

3. In the skit, what three ways did David use to worship God?

4. What other ways can you worship God?

More Bible Skits ©1994 Gospel Light. Permission granted to photocopy.

O Worship the King

CHARACTERS
DAVID

JOAB

ZIBA (ZEE-buh)

PRONUNCIATION GUIDE
Mephibosheth (muh-FIB-uh-sheth)

Tou (too)

JOAB: *(Hauls ZIBA into the court.)* Here! I found him, my lord!

DAVID: Joab! I asked you to BRING Ziba to me.

JOAB: Well? That's what I did.

DAVID: There are different ways of escorting a person. Now, Ziba...

ZIBA: *(Falls to his knees and pleads.)* Forgive me, my Lord. I didn't mean to do it. It wasn't my fault...

DAVID: Stop! Stop! Stop! What wasn't your fault?

ZIBA: Whatever it was that made you bring me here.

JOAB: Give me three minutes with him and he'll confess!

DAVID: Confess to WHAT?

JOAB: Whatever you want him to confess to.

DAVID: I don't want him to confess to anything!

JOAB: You don't?

ZIBA: You don't?

DAVID: No. Come. Get off your knees and sit here. *(ZIBA sits.)* Now. You were one of Saul's servants...

ZIBA: *(Falls to his knees.)* Forgive me, my lord. I was young and foolish. I didn't know what I was doing. Never would I do such a thing again...

DAVID: Stop! Stop! Stop! What's the matter with you?

ZIBA: I have a slight cold, but other than that...

DAVID: I mean, why are you acting so strangely? Get up and sit down.

JOAB: You heard the king! *(Pulls ZIBA up.)* Get to your feet and sit down. *(Forces ZIBA into chair.)*

DAVID: Thank you, Joab. But I think he could have managed himself. Now, Ziba. You were one of Saul's servants.

ZIBA *(cautiously)***:** Yes.

DAVID: So you should know if any of Saul's grandchildren are still alive.

ZIBA *(cautiously)***:** Yes.

DAVID: Well?

ZIBA: Well...

JOAB: Answer the king! Before I...

DAVID: Joab! Please. Tell me, Ziba. Are any still alive?

ZIBA: There is one, my lord. But he's no threat to you.

DAVID: Ah! So THAT'S it. Ziba, I mean no harm to him. I only ask because I wish to show kindness to him.

ZIBA: There is one named Mephibosheth. But he's lame, so you don't have to worry about him.

DAVID: I'm NOT worried about him. I told you. Because of my friendship with Jonathan, I want to show kindness to any of his sons who may still be living. Please, Ziba, go and bring him to me.

ZIBA: As you wish, my lord. *(Exits.)*

JOAB: I don't get it. *(Pauses.)* Oh! Now I get it. You are clever!

DAVID: What do you mean?

JOAB: He thought you wanted to harm this Muffy—whatever the kid's name is. So he's got him hidden and you couldn't find him. Now, you've got him convinced that you don't want to hurt the kid, so he'll come right to the palace. Then, you'll kill him.

DAVID: Why would I do that?

JOAB: Because that's what kings DO.

DAVID: Kings who don't worship God may do that. I do not.

JOAB: Sure you do.

DAVID: What?

JOAB: Sure you worship God. I've seen you pray and write poems to Him.

DAVID: I meant, other kings may kill the former king's grandchildren. I don't.

JOAB: Oh! See, I thought you said you didn't worship God. But what's worshiping God got to do with making a sound political decision?

DAVID: Everything! Worship is a part of life.

JOAB: Naw, it's only when you write poems to God. Like that "sing a new song to the Lord" one. I like that one. Has a real catchy tune.

DAVID: Oh, no. Worship is much more than that. Remember when King Tou sent me that gift of gold, silver and bronze!

JOAB: Yeah. *(Looks around.)* Whatever happened to it?

DAVID: As an act of worship, I gave it to the Lord.

JOAB: You mean it's in HEAVEN?

DAVID: No. It has been dedicated to the Lord, so it can only be used by the priests in the Tabernacle to help all of Israel worship God.

JOAB: That's a pretty expensive way to worship. I should think poetry would be enough.

DAVID: Nothing I could give would be enough. This was simply a token, a symbol to show God that I recognize where my strength comes from.

JOAB: OK, but what about this Messy-fish—whatever his name is? You're actually planning to let him live?

DAVID: Of course! He's Jonathan's son!

JOAB: Precisely my point.

DAVID: God gave me the best friend I ever had. Should I repay God for this kindness by destroying the son of that friend? Heaven forbid!

JOAB: But he's a threat.

DAVID: If God should choose to replace me on Israel's throne, so be it. But I will worship God by showing kindness to the son of Jonathan. He will be honored in this court as if he were my own son. Do I make myself clear?

JOAB: As clear as an open window on a cloudless summer day. I still don't understand it; but mine is not to reason why. I will obey your orders, as always, my king.

DAVID: Thank you, Joab. You are a good and trusted friend.

MAKE A WISH

SCRIPTURE: 1 Kings 3

SUGGESTED TOPICS: Wisdom; seeking God's guidance

BIBLE BACKGROUND

During the long reign of David, the nation of Israel was united and able to triumph over her surrounding enemies. After years of war, the country was ready to enjoy peace, and needed a strong successor on David's throne. In spite of the machinations of David's other sons, Solomon was crowned king. David's last words to Solomon charged him to do what God wants and to walk in His ways (see 1 Kings 2:1-3).

Solomon did not feel adequately equipped for the task of king. He was still a young man, but he remembered his father's words and sought to follow the Lord. He traveled to Gibeon and burned incense before the Lord. During the night, God appeared to him in a dream. Whatever Solomon asked, the Lord would give. He could have chosen a long life, the lives of his enemies, great riches; but, instead, he asked the Lord to grant him the wisdom he would need to rule God's people. Shortly thereafter, God's answer was put to the test.

PERFORMANCE TIPS

1. Suggested props: throne and crown for Solomon, doll to represent the living baby, sword for the soldier.
2. The soldier can be one actor or there can be many soldiers.
3. The two women argue vehemently. However, they always address the king respectfully. Rachel should be struggling to keep herself from crying when speaking with Solomon.
4. In spite of the chaos around him, Solomon should always remain calm.
5. Begin the skit by relating the story of Solomon's dream (see 1 Kings 3:5-14).

DISCUSSION QUESTIONS

1. Read Proverbs 9:10. What do you think it means?
2. Name some decisions in your life that need to be wise ones.
3. How can you have God's wisdom to guide you? What different ways could God speak to you to help you make decisions?
4. Can you expect God to help you be wise if you are not part of His family? Why or why not?

Make a Wish

CHARACTERS

SOLOMON

RACHEL

NAOMI (nay-OH-mee)

SOLDIERS

SOLOMON: Next case.

> (RACHEL and NAOMI come into court, noisily arguing. NAOMI carries baby.)

SOLDIER: Quiet! Cut the noise!

> (WOMEN stop arguing.)

SOLOMON: Thank you. Now, what seems to be the matter?

> (WOMEN speak loudly, at the same time.)

SOLDIER: Quiet! Cut the noise!

> (WOMEN stop arguing.)

SOLOMON: Thank you. One at a time, if you please. You.

RACHEL: Yes, Sire?

SOLOMON: What's the story?

NAOMI: Don't listen to her! She tells lies!

SOLOMON: She hasn't said anything yet.

NAOMI: But she will! She'll tell lies! She always does!

SOLOMON: Quiet. You'll have your chance to speak. Now then...

RACHEL: Rachel, Sire.

SOLOMON: Rachel. There seems to be a disagreement between the two of you.

RACHEL: Yes, Sire.

SOLOMON: Describe it. Briefly.

RACHEL: Well, we live in the same house, Naomi and I.

SOLOMON: Yes.

RACHEL: And we each have babies. Both about the same age. Just three days apart.

SOLOMON: Two babies. Three days' difference in age. Go on.

RACHEL: Last night, when we were asleep, Naomi rolled over...

NAOMI: She lies! I didn't roll over! I never roll over! I sleep like a log!

RACHEL: You did, too! You always do! You toss and turn all night, sometimes!

NAOMI: Do not! Do not! Liar...

SOLDIER: Quiet! Cut the noise! *(WOMEN stop arguing.)*

SOLOMON: Thank you. *(To NAOMI.)* Please keep quiet. You will have your say. Rachel, continue. You were saying?

RACHEL: Yes, Sire. Well, she rolled over in her sleep and smothered her baby.

NAOMI: She lies! I wouldn't...

SOLOMON: *(Holds up palm to interrupt NAOMI.)* Rachel?

RACHEL: She must have. Her baby died. She must have rolled over and accidentally smothered it. Then, during the night, she took my Timmy from my arms as I lay sleeping and replaced him with her dead son.

NAOMI: What a liar! She tells lies! She always lies about me!

SOLOMON: You will have your chance, madam. Rachel?

RACHEL: That's all, Sire. But you have to make her give me back my Timmy.

SOLOMON: I see. *(To NAOMI.)* Now then...

NAOMI: Naomi.

SOLOMON: Naomi. What have you to say?

NAOMI: Well, she told some truth. But mostly she told lies.

SOLOMON: Then YOU tell me the truth.

NAOMI: Well, we do live together. And we both have babies. But she's the one who always tosses and turns. She's the one who smothered her baby. Now she's trying to rob me of my Nathan.

RACHEL: No! That's not true! He's my Timmy!

SOLOMON: Please! You've had your say. Go on, Naomi.

NAOMI: There's nothing more to tell. Except for you to tell her to peddle her papers elsewhere.

SOLOMON: I see. Two babies. One alive, one dead. Both about the same age. I have it. Where are the fathers? They should be able to identify the babies.

SOLDIER: There ain't no men with these women, Sire.

SOLOMON: Well, have them brought in! Where do your husbands work?

RACHEL: Well...

NAOMI: Uhh...

More Bible Skits ©1994 Gospel Light. Permission granted to photocopy.

SOLOMON: I'm waiting. Where are your husbands?

RACHEL: I have no husband, Sire.

NAOMI: Nor do I.

SOLOMON: Oh. Wait here a moment. *(Leaves throne, walks a short distance from WOMEN and looks upward.)* Lord, I have asked you for wisdom. Please give me the wisdom to decide this case fairly. *(Returns to throne.)* Guard!

SOLDIER: Yes, Sire.

SOLOMON: Bring me a sword.

SOLDIER: Got one right here, Sire. *(Draws sword.)*

SOLOMON: It is my decision that we shall never know who is the rightful mother of the living child. Therefore, split it in two and give each woman half.

RACHEL: *(Screams.)* NO!

NAOMI: Sounds fair to me.

RACHEL: *(Shields baby in NAOMI's arms from SOLDIER.)* No, Sire! Don't kill Timmy! If she wants him, let her keep him! But don't kill him!

NAOMI: You see what she's like, Sire. She can't appreciate a fair decision.

SOLOMON: Guard. Put away your sword. Bring me the baby.

(SOLDIER takes baby from NAOMI and gives to SOLOMON.)

SOLOMON: Rachel, come here and take your child. You are truly his mother.

RACHEL: *(Takes baby.)* Oh, thank you, Sire! Thank you!

NAOMI: Well, gotta run. Bye. *(Exits running.)*

THE IMPOSSIBLE DREAM

SCRIPTURE: 1 Kings 5—7; 2 Chronicles 2:1—5:1

SUGGESTED TOPICS: Acting wisely; planning

BIBLE BACKGROUND

King David had wanted, with all his heart, to build a splendid place for people to come and worship the one, true God. But God had refused to grant David's desire. God's house was to be a house of peace, and David had spent his life as a man of war. However, God had promised to give David a son who would be a man of peace, a man who would be allowed to build the Temple (see 1 Chronicles 22:8-10).

Nonetheless, the prohibition against building the Temple did not restrict David from planning the Temple. David had laid out elaborate plans and set aside a goodly sum from his own property to commence construction. By the fourth year of Solomon's reign, David's dream was ready to be turned into reality. Construction of the Temple was about to begin.

PERFORMANCE TIPS

1. Suggested props: crown for Solomon, two sets of blueprints, two papers to represent the letter from Solomon to Hiram and vice versa.

2. While discussing the difficulties, Solomon and Benaiah should be tracing their fingers along different areas of the blueprints to show they are carefully studying the plans.

3. Consider reading aloud 1 Chronicles 22:8-10 prior to the skit.

DISCUSSION QUESTIONS

1. What difficulties did Solomon have to think about when planning to build the Temple? What might have happened if he didn't plan, but just plunged into the project?

2. What were some of the wise decisions Solomon made when planning the project?

3. What are some of the instructions God gives us to live our lives in His will?

4. Some of God's instructions are tough to obey. How can we show wisdom when called to make tough choices? What ways does God help us to make those choices?

THE IMPOSSIBLE DREAM

CHARACTERS

SOLOMON

BENAIAH (beh-NYE-ah)

SOLOMON: Benaiah!

BENAIAH: *(Bows.)* Always present. Ever awaiting your instruction, m'lord.

SOLOMON: I have a plan...

BENAIAH: A plan! How wonderful. I'm sure it's marvelous.

SOLOMON: ...that my father gave me. *(Unrolls blueprints.)* A plan to build a Temple in Jerusalem.

BENAIAH: Oh! *(Looks over SOLOMON's shoulder.)* That looks wonderful! It looks marvelous! It looks—impossible.

SOLOMON: Impossible? Surely not.

BENAIAH: Oh! *(Bows.)* Forgive me. Not impossible. Improbable?

SOLOMON: Explain yourself.

BENAIAH: Well, look at the size of it. Ninety feet long, thirty feet wide, forty-five feet high!

SOLOMON: Yes.

BENAIAH: Well, think of the COST. Where will we find the money?

SOLOMON: Gold and silver are as plentiful as stones in Jerusalem. Besides, Dad left a legacy to be used for construction. That'll give us a good start.

BENAIAH: True. But materials. Where will we get the materials? This is no mud-and-straw hut you have planned.

SOLOMON: True. But plans are already underway. Here's a copy of a letter I sent to King Hiram of Tyre. And here's his reply. *(Reads.)* "Pleased to hear that you have succeeded to your father's throne. Am sending timber as requested. Furthermore, am sending skilled woodworkers to assist you."

BENAIAH: Good! There's no finer lumber than the cedars of Lebanon. And no better woodworkers than those in Tyre. But we'll need general laborers. Got it! We'll go to war, take a bunch of prisoners—and THEY can do the laboring.

SOLOMON: Afraid not.

BENAIAH: No? But it's such a good plan. And with Egypt to help us, we can't lose.

SOLOMON: The Temple is to be built by a man of peace. The laborers will have to come from Israel.

BENAIAH: But it's impossible! You'll need THOUSANDS of workers!

SOLOMON: Thirty thousand should do it.

BENAIAH: Oh, I think we could probably get by with ten thousand. But where will we find ten thousand men who can be away for all that time?

SOLOMON: We can't. But ten thousand can be away for a month at a time. We'll work three shifts of ten thousand each. One month on the job, two months at home.

BENAIAH: *(Points to plan.)* But look at all that stone work. It can't be done! After those stones have been hewn and brought to Jerusalem, there'll have to be chipping and fitting. The rubble will take YEARS to haul away!

SOLOMON: The Lord has provided skilled stone masons. They assure me they will be able to make all necessary fittings at the quarry. No tool will be needed to fit the stones in Jerusalem.

BENAIAH: They ALL say that.

SOLOMON: I've seen their work. I think they can do it.

BENAIAH: But what about all the implements for use in the Temple? Where will you ever find them? We don't have a Temple supply house to run out to and buy what we need.

SOLOMON: We have many in use now in the Tabernacle. And what we don't have, we'll make. There are goldsmiths, silversmiths and iron workers. We have the necessary resources.

BENAIAH: It looks like you've figured everything out. But this will take YEARS.

SOLOMON: Seven years should do it. We should be finished just about the time of the Feast of Tabernacles. That will be an appropriate time for a Temple dedication.

BENAIAH: Well, m'lord, I guess so. If everything works exactly right. If nothing goes wrong. If everyone pulls his weight. And if we cancel all other building projects, we might do it.

SOLOMON: Speaking of other projects, did I show you the plans for my new house? *(Pulls out second set of plans.)* We'll be building it at the same time as the Temple. It's going to be one hundred and fifty feet long, seventy-five feet wide, forty-five feet high. Windows, windows, windows! See the porch? Pillars everywhere! And, of course, we'll need a special area for my Egyptian wife. The daughter of Pharaoh can't just sleep anywhere. And the harem room over here...

BENAIAH *(holding his head)***:** Aagggh! PLEASE, your majesty!

DECISIONS

SCRIPTURE: 1 Kings 3:1; 4:29-34; 9—11:12; 2 Chronicles 7:11—9:31

SUGGESTED TOPICS: Trusting in God; obeying God

BIBLE BACKGROUND

The early years of Solomon's reign were guided by the wisdom God gave him in answer to his request. While following God's wisdom, material riches abounded in Israel (see 1 Kings 10:14-29). However, as time went on, Solomon slowly replaced his reliance on God's wisdom with dependance on his own abilities. Instead of the great wisdom he had shown in the past, he began to make damaging mistakes, errors of faith which undermined his leadership. Eventually, God took the kingdom from his heirs. But one tribe was left to Solomon's son, out of respect for David, and because God had promised that the Messiah would come from the lineage of David.

PERFORMANCE TIPS

1. Suggested props: crown for Solomon, Bible-times costumes.
2. Begin the lesson with a discussion of the wealth of Solomon and the wisdom he had shown. Then introduce the skit by saying, "But Solomon had some tough decisions to make along the way."
3. After the skit, explain the choices Solomon made and the eventual consequences of his decisions.
4. Benaiah is constantly bowing. It's a habit he can't break.

DISCUSSION QUESTIONS

1. Does a wise person always make wise decisions? Why or why not?
2. What were some wise decisions Solomon made? What were some foolish decisions?
3. God's wisdom is available to all who will listen. How can you learn to listen to God?
4. Is it always easy to make right choices? Why or why not?

Decisions

CHARACTERS

SOLOMON

BENAIAH (beh-NYE-ah)

PRONUNCIATION GUIDE

rhetoric (RET-ur-ic)

SOLOMON: Benaiah!

BENAIAH *(walking and bowing):* Here I am, My King. May your name be glorified forever. May peace follow you all of your days. May your enemies be crushed underfoot. May all your works show your power and might to the world. May songs be sung of you in Israel forever. What is it that you wish? Your word is my command.

SOLOMON: I need your advice on something.

BENAIAH: *(Bows.)* Ask, O King, and I will give you what little I have to offer.

SOLOMON: Cut the humility bit.

BENAIAH: *(Straightens up.)* As you wish.

SOLOMON: Would you say that my kingdom is secure?

BENAIAH: But of course it is! Have you not already subdued all that would harm you within Israel? Your kingdom is the most secure kingdom in the history of Israel.

SOLOMON: THAT'S not saying much. There have only been two kings before me.

BENAIAH: But you are well loved by the people. They would be ready to go into battle with you at the drop of a turban, may all your enemies be trodden underfoot. *(Bows.)*

SOLOMON: But that's just it. I don't WANT them to go into battle.

BENAIAH: O King, may you live forever, do not say that! If you go into battle alone, you will not survive. Just because Gideon defeated the Midianites with only three hundred men, you should not even consider fighting an entire army by yourself.

SOLOMON: I did not say that I would fight by myself.

BENAIAH: Forgive me for being an ignorant dog, but I thought you did.

SOLOMON: I want to present two ideas to you. Tell me which you think best.

BENAIAH: I am here at your service, My King. *(Bows.)* May your name be glorif—

SOLOMON: Cut the rhetoric and listen!

BENAIAH: Yes, My King.

SOLOMON: Now, our most dangerous potential enemy is Egypt. What would happen if I were to declare war on Egypt and go into battle?

BENAIAH: Do not ask me this, My King, for the answer is too distressing. If you insist on going into battle alone, choose a weaker enemy than Egypt.

SOLOMON: Not me alone! If I led an army against Egypt, what would happen?

BENAIAH: This also distresses me, My King. Please do not make me answer!

SOLOMON: As your king, I ORDER you to answer.

BENAIAH: Promise you won't be angry.

SOLOMON: I will not be angry.

BENAIAH: Promise you won't fly into a rage and try to pin me to the wall with a spear.

SOLOMON: *I* don't do that kind of thing. SAUL did that kind of thing.

BENAIAH: Promise?

SOLOMON: I promise.

BENAIAH: Well, Egypt is a mighty warrior nation. Pharaoh is a shrewd military leader. Israel's army would be cut to shreds in the first day.

SOLOMON: That's pretty much my assessment, also. Let me ask you this.

BENAIAH: Anything, my lord.

SOLOMON: If I should need assistance in a battle and asked Pharaoh for help, what would be his response?

BENAIAH: Do not ask me to be a mind reader, My King. Who can know the mind of another man unless he is a magician, which is illegal in Israel.

SOLOMON: What do you THINK his response would be?

BENAIAH *(bowing)*: May all those who would curse you be cursed. May all your enemies be trodden underfoot. May he who belittles the king of Israel be cast...

SOLOMON: Enough! What would be his response?

BENAIAH: He would laugh in your face.

SOLOMON: That also agrees with my assessment of the situation.

BENAIAH: Begging the king's pardon, but why are you asking these questions?

SOLOMON: All in good time, Benaiah. Another question. What would be the best way to secure the borders of Israel from attack?

BENAIAH: That is easy, My King. Secure a treaty with Egypt. That way, if anyone should attack you, he would be attacking Egypt at the same time. Nobody in his right mind would attack Egypt! Unless, of course, you are planning to attack Egypt. Then it would be a noble and just war.

SOLOMON: I am NOT planning to attack Egypt.

BENAIAH: *(Wipes brow.)* That's a relief.

SOLOMON: However, how can I make a treaty with Pharaoh? If I ask for his help, he would laugh in my face, as you said.

BENAIAH: Is this a riddle? I was never very good at those.

SOLOMON: Pharaoh has a daughter.

BENAIAH: Yes, he does.

SOLOMON: If I were to marry her, then I would be Pharaoh's son-in-law. THAT would secure a treaty with Egypt, would it not?

BENAIAH: Yes! Of course! The PERFECT solution.

SOLOMON: Except that Israelites are not supposed to have foreign wives.

BENAIAH: I was right. It is a riddle.

SOLOMON: Now come the two ideas. One is to hope that my borders are secure and do nothing. The other is to marry Pharaoh's daughter to secure a treaty. Which is the best idea? Which would give the country more security? Would the people feel that I had betrayed them by marrying a foreign woman or would they see the advantages of having Egypt as an ally?

BENAIAH: You're the king. I am glad this is not MY decision.

SOLOMON: I was hoping you would give me some guidance.

BENAIAH: I couldn't even hazard a guess. But if it is any help, I'm sure that you will make the right decision. May the God of Israel give you wisdom. *(Bows and exits.)*

SOLOMON: Oh. Right. Thanks anyway. *(Rubs head.)* Oy! Decisions, decisions, decisions.

You Can Be King

SCRIPTURE: 1 Kings 12—14; 2 Chronicles 10—12

SUGGESTED TOPICS: Making wise choices; listening to wise advice; obeying God

BIBLE BACKGROUND

David was a man after God's own heart. He attempted to instill the same values in his son, Solomon, and succeeded to a great extent. Unfortunately, the son was not as close to God as was the father. Later in his life, Solomon built altars and high places for the gods of his idolatrous wives. The result of this ungodly behavior was a stern prophecy from God that the kingdom would be torn from Solomon's grasp. However, even in His anger, God showed His mercy. Because of David's heart and the promise God had sworn to David, the kingdom would not be entirely removed from Solomon's successors. The kingdom would be split. Ten tribes and the northern half of the kingdom would be taken away from Solomon's heir, but David's seed would retain the southern tribe of Judah and the portion of the kingdom containing the city of Jerusalem.

PERFORMANCE TIPS

1. Suggested props: microphone for Rezon, crowns to be awarded to Jeroboam and Rehoboam, chair for Ahijah.
2. Rezon speaks quickly, Jeroboam and Rehoboam speak more slowly, as if considering their answers.
3. Announcer can be an offstage personality, a voice only.
4. Other members of the class can be audience. Make an applause sign to signal for the cheering.

DISCUSSION QUESTIONS

1. What wise decisions did Jeroboam make? What unwise ones?
2. What wise decisions did Rehoboam make? What unwise ones?
3. What are some things a kid your age might choose to do to be popular? Which choices are wise, and which ones are unwise?
4. What should you do when you feel like making an unwise choice just to be popular?

You Can Be King

CHARACTERS

ANNOUNCER

REZON (REE-zahn)

REHOBOAM (REE-uh-BOH-am)

JEROBOAM (JER-uh-BOH-am)

AHIJAH (ah-HYE-jah)

AUDIENCE

ANNOUNCER: And now it's time for everyone's favorite show, the show that can make you ruler in your own house, the show that can give you a feeling of absolute authority, YOU CAN BE KING! And here's the man who gives you the reason to want to be king, REZON!

AUDIENCE: *(Cheers.)*

REZON: Thank you, thank you, thank you! You're too kind. Well, not really. I deserve it! After all, how many other people can help you become king? Well, audience, it's time to play "You Can Be King." Who are our contestants today?

ANNOUNCER: First, a man who knows what it's like to hold the reins of power. One of the sons of former king Solomon, REHOBOAM! *(AUDIENCE cheers as REHOBOAM enters.)* Next, a mighty man of valor, one who has had some experience at being in charge of the House of Joseph, JEROBOAM! *(AUDIENCE cheers as JEROBOAM enters.)*

REZON: Well, it sounds like we have two good contestants today. Two men used to making decisions. Let's find out a little bit about them. Rehoboam, it says here that you're a son of Solomon.

REHOBOAM: That's right. I've been raised all my life to be a king.

REZON: That's wonderful. A natural for our game if ever there was one. Jeroboam, it says you were in charge of the House of Joseph. One house doesn't sound like a big responsibility.

JEROBOAM: Well, that really means that I was governor over a tribe descended from Joseph. So it really was a big responsibility.

REZON: All right. Two worthy opponents. And let's meet our judge, the prophet Ahijah. *(AHIJAH waves and AUDIENCE cheers.)* OK. It's time to play "You Can Be King." You know the rules. You're given a skill-testing question. If you give the right answer, you score one hundred points! Ahijah judges whether or not answers are correct. His decision is final. Now, lets find out what kingdom we'll be playing for today.

ANNOUNCER: It's the Kingdom of ISRAEL! Yes, answer correctly and YOU could be the proud owner of this fabulous kingdom. Begun by Saul, consolidated and prospered under David and BOOMING under Solomon, this kingdom features beautiful beaches along the Great Sea, the fast-flowing River of Jordan, all the salt you could want from the Dead Sea and, of course, the fabulous city of Jerusalem and the breathtakingly beautiful Temple built by Solomon!

AUDIENCE: (Cheers.)

REZON: A prize, dare I say it, fit for a king! And it could be all yours. OK. First question to you, Rehoboam. Suppose your people come to you complaining of their heavy tax burden. What would you do?

REHOBOAM: That's a tough question. First, I'd take time to consider. Say, three days. I'd consult with my advisors. Then, I'd make my decision.

REZON: And your decision would be?

REHOBOAM: My three days aren't up yet.

REZON: Sorry, you don't have three days. Only one minute. What would you do?

REHOBOAM: Well, the old men would probably advise that I lower taxes. But my young advisors would probably say, "Why lower taxes? That will only lower your income and make the people think you're weak. Stick it to them! Don't lower taxes; raise them!" That's what I'd do. I'd raise the taxes higher.

REZON: It sounds like a good decision to me, but I'm not the judge. Ahijah?

AHIJAH: You should have listened to the older men. Such action as this will only infuriate your people. It could lead to a revolution. No points.

REZON: Too bad, but you can't be right all the time. Jeroboam, suppose a prophet called you to lead a nation. How would you get the people to follow you?

JEROBOAM: Well, first I'd find something the people didn't like. Then, I'd call on the king with a large group of men. We'd demand changes. If the king made the changes, I'd be a hero and be in position to take over when he died. If he didn't, I could promise to make the changes and the people would follow me.

REZON: That almost sounds like treason. What about it, judge?

AHIJAH: You have spoken wisely. It is much easier to lead if your people follow willingly. One hundred points.

REZON: Rehoboam, you've got some catching up to do! Second question: Suppose you were king of Israel and your people rebelled. What would you do?

REHOBOAM: Man, that's tough. My first reaction would be to gather up an army and quell the revolt. Kill the revolutionaries. But all the people are related and God might not want us to fight. I'd...

REZON: Yes?

REHOBOAM: I'd let those who wanted to separate leave and concentrate on improving relations with those who remained loyal.

REZON: Not very decisive. I would have thought the king would be tougher. Ahijah?

AHIJAH: The Lord God of Israel loves His people. He would not want them fighting among themselves. You have chosen wisely. One hundred points.

REZON: Back to you, Jeroboam. You have a country, but the people are used to going out of your country to worship their God. What do you do?

JEROBOAM: Well, that's easy! You don't want all that money leaving the country. So you make a new place to worship. Just to make sure that the people will come to the new place, you make new gods. Calves of gold are always good.

REZON: Keep the money where it belongs. Good answer. Right, Ahijah?

AHIJAH: Only one nation has a single place of worship. That nation is Israel. The God of Abraham, Isaac and Jacob does not approve of idol worship. Since He gave you the power, you should obey Him. No points.

REZON: We're down to our last questions. Rehoboam, suppose the king of Egypt attacked you and took away all the gold and silver from the Temple. What would you do?

REHOBOAM: What COULD I do? Nobody can stand up to Egypt. I'd let them go and replace them with brass or bronze. Much less valuable. And I'd encourage the people to worship other gods so there wouldn't be so much treasure all in one place.

REZON: Sensible. Ahijah?

AHIJAH: You were not listening to the previous answer. The God of Israel would not approve and He is the One who gives power to princes. No points.

REZON: Last question, Jeroboam. Say you have had an altar built, and a prophet of God appears. He says God disapproves and will destroy the altar. You lay your hand on the altar and your hand shrivels up and the altar falls apart. What do you do?

JEROBOAM: First, I'd get the prophet to heal my hand by promising to repent. Then, when my hand was healed, I'd do whatever I wanted. After all, this is a one-in-a-million thing.

REZON: *(Nods head.)* Play the odds. Rule with might. Ahijah?

AHIJAH: *(Shakes head.)* You have learned little. The Lord God's warnings should not be scorned. No points.

REZON: Well! We're just about out of time. Ahijah's adding up the points. And the winner is?

AHIJAH: It's a tie. One hundred points to one hundred points.

REZON: A tie? How will we award the prize?

AHIJAH: The prize will be split. Each will be awarded a crown. *(REZON takes crown to JEROBOAM.)* Jeroboam, you will be given ten of the tribes of Israel. Most of the people will follow you. *(REZON takes crown to REHOBOAM.)* Rehoboam, although you will not rule over most of the people, you will retain the tribe of Judah. With it, you will rule over the city of Jerusalem and thereby have most of the wealth.

REZON: A fair compromise. We're out of time. Join us again tomorrow when we play "YOU CAN BE KING!"

AUDIENCE: *(Cheers.)*

More Bible Skits ©1994 Gospel Light. Permission granted to photocopy.

RULE THE WORLD

SCRIPTURE: 1 Kings 16:29-34; Proverbs 20:11

SUGGESTED TOPICS: Using one's influence

BIBLE BACKGROUND

Throughout the history of Israel's divided kingdom, most of the rulers seemed intent to wipe out any memory of the God of Abraham, Isaac and Jacob. Idol worship seemed so much easier than devotion to the true God. Although many kings and queens led Israel astray, none so epitomizes evil as does Jezebel. The name still conjures up visions of a vicious, scheming woman, one who is unworthy of trust. Using her influence over King Ahab, Jezebel turned the nation of Israel into a nation of idol worshipers. The prophets of Baal dined at her table. Against the power of this decadent royal couple stood a man of God, Elijah.

PERFORMANCE TIPS

1. Suggested props: lab coat, test tube and other laboratory equipment, white jelly beans for "eye of newt."
2. The mad scientist should alternate between periods of calmness and raving lunacy.
3. The assistant fawns over the scientist. The scientist is his god.

DISCUSSION QUESTIONS

1. What influence does the mad scientist have? What influence does he want to have?
2. What people influence the world today?
3. Who influences your personal life? In what ways?
4. How can you recognize how other people are influencing you?
5. Read Proverbs 20:11. What kind of influence can a kid your age have?
6. Who do you influence? In what ways?
7. Name a good way you can influence others.

RULE THE WORLD

CHARACTERS
MAD SCIENTIST
ASSISTANT

SCIENTIST: Have you got it?

ASSISTANT: Yes, Master.

SCIENTIST: Just as I ordered?

ASSISTANT: To the smallest detail, Master.

SCIENTIST: At last. My dream shall be achieved!

ASSISTANT: Oh, Master. This is so exciting!

SCIENTIST: Yes. With this last ingredient, my invention will be complete. And with its completion, I shall—dare I say it?

ASSISTANT: Please, Master, say it! It's so exciting.

SCIENTIST: With its completion, I shall...rule the world.

ASSISTANT: Oh, Master. When you rule the world, can I be prime minister?

SCIENTIST: Of course not. There will only be room for one ruler. Me.

ASSISTANT: Forgive me, Master. I lost my head.

SCIENTIST: If you keep up these ideas of grandeur, that can be arranged.

ASSISTANT: I would rather it stay where it is.

SCIENTIST: Then forget ruling and follow.

ASSISTANT: Of course, Master. You lead, I follow.

SCIENTIST: Good. Now, give me the final ingredient. Then I shall rule the world.

ASSISTANT: Here it is, Master. But how can this let you rule the world?

SCIENTIST: By adding this last ingredient, I shall have a solution that is absolutely potent. So I shall be an absolute potentate!

ASSISTANT: Oh, Master, you are so brilliant.

SCIENTIST: Yes, I am.

ASSISTANT: Please explain it to me again.

SCIENTIST: Very well. First, I take ten milligrams of sodium hydroxide.

ASSISTANT: This is so exciting.

SCIENTIST: Then, I take one hundred milligrams of auric sulphate.

ASSISTANT: You are so brilliant. You are my idol.

SCIENTIST: As well I should be. Then, a pinch of potassium pentothal...

ASSISTANT: How alliterative.

SCIENTIST: Now, I shall add the final ingredient, eye of newt, and I shall, dare I say it?

ASSISTANT: Say it! Say it!

SCIENTIST: I shall...rule the world.

ASSISTANT: But, Master. What will this invention do?

SCIENTIST: What will it DO? Why, it will dissolve anything it touches!

ASSISTANT: Oh!

SCIENTIST: Does China have nuclear missiles? Hah! I laugh at nuclear missiles.

ASSISTANT: But, Master...

SCIENTIST: Does Turkey have an atomic bomb? Hah! I laugh at atomic bombs.

ASSISTANT: But, Master...

SCIENTIST: Does (name of your country) have (name of current leader)? Hmm. That is scary. No matter. I laugh. Hah!

ASSISTANT: But, Master...

SCIENTIST: Why must you interrupt my brilliant speech? With this invention, all nations must bow to me. Whatever *I* say, THEY must do. I shall...rule the world.

ASSISTANT: But, Master...

SCIENTIST: What?

ASSISTANT: If it will dissolve ANYthing, how will you store it?

SCIENTIST: Hmm. That is a tricky question. Store it. *(Pauses.)* I have it! I will invent a material that will never dissolve! And with an invention such as that, I shall...rule the world.

ASSISTANT: That's my master. He always has an answer. What shall I do with the newt's eyes?

SCIENTIST: *(Takes one from jar and eats it.)* Keep them. They'll make a marvelous casserole for supper tonight.

ASSISTANT: Oh, Master.

Ahab's Mount Carmel Press Conference

SCRIPTURE: 1 Kings 18; 19:1

SUGGESTED TOPICS: Trusting God; listening to God; obeying God; courage

BIBLE BACKGROUND

Under the evil influence of Queen Jezebel, King Ahab had instituted idol worship in Israel. As a sign that He alone was the only true God, Jehovah withheld rain from Israel for three years. Since Elijah was God's prophet who foretold this disaster, Ahab and Jezebel blamed Elijah for all of Israel's problems. They hunted everywhere for him, wishing to execute him. They were shocked when Elijah came out of hiding and proposed an extraordinary showdown between Baal and Jehovah.

PERFORMANCE TIPS

1. Suggested props: podium for Ahab to stand behind, notebooks for the reporters.
2. Ahab's opening address is long. Give your actor time to look over the part. If performing the skit from memory, Ahab could be allowed to read the opening address.
3. Prior to performing the skit, discuss press conferences and their purposes with the class. Be sure they understand that some press conferences are not intended to give out information but to give someone a chance to alibi a situation which might make him look bad.
4. After the press conference, have the class explain what they understand happened. Be prepared to fill in parts the class might have missed.

DISCUSSION QUESTIONS

1. What do you think the word "influence" means?
2. How did Ahab and Jezebel influence their country?
3. How did Elijah influence the country?
4. What things influence a kid your age to do good things? evil things?
5. Name ways you can pay attention to the good influences and ignore the bad ones.

AHAB'S MOUNT CARMEL PRESS CONFERENCE

CHARACTERS
AHAB
REPORTER ONE
REPORTER TWO

PRONUNCIATION GUIDE
Baal (bale)
Elijah (ee-LIE-juh)
Hamath (HAY-math)
Jezebel (JEZ-uh-bel)
Obadiah (OH-buh-DIE-uh)

AHAB: I want to thank all of you for coming out—well, both of you—on such a rainy and stormy night as we're having tonight. I haven't seen rain like this for over three years, ha, ha. Before I entertain questions from you, I would like to read a prepared statement that should do away with many unnecessary questions that would only waste our time. *(Clears throat.)*

"For three years now, Israel has been without rain and has been experiencing one of the darkest hours in its history. This administration recognizes the importance of the family farm to our illustrious nation's economy and has been spending significant resources to end the drought that has imperiled the livelihood of this significant factor of our great nation. Although some of the experiments attempted to alleviate the drought were resoundingly unsuccessful, this is not to say that they were a waste of taxpayers' money. If nothing else, they have been entered into the *Chronicles of King Ahab* and it will not be necessary for other kings to try these procedures should a similar situation occur.

"Of particular note was the cloud-seeding experiment suggested by Hamath, minister of science. The press was quick to ridicule the minister for this timely experiment, implying that firing arrows at the clouds was a waste of the kingdom's money and manpower. Although this experiment did not bring forth the desired rain, it did lead to major improvements in the bow and the strength of the bowmen, which should keep Israel in the fore of military might for decades to come.

"We are pleased to announce that the terrible drought which has been afflicting the country has come to an end. Contrary to the mutterings of certain doomsayers, this is NOT signaling a forthcoming flood of proportions not seen since the days of Noah.

On the contrary, this rain is the very thing this country has needed for the past three years. In the event of any flooding in the lowlands which might imperil life of person or animal, the military is on the alert and will respond with the speed and diligence that has made Israel's proud fighting man the envy of the surrounding nations.

"Although we are naturally pleased with the end of the drought, we are also saddened by the senseless death of eight hundred and fifty kindly and gentle men of Israel. I am, of course, referring to the prophets of Baal and the groves who had been blamed by certain rabble-rousers and publicity-seekers for Israel's problems. This only shows what can happen when justice falls into the hands of a mob instead of resting in the duly constituted authority of the king. In light of the large number of men responsible for the death of these prophets and the resulting disaster which would befall the country if all should be arrested and imprisoned, they are being given a full pardon by this administration. The only one who will be punished, as an example to the many, is the ringleader of the mob, Elijah—if we ever catch him. Although his whereabouts are unknown at this time, Israel's finest soldiers are out scouring the countryside for him at this very moment."

That is the end of the prepared statement. I will now entertain any questions that you gentlemen might have.

REPORTER ONE: Is it your contention, O King, that the drought we have experienced was not caused by Israel's sin but by some as yet unknown natural cause?

AHAB: Could you elaborate on that phrase you used, "Israel's sin"?

REPORTER ONE: Certainly. I am referring to the fact that most of Israel has stopped following the God of Abraham, Isaac and Jacob and is, instead, bowing down to idols, most of which are championed by the queen, Jezebel.

AHAB: In the first place, I must caution you about your lack of honor for the name of the queen. That is treason. I am sure you meant no harm so I will overlook it this time. But don't let it happen again. Concerning the worship of gods in Israel: Every nation in the world worships many gods. The backwardness of Israel in worshiping only one god has held it back from occupying its true place as one of the great nations of the world. The queen and myself have simply been trying to correct this problem and to enlighten the people under our control—er, authority.

REPORTER TWO: I understand that Elijah has been an outlaw in Israel for many years, but according to reports received by our editor, Elijah was in full view of the king and his soldiers today at Mount Carmel and was not arrested at that time. Would the king please explain why a known outlaw was not taken into custody?

AHAB: I would be delighted to answer your question. You know Obadiah....

REPORTER TWO: Certainly. He is one of your servants.

AHAB: He is one of my most TRUSTED servants. As you know, he is one of the keenest-eyed men in all of Israel. He and I were out searching for water, a little brook or a minor fountain, or perhaps some green grass to feed the livestock to keep them alive for a short time.

REPORTER TWO: I wouldn't think you'd need a keen-eyed man for that. Surely any green would stand out like a sore thumb in this land where everything has turned brown?

AHAB: At any rate, Obadiah ran into this Elijah. As you know, Obadiah is not a soldier or one of my guards. Being the brave man that he is, Obadiah was ready to attempt a citizen's arrest of this notorious criminal....

REPORTER TWO: I had never heard that Elijah had ever hurt anyone.

AHAB: But before he could make the arrest, Elijah told him to go and tell me that he, Elijah, wanted to meet with me. Naturally, Obadiah was reluctant to leave a known criminal, thinking that he might hide again, but my faithful servant did bring me the message that Elijah wanted to meet with me. I considered coming for my soldiers but decided that I would be able to handle this arrest myself.

REPORTER ONE: Concerning Obadiah's reluctance to leave Elijah and take his message to you: There is a rumor that if you had gone to meet with Elijah and he was not there, your ferocious anger would have been kindled and you would have taken it out on Obadiah, possibly killing him on the spot for bringing you a false report. Would you comment on that, please?

AHAB: I have not finished answering the previous question, but I cannot leave so vicious a rumor unanswered. All who know me, those close to me, know that I have been maligned by my political opponents. In truth, I am a gentle man, and had Elijah not been there, I would have reprimanded Obadiah for leaving a known criminal to run free, but I would have understood his motives and acted accordingly.

REPORTER TWO: Are we to understand, then, that you saw this outlaw not only at Mount Carmel, but also earlier in the week?

AHAB: Yes. I met with him.

REPORTER TWO: And yet you did not arrest him at that time. Could you please explain your motives in allowing him to go free?

AHAB: That would be simplicity itself. At our meeting, he gave me to understand that all of Israel's troubles could be solved if I would meet him at Mount Carmel with the four hundred and fifty prophets of Baal and the four hundred prophets of the groves. Naturally, Israel's troubles were all related to the drought that had been in existence for the past three years. Because we had been dealing with this problem unsuccessfully for so long, I thought it in the best interests of Israel to meet with him and the other prophets at Mount Carmel.

REPORTER ONE: Are you saying that Elijah is a prophet? I thought he was an outlaw. Which is it?

AHAB: I was merely patronizing him. Of course he is not a REAL prophet, but he likes to think of himself as one. I was merely stating his point of view.

REPORTER TWO: But all of Israel knows Elijah does not believe that the prophets who eat at the queen's table are true prophets. Didn't you question his motives in wanting to meet with them? Didn't you think it strange that he also wanted you to summon all of Israel to witness what would happen at Mount Carmel?

AHAB: Certainly I was curious about his wanting all the other prophets there. But I restrained my curiosity for two reasons. First, any chance of ending the drought had to be taken, even if it was being spearheaded by a criminal. Second, I was hoping that he'd come to his senses and was gathering a giant prayer meeting to implore the gods to send rain. And I did not have to order the people of Israel to come. Their curiosity was so aroused, I doubt I would have been able to keep them away.

REPORTER ONE: Once he started to speak, did you not realize that he was hoping to incite a riot? His very manner suggested that he wanted mob rule to be the order of the day, did it not? Weren't you worried by his attitude?

AHAB: Not at all. I knew he was playing for a showdown, but there were many soldiers there. Also, I knew that when his God failed to provide relief for the people, they would realize that Elijah was just another religious fanatic whose day had finally ended. I had hoped that this would put an end to the dangerous brand of religious fervor that he advocated. Unfortunately, I miscalculated. But it was an honest error that any king seeking the best for his subjects would have made.

REPORTER TWO: Would the king please comment on his feelings about the show put on by the prophets of Baal at Mount Carmel today?

AHAB: It was one of the most impressive spectacles I have ever witnessed in my life. No adjective in our language could adequately describe my feelings at the time. I suppose "glorious" is the closest—the dancing, the singing, the cutting themselves with knives. Of course, any king loves to see the sight of blood—unless it's his own or that of his soldiers.

REPORTER TWO: Would the king then explain why, if he was so impressed with the performance of the prophets of Baal, he allowed this Elijah to make fools of them? To laugh at them? To imply that they were wasting their time trying to arouse a god that could not hear?

AHAB: I was, of course, letting him dig his own grave. Everybody there knew the test set out was impossible. The longer I let him ridicule the prophets of Baal, the greater would be his downfall when he also failed. It was simple psychology that any king worth his salt would have used.

REPORTER ONE: Would the king please express his thoughts about the amount of water Elijah wasted when Israel was in the middle of the worst drought in its history? How could the king stand idly by while Elijah had twelve barrels of water poured on his altar? Did not the king feel that the water could be better used elsewhere?

AHAB: No. What amazed me was that the people of Israel did not see that the prophets of Baal must have succeeded. Not in getting fire but having water appear instead. I have no idea where so much water was found. That is just another example of what can happen when a large number of good men gather to pray.

REPORTER ONE: Then you're saying the prophets of Baal made the water appear?

AHAB: I certainly can't think of where else it might have come from. Can you?

REPORTER ONE: Discretion being the better part of valor, I would not even suggest to the king that maybe Elijah's God produced it for him.

AHAB: You are wise not to suggest such a possibility to me.

REPORTER TWO: When the fire appeared from heaven and consumed not only the sacrifice that Elijah had placed on his altar but also the altar itself, the water running around the altar and the dust, what were your feelings?

AHAB: Naturally, I was awestruck. If it would not have been undignified, I would have fallen to the ground with the rest of the people of Israel.

REPORTER ONE: Would the king explain why he did not stop the senseless slaughter of the unsuccessful prophets on the mountain? Why did you not exert your authority and make the people go home?

AHAB: You were there. You saw how the mob suddenly followed everything that Elijah suggested. There were too many people and not enough soldiers to stop the ensuing slaughter. You were lucky that Elijah had a grudge against Baal's prophets and not reporters.

REPORTER ONE: *(Aside.)* Or kings.

REPORTER TWO: Would the king please explain why it took so long to arrive back in Jezreel after the catastrophic violence that took place?

AHAB: I had to stop and think. There was much to ponder concerning what was to be done in the aftermath. With all those people there, it was impossible to arrest Elijah. I could not punish all of the participants in the massacre. I had to decide what to do.

REPORTER ONE: There is a rumor that the reason the king took so long to arrive back in Jezreel is that he was afraid to face Jezebel and tell her that her favorite prophets had all been slain at the command of Elijah. Would the king care to comment?

AHAB: That is simply another of the vicious rumors started by my political opponents in an attempt to embarrass me and to make me a laughingstock in Israel. It is a ploy which shall never succeed because it is unfounded. Imagine any man, much less the king, being afraid of his wife. This press conference is now over. Thank you for coming.

REPORTERS *(together)*: Thank you, Your Majesty. *(REPORTERS exit.)*

AHAB: Now then, how AM I going to explain this to Jezebel?

Food for Thought

SCRIPTURE: 2 Kings 2:1-22; 4:38-44

SUGGESTED TOPICS: Positive influences; complaining; trusting God

BIBLE BACKGROUND

Elijah took a young student, Elisha, under his wing. By observing Elijah in the crucible of the world, Elisha learned that God's promises were true and could be trusted. When the time came for Elijah to be taken from this world, Elisha refused to abandon his mentor and friend. The faithful Elisha received Elijah's mantle and became God's voice in Israel.

Part of Elisha's role was teacher to a group of students. Likely, they were all attentive, realizing the importance of their teacher's words. However, human nature seems to try to find fault. The complaining student in the skit is typical of the common human tendency to criticize.

PERFORMANCE TIPS

1. Suggested props: Bible-times costumes, two chairs.

2. Student One is a complainer. His whining voice and frequent sighs should indicate this.

3. Student Two is enthusiastic. His voice and energetic body language should indicate this.

4. Students could pantomime gathering firewood, cleaning house or some other manual task as they talk.

DISCUSSION QUESTIONS

1. Why do people complain?

2. What things do kids your age complain about? Are those things really that bad?

3. Think of all the good things you have. Do you give thanks for them as often as you complain about the things you don't like?

4. Who or what are some of the teachers God has given to you? What sorts of things do you learn from them?

5. What can you do to thank the people who are good influences on you?

FOOD FOR THOUGHT

CHARACTERS

STUDENT ONE
STUDENT TWO

PRONUNCIATION GUIDE

Elisha (ee-LIE-shuh)

STUDENT ONE: *(Sighs heavily.)* I sure get tired of the same old food, day after day.

STUDENT TWO: Why complain? Many people have no food at all.

STUDENT ONE: Yeah. But all we get these days seems to be bread.

STUDENT TWO: We have other things.

STUDENT ONE: Yeah, like yesterday. Poisoned stew.

STUDENT TWO: Well, it started out poisoned, but Elisha fixed it. Then it was delicious!

STUDENT ONE: We were lucky we weren't all killed.

STUDENT TWO: We weren't LUCKY—we're with Elisha. And GOD is with Elisha.

STUDENT ONE: If we aren't lucky, what are we?

STUDENT TWO: We're BLESSED.

STUDENT ONE: Hah! Blessed. Sure.

STUDENT TWO: Sure we are. Even if we didn't have enough to eat, think of the other things we have.

STUDENT ONE: Name one.

STUDENT TWO: Most importantly, Elisha's teaching.

STUDENT ONE: It's just like the food—same thing day after day! *(Rolls eyes.)* Follow God. Follow God. Follow God. Why can't we have something different?

STUDENT TWO: We have the best, and you want something different?

STUDENT ONE: Well, yeah. How about a MIRACLE? I keep hearing about them, but I don't see any.

STUDENT TWO: You wouldn't know a miracle if it leapt out and bit you! You've seen lots of miracles.

STUDENT ONE: Oh yeah? Like what?

STUDENT TWO: Like what? You were almost poisoned yesterday. Everyone knew the stew had been poisoned and we would all die. But DID we?

STUDENT ONE: You're telling the story. *(Sarcastically.)* DID we die?

STUDENT TWO: Of course not. We're alive, aren't we?

STUDENT ONE: If you can call this living.

STUDENT TWO: This is the best life ANYONE could have! Learning from a man of God!

STUDENT ONE: Yeah? Just wait until the food runs out. Then we'll see who's so happy to be learning from Elisha. If your belly wasn't full, your mind wouldn't care.

STUDENT TWO: That's where you're wrong. But I'll never get a chance to prove it— because Elisha always makes sure our needs are met.

STUDENT ONE: He's not meeting MY needs.

STUDENT TWO: Sure he is! He may not be meeting all your WANTS, but he's meeting your NEEDS.

STUDENT ONE: Needs, wants—same thing to me. *(Sarcastically.)* But I can hardly wait for supper.

STUDENT TWO: Why? I thought you said you were tired of the same thing.

STUDENT ONE: Oh, tonight will be different. I saw supper arrive.

STUDENT TWO: What is it?

STUDENT ONE: Bread and grain.

STUDENT TWO: That sounds like what we usually have.

STUDENT ONE: The quantity is different. Tonight, there won't be enough for HALF the people here. But, since you don't care about food as long as Elisha is teaching, I'll have YOUR share.

STUDENT TWO: Fair enough. You eat until you're full. If there's any left over, I'll eat.

STUDENT ONE: *(Laughs.)* Tonight, you starve. And tomorrow during classes, your little tummy will be growling. We'll see if you pay attention to teaching tomorrow.

STUDENT TWO: *(Rises.)* There's the dinner bell. Let's go. We'll feed the body tonight and the mind tomorrow.

STUDENT ONE: You mean, I'LL feed the body tonight. Who KNOWS what we'll get tomorrow!

MAD ABOUT ELISHA

SCRIPTURE: 2 Kings 6:24,25,31-33; 7:1-20; 13:14-19

SUGGESTED TOPICS: Setting a good example; obedience to God

BIBLE BACKGROUND

The mantle of Elijah had fallen upon Elisha. He was now the most influential prophet in Israel. He could have used this position for great personal power and wealth. Many prophets were welcomed at the king's court, provided they would tell the king what he wanted to hear. Elisha, however, remained true to his calling. In spite of personal danger, he remained faithful to the God he was called to serve. Elisha's faithfulness resulted in God's supernatural protection for him (see 2 Kings 6:17). The king of Syria wanted Elisha dead because he believed Elisha was responsible for Israel's repeated success in battles against Syria. Ironically, the king of Israel later blamed all of Israel's problems on Elisha and also sought to kill him.

PERFORMANCE TIPS

1. Suggested props: trench coat and notebook for Dan, crown for the king.

2. The king is under a lot of pressure. He should appear short-tempered and impatient.

3. Dan is methodically doing his job. His speech should be matter-of-fact, almost monotone.

4. Finish the story by telling about God's miraculous intervention on Israel's behalf.

DISCUSSION QUESTIONS

1. The king blamed Elisha for Israel's problems. Was Elisha to blame? Why or why not?

2. How was Elisha a good influence on those he met?

3. Read 1 Timothy 4:12. How can you be a good influence on the people you meet?

MAD ABOUT ELISHA

CHARACTERS

DAN

KING

PRONUNCIATION GUIDE

bunco (BUN-coe)
Dothan (DOE-thun)
Samaria (suh-MARE-ee-uh)
Syrian (SEER-ee-un)

DAN *(facing audience)*: This is Samaria,
known to us as "The City." In The City are a million stories—
well, a few thousand, anyway. This is one of them. My name is Dan. I'm a policeman.
The following story is true. Really. I'm a policeman. Would I lie to you? It all started
when I was summoned to the king's palace...*(Turns to KING and pulls out notebook.)*

KING: Dan, I've been told you're the best man on the Samaritan police force.

DAN: I'm happy that you've heard such good reports, Your Majesty, but I'm sure you
didn't summon me here to tell me that.

KING: You're right. I didn't. I need your help.

DAN: What seems to be the problem, Your Majesty?

KING: Elisha!

DAN: Bless you. That's quite a cold you have there. But I'm not a physician. You need a
doctor, not a policeman.

KING: I don't have a cold. My PROBLEM is a man named Elisha.

DAN: Has he been threatening you? Threats are not colds. Threats would be a police
problem. *(Flips open notebook and begins to take notes.)* How long has this—could you
spell the name of the man who's been threatening you?

KING: E-L-I-S-H-A!

DAN: Thank you. How long has he been threatening you?

KING: He hasn't ACTUALLY been THREATENING me.

DAN: Maybe you'd better give me the facts, sir. Just the facts. Who is this Elisha?

KING: He's a prophet.

DAN: You mean like a fortune-teller? You've called the wrong department, Your Majesty.
You should have called bunco. I usually deal with more violent crimes.

KING: No! Elisha is not like a fortune-teller. Sometimes he DOES predict the future; and
when he predicts something, it comes TRUE.

DAN: That would make a bunco rap tough to fasten on him. If you don't want him
arrested as some sort of con man, what do you want? Just the facts, Your Majesty.

KING: I'm not sure what I want. That's why I need your help. Maybe if I tell you what happened, you'd be better able to advise me.

DAN: That's a good idea. Facts are always useful. What has this prophet done to hurt you?

KING: It started some time ago when the Syrian army was encamped against the town of Dothan.

DAN: If he was fighting for the Syrians, then a charge of treason would be appropriate. By the way, you wouldn't happen to have a spare cup of coffee, would you?

KING: No. I wouldn't.

DAN: OK. Back to Elisha. Fighting for the Syrians would be treason. That should be no problem to pin on him.

KING: He wasn't fighting for the Syrians.

DAN: Oh. Then treason's no good. What was this guy doing?

KING: He was the reason the Syrians were attacking Dothan. They wanted to KILL him.

DAN: This Elisha sounds like one terrific troublemaker. Both the king of Syria and the king of Israel want to kill him. That's the first thing you two have ever agreed on, isn't it? How about some fruit?

KING: No. I don't think fruit comes into the story anywhere.

DAN: I meant to eat. *(Looks around.)* Do you have any spare fruit around? It doesn't have to be a lot of fruit. A handful of grapes would do. Even raisins.

KING: No, I don't have any spare fruit! Can we get on with this?

DAN: Certainly. What happened at Dothan?

KING: The Syrian army was BLINDED. Couldn't see their spears in front of their faces!

DAN: And this Elisha had something to do with it?

KING: He is rumored to be responsible for it. Yes.

DAN: Then I think we've got him. Assault causing bodily harm. Should be good for five to ten in the dungeon. Sort of ironic.

KING: What is?

DAN: He blinds an army but he's the one who ends up in the dark! *(Chuckles.)*

KING: I don't think we can charge him with anything for blinding the Syrian army. Hurting Syrians is not a crime in Israel.

DAN: You're right. I guess that's why you're king and I'm not. Let's continue. What did he do with this army of blind men?

KING: He led them into Samaria.

DAN: Ah! Illegal immigration! Probably charged each one a pretty price for the privilege. I'm not sure whose jurisdiction this falls under.

KING: They weren't immigrating. He led them here to be my prisoners!

DAN: Got him—slave trading! *(Pauses.)* No. That's not a crime yet. What happened to these prisoners?

KING: I was ready to kill them. I figured THAT would teach the king of Syria to send an army against Israel. But Elisha wouldn't let me!

DAN: He physically restrained you? Common assault should stick for that.

KING: No. He didn't touch me. He just told me that I shouldn't kill them.

DAN: What did you do then, sir? Just the facts, please. Did you torture them?

KING: No. Elisha told me to give them bread and water and to send them back to Syria.

DAN: Bread?

KING: Yes, bread.

DAN: Where?

KING: Well, it's gone now. They ate it!

DAN: No, I mean now. Have you any bread to spare?

KING *(glaring)*: No, I don't!

DAN: It doesn't have to be good bread. If it's a little moldy, that would be fine with me. I missed breakfast this morning.

KING: I don't have any bread to spare! Stop worrying about your stomach and start worrying about my problem!

DAN: So far, I don't see that he's caused you any problems.

KING: You don't see any PROBLEMS? Look around you! We're having the worst famine in our history in this city. People are eating their own children to stay alive, and you don't see that he's causing any PROBLEMS?

DAN: Black marketing. While the city is starving, he's making a big profit by selling storeholds of food at steep prices. Rather ironic.

KING: How so?

DAN: While the people starve, the prophet profits. *(Laughs at own joke.)*

KING *(irritated)*: He's NOT profiting. He's NOT selling food on the black market! He DOESN'T have food stashed away.

DAN: Then how do you figure that he's responsible for the famine?

KING: The famine is caused by the Syrian army camped around Samaria. If Elisha hadn't made me release them before, they wouldn't be here NOW.

DAN: Strange. I don't remember a large group of Syrians being around here recently. When did you release this army?

KING: Oh, years and years ago.

DAN: Then we can't charge him on that one. The statute of limitations would have already expired.

KING: Well, you have to do SOMETHING about him! You're the police!

DAN: That's the problem. I have to uphold the law. He hasn't broken it. If he were in the palace and you had him executed, that would solve your problem.

KING: But then you'd come and arrest me for murder.

DAN: No, I couldn't do that. The king's palace is outside of my jurisdiction. Anything that happens inside with the king's consent is legal. Well, if there are no more facts, I think I'll go and try to find a little something to eat.

KING: You do that. *(Calls in other direction.)* Servant! Come here! I want you to take a message to Elisha!

HE AROSE

SCRIPTURE: Matthew 26:1-5,47-68; 27:11-66

SUGGESTED TOPICS: Jesus' resurrection

BIBLE BACKGROUND

Ghandi once said Christianity was exactly what India needed—if Christians truly believed what they said. His implication was that India could have her problems solved if Christians acted the way they said they believed; the central truth of Christianity was unimportant to him. The apostle Paul is not so charitable to Christians as Ghandi. To Paul, the importance of Christianity was not that people acted differently if they believed; the importance lay in its truth. "If there is not resurrection of the dead, then Christ is not risen. If Christ is not risen, our preaching and your faith are worthless. We would be false witnesses and you would still be lost in your sins" (see 1 Corinthians 15:13-17). To disprove Christianity, one must disprove the resurrection.

For centuries, people have tried to find reasonable explanations for the empty tomb. Various possibilities other than Jesus' resurrection have been proposed: "The disciples stole the body"; "He wasn't really dead, so the coolness of the tomb revived Him and He got up and left"; "He never really existed, it's all just a story." When examined closely, none of the alternative explanations hold water. Christians can rejoice in the confidence of a loving God who came to die so that our sins might be forgiven and rose, victorious over death.

PERFORMANCE TIPS

1. Suggested props: Bible-times costumes, table and chairs for Annas and Alexander.

2. These are shrewd men. Annas and Alexander are not as quick to catch on to things as Caiaphas, but they are not stupid.

3. Caiaphas paces throughout the skit. He is tense and eager to go.

DISCUSSION QUESTIONS

1. Why is Jesus' resurrection important?

2. Do you agree with this statement: "It's not important what you believe, only that you believe something." Why or why not?

3. What evidence do we have that the resurrection is a fact?

4. Some people believe Jesus' disciples stole the body and said Jesus rose. Why can we know this is not true?

HE AROSE

CHARACTERS
CAIAPHAS (KYE-uh-fus)
ANNAS
ALEXANDER

PRONUNCIATION GUIDE
Nicodemus (NICK-uh-DEE-mus)
Zebedee (ZEB-uh-dee)

CAIAPHAS: *(Rubs forehead.)* What a day!

ANNAS: *(Yawns.)* I've never been so tired in my life.

ALEXANDER: But at least it's over.

CAIAPHAS: Not yet, it isn't.

ANNAS: What do you mean?

ALEXANDER: The blasphemer, Jesus, has been crucified.

ANNAS: He's crucified and dead! You saw the blood and water spill from His side.

ALEXANDER: He'll be put into Joseph's tomb and that's the end of it.

CAIAPHAS: Not quite. We must go and see Pilate again.

ANNAS: Why? I don't like him.

ALEXANDER: And he doesn't like us. Look what he wrote on the charge sheet against Jesus. "This is Jesus, the King of the Jews."

ANNAS: And we couldn't get him to change it. It wouldn't have been so hard to have it say, "This is Jesus, who SAID He was the King of the Jews."

CAIAPHAS: Yes, he could have done that. *(Clenches fists.)* I'll never forgive him for it. I'll find a way to make him pay for that insult.

ALEXANDER: I still don't understand why Pilate had Jesus crucified.

ANNAS: Because He's a blasphemer. That requires death.

ALEXANDER: But PILATE doesn't care about blasphemy.

CAIAPHAS: But he cares about his own neck.

ANNAS: What do you mean?

CAIAPHAS: When we brought Jesus to Pilate for sentencing, did you think he would have Him killed because WE wanted it?

ANNAS: Why not? The man was guilty! He needed to be killed.

ALEXANDER: I WAS surprised. Pilate's never had any sensitivity to important religious matters in the past.

CAIAPHAS: I doubted he would pass sentence. That's why I had another plan waiting. Do you think I spoke to Pilate on the spur of the moment, without planning what I would say?

ANNAS: You mean you wrote out your speech beforehand?

ALEXANDER: You memorized it?

CAIAPHAS: Not exactly. But as we led Jesus to Pilate's court, I made preparations in case Pilate would not sentence Jesus to death.

ANNAS: I never quite understood that.

ALEXANDER: Neither did I. But it worked.

CAIAPHAS: Let me explain. Jesus claimed to be God. That's why WE sentenced Him to death.

ALEXANDER: Sure, but Pilate wouldn't care about that. Pilate doesn't care about religion.

ANNAS: He should!

CAIAPHAS: But he doesn't. But Pilate DOES care about politics. If Jesus claimed to be our God, He ALSO claimed to be our King! *(Gets blank stares from ANNAS and ALEXANDER.)* But only CAESAR can appoint a king.

ANNAS: Ah, now I see!

ALEXANDER: *(Strokes beard.)* By claiming to be King, Jesus committed treason against ROME!

CAIAPHAS: Precisely. Come, we must go and see Pilate.

ANNAS: He won't want to see us.

ALEXANDER: He was upset when you pressured him into crucifying Jesus.

CAIAPHAS: I don't care. We have more pressing issues.

ANNAS: Like what?

ALEXANDER: It's almost the Sabbath. Can't it wait for a few days?

CAIAPHAS: No. It must be done immediately!

ANNAS: What is so important that we must risk breaking the Sabbath?

CAIAPHAS: Do you remember the blasphemer claiming He would not remain in the grave?

ALEXANDER: A fool's boast. Dead is dead.

ANNAS: Those two traitors, Joseph and Nicodemus, will see to it that He's buried. They may not do a perfect job, but they'll use enough spices and linen to secure the body.

CAIAPHAS: But what if someone else decides to MOVE the body?

ALEXANDER: Who would disturb the body? Everyone knows who's buried there. Grave robbers aren't going to break into the tomb of a poor carpenter and preacher. There's nothing worth stealing.

CAIAPHAS: What about His disciples?

ANNAS: They all ran away. They're just a pack of cowards.

CAIAPHAS: I think I saw one near the Cross. John, the son of Zebedee.

ALEXANDER: He won't cause any trouble. He'll just go back to fishing.

CAIAPHAS: But suppose. What if the disciples suddenly find some courage? They might go and move the body and claim Jesus rose from the dead!

ANNAS: Why would they do that? There's no profit in it for them.

CAIAPHAS: They might do it in memory of their Master. Make people think He was more than just an ordinary man.

ALEXANDER: It sounds far-fetched to me. Not a chance in a hundred.

CAIAPHAS: But can we take that one chance?

ANNAS: What do you suggest we do? Sit by the tomb until Pentecost?

CAIAPHAS: No, but Pilate could assign a guard for the tomb.

ALEXANDER: The way he feels about us, right NOW? If we went and asked for a guard, he'd say, "Go peddle your papers!" or something like that.

CAIAPHAS: Of course he would.

ANNAS: So, you're saying we should go to Pilate so he can insult us?

CAIAPHAS: Not at all. We go in a position of strength. Remember, politics.

ANNAS: I'm a priest, not a politician.

ALEXANDER: These days, one must be both. How do we convince Pilate?

CAIAPHAS: We tell him that if Jesus' disciples steal the body, they will claim Jesus rose from the dead.

ANNAS: How will that convince Pilate? He'll say, "What utter nonsense!"

ALEXANDER: True. And probably have us thrown out.

CAIAPHAS: Pilate is smarter than that. He has studied our beliefs.

ANNAS: Not so you'd notice.

ALEXANDER: Hasn't changed him one bit. He's the same arrogant Roman dog he always was.

CAIAPHAS: Let me ask you, if Rome had crucified the REAL Messiah, what would the people of Israel do?

ANNAS: That's simple. They'd riot.

ALEXANDER: Ahh! Now I see.

CAIAPHAS: Pilate can't take that chance. A riot in Israel and he'll be back in Rome, facing a court-martial. He'd be disgraced, maybe even killed.

ANNAS: I have to hand it to you, Caiaphas. You think of everything.

CAIAPHAS: In this job, one must. That's what being high priest is all about.

ALEXANDER: Hey! If we can get a guard, maybe we can even have the tomb sealed.

CAIAPHAS: Sealed with a Roman seal. NOBODY'S going to touch THAT. Good thinking. Come! Let's go before it's too late. Jesus' body MUST stay in that tomb.

TRUST AND OBEY

SCRIPTURE: 2 Kings 15:1-7; 2 Chronicles 26; Isaiah 6

SUGGESTED TOPICS: Obedience to God; pride; consequences of sin

BIBLE BACKGROUND

After the split of the kingdom of Israel into Israel and Judah, a series of kings held power for varying amounts of time. All the kings of Israel and many of the kings of Judah had evil reigns, leading their people into idolatry. As a result, the job of prophet in Israel or Judah was hazardous. The king would inquire of the prophet, "Should I go to battle?" If the prophet told him "No, the Lord is not with you," the king might easily order the prophet killed as a traitor to the crown. If he said yes, and the king lost but was able to return, the prophet might be killed for lying to the king. Occasionally, a good king arose in Judah; one who would listen to the prophets of God and act accordingly.

However, even a good king can forget his position in life and allow his successes to go to his head. Uzziah was such a king. 2 Chronicles 26:4 states that Uzziah did what was right in the sight of the Lord. The verses that follow list his considerable accomplishments. The list continues until verse 16 which begins with the dreaded word "but." We find that Uzziah, when he was strong, lifted up his heart to destruction. Against all advice, Uzziah tried to usurp the rightful role of God's priest, and he paid dearly for his folly.

PERFORMANCE TIPS

1. Suggested props: a crown and throne for Uzziah, a large book for Jeiel, a bottle to represent the incense, a curtain or sheet to mark the Holy of Holies.

2. The stage could be divided into two parts: the throne room and the Temple. If your stage is too small, have Uzziah and Jeiel walk while the scene changes from the throne room to the Temple.

3. Uzziah should be played as smug and self-satisfied.

4. Jeiel is always deferential toward Uzziah and bows often, out of habit. But he is sarcastic behind Uzziah's back.

5. The high priest takes his job seriously. He is not impressed with human kings.

6. After the skit, read or tell the story in Isaiah 6 to contrast the two men's attitudes toward God.

DISCUSSION QUESTIONS

1. What were some of the sins Uzziah committed? (Remember, sin means "missing the mark.")

2. What was Uzziah's attitude when his sin was pointed out to him?

3. The high priest's responses to King Uzziah were taken from Job 38 and 39. (Assign short passages to students to read and paraphrase.) What should Uzziah's attitude have been?

4. Read Isaiah 6:5. What was Isaiah's attitude when reminded of his sin?

5. We all sin and need to be corrected. How do you react when somebody points out something you have done wrong?

6. How can you learn to be more like Isaiah? Think of practical things you can do each day.

TRUST AND OBEY

CHARACTERS

UZZIAH (yoo-ZYE-ah)

HIGH PRIEST

JEIEL (JAY-el)

UZZIAH: Where is Jeiel? I want my scribe! Where is he?

JEIEL: *(Runs in, bowing.)* Coming hastily, O Mighty Monarch.

UZZIAH: Have you got the *Book of the Chronicles of Uzziah*?

JEIEL: In my hand. Held most preciously, O Righteous Ruler.

UZZIAH: Good. I feel in need of some good literature. Read about the things I have done.

JEIEL: Where would you have me begin, O Powerful Potentate?

UZZIAH: Anywhere at all. The beginning is always a good place.

JEIEL: And at what point should I cease reading, O Kindly King?

UZZIAH: Just keep reading. I'll tell you when I get tired.

JEIEL *(softly, to audience)***:** Oh dear. The whole book, again.

UZZIAH: What was that?

JEIEL: I said, "Good cheer. Uzziah reigns."

UZZIAH: Very good. Begin.

JEIEL: Ahem. *(Reads.)* "Uzziah's celebrated reign began in his sixteenth year of life. Son of good King Amaziah and Queen Jecoliah..."

UZZIAH: You can skip the family history. That stuff always bores me.

JEIEL: But of course, Munificent Majesty.

UZZIAH: Continue with the good stuff.

JEIEL: "Having sought the Lord God, the God of Abraham, Isaac and Jacob, He who brought us up from the land of Egypt in the days of Moses..."

UZZIAH: Let me see that book. *(JEIEL hands book to UZZIAH.)* That part could be edited a bit. Let's cross out all that bit about Abraham, Isaac, Jacob and Moses.

JEIEL: As you wish, Illustrious Imperator. *(Aside.)* I don't know what that means, but it sounds good. *(Crosses out part of writing.)*

UZZIAH: Continue.

JEIEL: "Mighty Uzziah, Conqueror of Nations, Worker of Wisdom, went to battle..."

UZZIAH: *(Interrupts.)* Is that ALL?

JEIEL: No, Supreme Ruler of All He Surveys. There is much more about your deeds.

UZZIAH: I mean, descriptions of me. There's only two.

JEIEL: Yes.

More Bible Skits ©1994 Gospel Light. Permission granted to photocopy.

UZZIAH: Well, we crossed out all of that Abraham, Isaac, Jacob, Moses stuff. So we can put in more about me. See to it when you leave.

JEIEL: Your every wish is my command, O Living Legend.

UZZIAH: Continue.

JEIEL: "...went to battle. Under his Fabulous Feet, Uzziah trampled the grapes of Philistine manhood into the sweet wine of success to be savored upon the lips of His Illustrious Highness..."

UZZIAH: What's all that mean?

JEIEL: It is a poetic way to say you conquered the Philistines, O Conquering Commander in Chief. I could change it to say "Uzziah conquered Philistia."

UZZIAH: No, the other way sounds better. Continue.

JEIEL: "The deeds of His Royal Highness, Emperor of the Minions, Protector of the Defenseless, Wielder of the Weapons of War, have spread across the breadth of the world. The Ammonites..."

UZZIAH: You can skip that part. Go on to my building projects.

JEIEL: *(Aside.)* Good. The abridged version.

UZZIAH: What was that?

JEIEL: I said, "Good bridges"—referring to your most capable construction.

UZZIAH *(surprised)*: Have I built bridges? I must have. I've done everything else. *(Waves hand.)* Continue.

JEIEL: "Uzziah, Builder of Billions, Mason of Might, Woodworker of Wonder, set his hand to the ageless aggrandizement of His Noble Nation..."

UZZIAH: I like that, "Woodworker of Wonder." By the way, send in the royal physician when you leave. I got a splinter in my finger from the throne.

JEIEL: As my feet leave the throne room, my lips shall impart your most majestic message.

UZZIAH: Continue.

JEIEL: "...tirelessly toiling, the Undaunted Uzziah effortlessly erected towers at the Corner Gate, at the Valley Gate and at the turning of the wall. Fearlessly fortifying the formidable fortresses, His Most Unrelenting Uzziah has prospered the portals of the House of Judah with peace everlasting."

UZZIAH: Stop! Something has occurred to me.

JEIEL: Yes, Omnipotent One.

UZZIAH: All this has happened because I sought the advice of the Lord?

JEIEL: I believe that is in the preface. I can erase that part, should you wish.

UZZIAH: No! It's not that. But what have I done to give thanks? Have I offered thanks at the Temple?

JEIEL: Most assuredly, Majestic Majesty. Every year, you and all the people gather to give the sacrifices to God...

UZZIAH: I'm not talking about that! How utterly boring, sacrificing with the RABBLE. I should do something special. After all, God will surely be pleased with a thank offering from ME. I'm so important! Not like the common people.

JEIEL: *(Aside.)* May the Lord be praised.

UZZIAH: What was that?

JEIEL: I said, "Magnificently raised." Above the level of the common people.

UZZIAH: Quite. Come with me. We'll go to the Temple now.

   (UZZIAH and JEIEL go to the Temple.)

UZZIAH: High Priest! Thank your lucky stars. I have come to sacrifice.

HIGH PRIEST: Have I missed something? Is it time for the sacrifice, already?

UZZIAH: No! This is a special sacrifice, because I'M special.

HIGH PRIEST: This is not the attitude one should have before God.

JEIEL: Careful, High Priest. You're speaking to His Imperial Majesty.

HIGH PRIEST: Then he should stop sounding like His Doddering Donkey. Come to the Lord with thanksgiving and with a humble spirit.

UZZIAH: Nonsense. Humility is fine for those who should be humble, but I'm special. I'm important. I am the KING. I am the Great Builder!

HIGH PRIEST: Where were you when Jehovah laid the foundations of the earth? Have you the ability to measure the earth? Have you stretched a measuring line across its width?

JEIEL *(quietly, to HIGH PRIEST)*: Careful. Don't get him angry!

UZZIAH: I am Uzziah, King of Judah! I have laid waste to vast nations.

HIGH PRIEST: Have you taken hold of the ends of the earth, that the wicked could be shaken out? Have the gates of death been opened to you?

JEIEL: *(To HIGH PRIEST.)* Don't make him angry. You won't LIKE him when he's angry!

UZZIAH: Not since the days of Solomon has such wealth been seen in Judah! I have great herds of sheep and oxen! Vast numbers of horses!

HIGH PRIEST: Who set the wild donkey free? His pasture includes all the mountains. Will the wild ox allow itself to be tamed by you? Have you given the horse its strength? Do hawks and eagles fly because you command them?

JEIEL: *(Rolls eyes.)* Too late. He's mad.

UZZIAH: I WILL sacrifice and the Lord WILL be pleased. He will be pleased because *I* am making the sacrifice.

HIGH PRIEST: *(Crosses arms.)* When you have this attitude, you cannot sacrifice.

UZZIAH: Who says I can't! Give me that incense! *(Grabs incense and exits.)* I will burn incense to God!

HIGH PRIEST *(shocked)*: No! You must not! You must not go into the Holy Place! Only the sons of Aaron have been appointed to enter and burn incense. You are trespassing! *(Runs after UZZIAH.)* What you are doing will neither bring honor to God nor to yourself.

   (UZZIAH stomps into the Holy Place.)

UZZIAH *(screaming)*: AAH! *(Stumbles out of the Holy Place.)*

JEIEL: What is it, my king? What's wrong?

HIGH PRIEST: *(Jumps back.)* It's leprosy! Quick! Cast him out of the Temple! The Temple must not be defiled!

JEIEL *(leading a defeated UZZIAH)*: Don't worry, Leprous Leader. I'll find some way to write this out so that it will sound good.

HECKLING HEZEKIAH

SCRIPTURE: 2 Kings 18; 2 Chronicles 32:1-19; Isaiah 36

SUGGESTED TOPICS: Trusting in God; revering God; discouragement; courage

BIBLE BACKGROUND

Hezekiah inherited a mess. His father, Ahaz, had made Judah a nation of idolatry during his sixteen-year reign. Because Syria and Israel had joined forces against him, Ahaz made a pact with the strongest nation of the time, Assyria. As a present to Tiglath-pilesar, King of Assyria, Ahaz sent a tribute which included all the silver and gold in the Temple as well as what he himself owned. In spite of the alliance, Judah was beset on all sides (see 2 Chronicles 28:16-22). At the time of Ahaz's death, the Temple of God had been closed up and altars to every heathen god imaginable were set up throughout the land. Children were being sacrificed to appease the strange gods.

In spite of the actions of his father (or perhaps because of them), Hezekiah began his twenty-nine-year reign in a very different manner. In the first month, he reopened the Temple and had it cleansed. He tore down all the altars and high places for idol worship. He commanded Judah to come together for a great sacrifice to God, to ask Him to remove their sin. He reinstituted the Passover. Also, he stopped paying tribute to Assyria. After fourteen years, Assyria's new king, Sennacherib, decided enough was enough and launched a major campaign against Hezekiah.

PERFORMANCE TIPS

1. Suggested props: a crown and a chair for Sennacherib, a writing pad for the counselors, a very large book for Rabshakeh, weapons (swords, spears, shields, etc.).

2. Set Sennacherib's camp to one side of the stage. Soldiers and counselors will enter from the near wings. Jerusalem will be offstage in the far wings.

3. When Rabshakeh addresses the people of Jerusalem, he should walk to the opposite side of the stage from Sennacherib. He can simulate shouting by cupping his hands widely around his mouth.

4. Prior to the skit, tell about the cleansing of the Temple, the revival in Judah and the fact that Hezekiah stopped paying tribute. After the skit, ask "What would you do if you had to go to war against the strongest country in the world when your army was one of the weakest?" Then read or tell about Hezekiah's prayer, Isaiah's counsel and God's answer.

DISCUSSION QUESTIONS

1. Why would Hezekiah insist on offering a sacrifice for the sins of the whole country of Judah?

2. Why does God hate idol worship so much? (Read 2 Chronicles 28:3 to see part of the answer.)

3. We don't worship statues of idols, but sometimes we have other gods. What other gods do we allow to creep into our lives?

4. One of Satan's strongest weapons is discouragement. What is discouragement? Why does Satan use it as a weapon?

5. How can God help you overcome discouragement? How can other people help? How can you help others?

HECKLING HEZEKIAH

CHARACTERS
SENNACHERIB (seh-NACK-er-ib)
SOLDIER ONE
SOLDIER TWO
SOLDIER THREE
COUNSELOR ONE
COUNSELOR TWO
COUNSELOR THREE
RABSHAKEH (rab-SHAY-keh)

PRONUNCIATION GUIDE
Assyria (uh-SEER-ee-uh)
Hezekiah (hez-uh-KY-uh)

SOLDIER ONE: O Mighty King Sennacherib, may you live forever.

SENNACHERIB: Speak.

SOLDIER ONE: We have returned from our scouting expedition.

SOLDIER TWO: The city of Jerusalem is just beyond that next hill.

SOLDIER THREE: But our advance scouting reports were wrong.

SENNACHERIB: WRONG?

SOLDIER THREE: "Wrong" is maybe a bit harsh. Let's say "Mistaken."

SENNACHERIB: WRONG?

SOLDIER THREE: OK. Wrong.

SENNACHERIB: In what WAY were they wrong?

SOLDIER ONE: We were told there would be plenty of water flowing down from springs near Jerusalem.

SOLDIER TWO: We were told we would have all we needed to drink.

SOLDIER THREE: But the water is dried up. I think the people might have built a dam in Jerusalem to stop the water.

SENNACHERIB: The scurvy dogs! How dare they? Water is sacred! Counselor!

COUNSELOR ONE: *(Enters.)* Yes, Sire.

SENNACHERIB: Make a note. "Amend the rules of war: Changing the course of waterways will henceforth be prohibited." Got that?

More Bible Skits ©1994 Gospel Light. Permission granted to photocopy.

COUNSELOR ONE: In its entirety, my lord. *(Exits.)*

SENNACHERIB: So. Hezekiah thinks he can stop me by shutting down one little waterway, does he? We're close enough to water and have enough men to shuttle the water back and forth. We'll have enough. Well? Are you still here?

SOLDIER ONE: There's more, Sire.

SENNACHERIB: More?

SOLDIER TWO: Yes, Sire. You remember the reports about the city walls?

SENNACHERIB: Certainly. They're in need of repair.

SOLDIER THREE: No longer, Sire. The inner wall has been built up to the towers.

SENNACHERIB: What do you mean, INNER wall?

SOLDIER ONE: They've built another wall outside of the first, Sire.

SENNACHERIB: A second wall? Counselor!

COUNSELOR TWO: *(Enters.)* Sire?

SENNACHERIB: Make a note. "In conjunction with the *Rules of War*, Article 5, Paragraph 7, Subparagraph 25. No additional fortifications shall be made to capital cities once war has been declared." Got that?

COUNSELOR TWO: From your lips to the page, my lord. *(Exits.)*

SENNACHERIB: Good. Well, Hezekiah's plans will do him no good. I'm the world champion of wall destruction. Any other problems?

SOLDIER ONE: No, O Mighty King.

SOLDIER TWO: None, O Valiant Warrior.

SOLDIER THREE: All is now well, O Terror of the Nations. *(SOLDIERS exit.)*

SENNACHERIB: Counselors!

COUNSELOR ONE: *(Enters.)* We come.

COUNSELOR TWO: *(Enters.)* Most hastily.

COUNSELOR THREE: *(Enters.)* Ever eager to serve.

SENNACHERIB: Yeah, yeah, yeah. What's the latest on our data about Judah?

COUNSELOR ONE: They have fallen away from the true faith. No longer do they worship many gods. They only worship one God.

SENNACHERIB: One God? Why, that's blasphemy! If I only worshiped one God, I'd be the laughingstock of the world.

COUNSELOR TWO: We know they have completely cleaned and repaired the Temple in Jerusalem. Hezekiah has ordered all of the high places to be destroyed. All worship will only happen in the Temple.

SENNACHERIB: And people call ME cruel. How are all the old people supposed to get to Jerusalem for worship?

COUNSELOR THREE: We have also learned that Hezekiah ordered sacrifices to this one God to ask forgiveness for the sin of Judah.

SENNACHERIB: He's not much of a psychologist. You're not supposed to tell people they've done bad things. You're just supposed to call it "alternative lifestyles." Any word on the payment of tribute?

COUNSELOR ONE: Yes, my lord. He has sent a tribute of silver and gold.

SENNACHERIB: The full amount? Three hundred talents of silver and thirty talents of gold?

COUNSELOR TWO: If not the full amount, very close to it.

SENNACHERIB: Ridiculous. Hezekiah hasn't got that much. Where did he get it?

COUNSELOR THREE: Our reports say he took all the gold and silver from the Temple treasury. All the gold and silver vessels from the Temple. He even cut the gold from the doors and the pillars.

SENNACHERIB: Hmm. Get me my lawyer!

RABSHAKEH: *(Enters.)* Here I am.

SENNACHERIB: I sent an ultimatum to Hezekiah. I told him, "Send me three hundred talents of silver and thirty talents of gold or I'll destroy you." And he sent me a bunch of gold and silver.

RABSHAKEH: Then, what's the problem?

SENNACHERIB: The problem is, I WANT to destroy him.

RABSHAKEH: Ah, I see. Let me consult a little volume I have with me. *(Two men carry out huge book. RABSHAKEH thumbs through it.)* Here it is. Torts.

SENNACHERIB: None for me, thanks. I'm watching the old waistline.

RABSHAKEH: Not dessert—damages for wrongful actions. His refusing to pay before you got here caused you to suffer grievous personal loss.

SENNACHERIB: It did?

RABSHAKEH: Work with me on this.

SENNACHERIB: Oh, it did. IT DID!

RABSHAKEH: Therefore, you're going to damage him for his wrongful actions.

SENNACHERIB: Excellent! I'll destroy him now.

RABSHAKEH: Let's do this by the book, shall we? We'll have to inform him of your intent. We also want to destroy his confidence at the same time. How about you leave this to me?

SENNACHERIB: You're the expert.

(RABSHAKEH walks to far side to show he has walked some distance.)

RABSHAKEH: Hey, Judeans! You in Jerusalem! I've got a message for Hezekiah from Sennacherib. Here's the message: Hey! Stupid! What's the matter with you?

SENNACHERIB: *(Stands where RABSHAKEH left him and delivers rest of lines to audience.)* Couldn't have put it better, myself.

RABSHAKEH: Who do you think is going to help you if the mighty king of Assyria is against you?

SENNACHERIB: He could have been a little more forceful. Mighty king of Assyria, Ruler of the Universe, Conqueror of All that Lives, Destroyer of Dogs Who Don't Pay Up. Things like that.

RABSHAKEH: Maybe you're planning to trust Egypt?

SENNACHERIB: He might be. Egypt is pretty strong.

RABSHAKEH: I say, hah! Egypt's strength is the same as a broken stick! If you lean on Egypt, you'll impale yourself!

SENNACHERIB: Nice touch.

RABSHAKEH: Maybe you're planning to trust in God? What? You got a penny that says "In God We Trust"? How can you trust God when Hezekiah destroyed all His places of worship?

SENNACHERIB: That'll teach Hezekiah to be a blasphemer.

RABSHAKEH: OK, here's the deal! You give us a damage deposit, say a few hostages, and Sennacherib will give you two thousand horses!

SENNACHERIB: Why would I do that?

RABSHAKEH: But only if you have enough soldiers to ride them!

SENNACHERIB: Oh! Excellent!

RABSHAKEH: Even if you have two thousand horsemen, do you think you could stop one Assyrian chariot? Hah! We're men of war! You are farmers!

SENNACHERIB: What do farmers have to do with anything? Some farmers are pretty tough.

RABSHAKEH: God told me to go up against Jerusalem and destroy it! Don't let Hezekiah fool you, Judeans! He can't save you!

SENNACHERIB: Good. Talk right to the people. Make them lose heart.

RABSHAKEH: OK! Here's the deal! Surrender to me, the king of Assyria! Bring me presents to show you really mean it! Then I will not harm you! Everyone will have his own farm and will live!

SENNACHERIB: THAT'S where the farms come in.

RABSHAKEH: Don't let Hezekiah fool you by telling you God will save you! What about the gods of all the other countries I have conquered? They couldn't stop me! And Hezekiah's God is no different! Surrender and live! Rebel and die!

SENNACHERIB: That was a good job. Now, I just have to wait a bit for the people to start fleeing the city. Then, I destroy it and all within. *(Laughs wickedly.)*

STANDING FIRM

SCRIPTURE: 1 Corinthians 15:58

SUGGESTED TOPICS: Holding fast to the truth; obeying God; courage

BIBLE BACKGROUND

Jeremiah's tenure as prophet in Judah seemed to have come at an auspicious time. Under the leadership of Josiah, the Temple had been restored and the Book of the Law had been found, producing a revival of worship of the one true God. Josiah's reign continued for eighteen years after God called Jeremiah. Unfortunately, all the laws in the world cannot change the hearts of people. Although changes in worship were made, they were largely superficial; the underlying sin of Judah remained unresolved. When Josiah was killed in battle, his son Jehoahaz reigned for only three months, then was forcibly replaced by the king of Egypt. The remaining kings of Judah did evil in the sight of the Lord until Judah was taken into captivity by Nebuchadnezzar, and Judah was no more.

From a worldly perspective, Jeremiah's ministry was a failure. He called a callous nation to repent, warning of the dire consequences if it refused. But his message was unpopular, so Judah turned to other prophets who would say what she wished to hear. Undaunted by beatings and imprisonment, Jeremiah still proclaimed the word of God, continuing to call the people to repentance even after the nation had fallen.

PERFORMANCE TIPS

1. Suggested props: table and chairs, stack of books to represent legal books.
2. John has no courage to match his convictions. He just wants to be liked.
3. Janet should be portrayed as sarcastic when she speaks to Jacqueline.
4. Jacqueline is polite but firm. She knows she's right.

DISCUSSION QUESTIONS

1. What do you think will happen to Jacqueline because of her stand?
2. What are some things you are asked to do to be popular? How can you resist doing those things which are wrong?
3. What are some ways to determine if an action is right or wrong?
4. What could you do if a friend asked you to do something wrong? What could you say?

Standing Firm

CHARACTERS
JACQUELINE
JANET
JOHN
JAKE

PRONUNCIATION GUIDE
Behemoth (buh-HEE-muth)
Megaloth (MEG-uh-loth)

JAKE: *(Stands.)* As senior partner in this law firm, I've called this meeting to discuss an unfortunate problem with one of our clients, Megaloth Industries.

JACQUELINE: *(Aside to Janet.)* That's one of our biggest clients.

JANET: *(To Jacqueline.)* Yeah. We make at least a hundred thousand dollars a year from them.

JAKE: Naturally, what concerns Megaloth concerns us.

JOHN: As well it should. The affairs of our clients are our sacred trust.

JACQUELINE: What seems to be their problem?

JAKE: At great expense, they have developed a new product. One that will revolutionize the lives of everyone in this great land...

JANET: Excuse me, sir. But you're beginning to sound like an ad executive.

JAKE: Sorry. It's just that the unfairness of the situation upsets me.

JOHN: I can understand that. You're a sensitive man

JACQUELINE: Their problem?

JAKE: It's actually a multiple problem. Part of the problem is their largest competitor: Behemoth, Incorporated.

JANET: What's that giant trying to do? Squash the little man, again?

JAKE: Actually, Behemoth says Megaloth stole the idea from them.

JOHN: Well! The nerve of those liars!

JACQUELINE: So our job is to prove who actually developed the idea first.

JAKE: No. We DON'T want to do that.

JANET *(confused)***:** Why is that, sir?

JAKE: Because Behemoth DID develop it. Megaloth simply stole the idea and adapted it to their needs. What we need is a legal stratagem to confuse the issue until Megaloth can get their product out.

JOHN: OK. How can we do that?

JACQUELINE: We can't.

JAKE: And why do you say that?

JACQUELINE: Because it's WRONG.

JOHN: She does have a point there.

JANET: Don't be a fool, Jackie. BEHEMOTH isn't paying us. Megaloth is!

JOHN: Precisely! Just what I was going to say.

JAKE: Good. Then we're all agreed.

JACQUELINE: No, we're not all agreed. We can't do it. It's wrong.

JANET: *(Sighs.)* Miss Goody-Two-Shoes. I knew we shouldn't have taken you in.

JAKE: What seems to be your problem?

JACQUELINE: It's against the LAW. We KNOW our client stole the idea. We can't help them profit from it.

JOHN: Good point. Ethics and all that.

JANET: You want us to lose a six-figure client? They don't grow on trees, you know.

JAKE: Besides, this is nothing new to business. It's done all the time.

JACQUELINE: Not by me. It's wrong.

JANET: What's wrong with helping a client make a few bucks?

JACQUELINE: How can I make you people understand? It's a sick bird!

JAKE, JOHN and JANET: What?

JACQUELINE: It's a sick bird. Ill eagle.

JAKE and JANET: *(Groan.)*

JOHN: *(Catches on slowly.)* Ill eagle...sick bird—ha! Very good!

JAKE: Let me point out to our esteemed associate that our job is to protect our clients.

JACQUELINE: Agreed. But our job is NOT to subvert the law. If anybody respects the law, lawyers should.

JOHN: Hear, hear! *(Applauds but stops as JAKE and JANET stare at him.)*

JANET: Of COURSE we respect the law. But it's very vague on this point.

JAKE: Precisely. We simply have to ignore the portions we don't like and concentrate on those we do.

JANET: Certain considerations must bow to others.

JACQUELINE: In other words, if the fee is big enough, look the other way?

JAKE: I knew you'd see it. Janet, get right on it. Find anything that will help us.

JACQUELINE: I DON'T see it! I disagree!

JANET: No problem, sir. I've got a few tricks Behemoth has never seen.

JOHN: You said it was a multiple problem, sir?

JAKE: Yes. The government seems to be a little uncomfortable with Megaloth's version of the product. What was the term they used? "Environmentally unfriendly."

JACQUELINE: You mean, it's a POLLUTANT?

JAKE: Pollutant is such an UGLY word. *(Slowly and distinctly.)* Environmentally unfriendly.

JACQUELINE: If you call a pile of manure a bed of roses, it still stinks.

JOHN: Manure. Roses. Stinks. That's good. Very funny.

JANET: Worried about the whales again? Color Jackie green.

JAKE: It IS a point to consider.

JACQUELINE: Thank you, sir.

JAKE: But the point is, how much is too much? John, you're the best man for this. We have to prove that Megaloth's product is no more harmful than something else in common use.

JOHN: How harmful is it?

JAKE: Very. So find an analogy that will confuse people.

JACQUELINE: *(Shakes head.)* I don't believe it.

JOHN: I haven't even FOUND it yet. How can you not believe it?

JANET: Jackie Greenpeace here means she finds our callous behavior intolerable.

JACQUELINE: *(Smiles sweetly.)* Thank you. I couldn't have worded it better.

JANET: Look, little girl. Wake up and smell the coffee. Refusing to help our client will not save the humpbacks. HELPING them will save our JOBS.

JAKE: You have a way of finding the crux and stating it well.

JANET: Thank you, sir.

JACQUELINE: Don't you care about anything but money?

JANET: Of course, I do. Jewels, clothes, cars.

JOHN: *(Snaps fingers.)* That's IT! Does less harm to the environment than the exhaust from one vehicle!

JAKE: But it doesn't hurt the atmosphere. It ruins the WATER.

JOHN: That's the beauty of the argument. By comparing water pollution with air pollution, we've confused the issue. It'll take years to sort out. No politician wants to wrestle with a problem for years. They'll let it through.

JACQUELINE: But is the statement true?

JOHN: Who CARES if it's true? It'll WORK. That's the issue.

JACQUELINE: What ever happened to truth?

JANET: It disappeared with beauty. Lighten up.

JAKE: Good. Everything is settled. Back to work. Oh, Jacqueline, see me in my office. We have to reevaluate your position with the firm.

THE WRITING ON THE WALL

SCRIPTURE: Daniel 5

SUGGESTED TOPICS: Obeying God; honesty; courage

BIBLE BACKGROUND

Because of the sin of Israel and Judah, God allowed both to be taken into captivity by Assyria and Babylon respectively. When Babylon conquered a country, the royalty, nobility and well-educated were either killed or carried off in captivity. These captives were then trained in the ways of the Chaldeans so they could serve the king of Babylon. The commoners were left to tend the land under the supervision of governors placed there by Babylon.

Among the young men who were carried off for training was Daniel. In spite of the attempts of Babylon to indoctrinate him into its culture, he remained faithful to the God of Israel. His responsible actions were honored by God who granted him such great wisdom and insight that he soon rose to a position of influence and respect in Babylon. For many years, Daniel served as a trusted advisor to King Nebuchadnezzar, but when Belshazzar succeeded to the throne, Daniel's value was overlooked until the night of a fateful banquet.

PERFORMANCE TIPS

1. Suggested props: table, dishes (preferably unbreakable, some wrapped in foil to simulate gold and silver), chairs, crown for Belshazzar.
2. When repeating the name of Nebuchadnezzar, the tone should be solemn, honoring his memory.
3. For comedic purposes, Belshazzar and the wise men can let their knees knock in an exaggerated manner when they see the writing on the wall.
4. If you wish, continue the skit by having Daniel enter and interpret the writing. If not, finish the story either by reading it from the Bible or simply telling it.
5. Consider introducing the skit by telling the story of Daniel's instruction in Babylonian ways and the telling of Nebuchadnezzar's dream. Explain that the new king either didn't know about Daniel or had forgotten how much he had helped Nebuchadnezzar.

DISCUSSION QUESTIONS

1. In Daniel 1, Daniel and his three friends refused to eat certain things from the king's table. Why?
2. If the king had been angry about this, what might have happened to the four young men?
3. Belshazzar did not know about Daniel, even though he had helped Belshazzar's father. Why might Belshazzar have forgotten about Daniel?
4. What was Daniel's reward for telling the meaning of the writing? What was the danger in telling Belshazzar what the writing meant?
5. What are some situations in which a kid your age might need courage? How can someone find the necessary courage?

More Bible Skits ©1994 Gospel Light. Permission granted to photocopy.

THE WRITING ON THE WALL

CHARACTERS

BELSHAZZAR (bell-SHAZ-ur)
WISE MAN ONE
WISE MAN TWO
WISE MAN THREE
SERVANT
QUEEN

PRONUNCIATION GUIDE

Mene (MEE-nee)
Nebuchadnezzar (NEB-uh-kad-NEZ-er)
Parsin (PAR-sun)
Tekel (TEE-kul)

BELSHAZZAR: Gentlemen, gentlemen, gentlemen! Unaccustomed as I am to public speaking, nonetheless I say this: Eat, drink, be merry! For tomorrow we diet! But seriously, eat and drink all you want. This feast has seven days. Or more, if we're having FUN. Thank you. *(Sits down beside WISE MAN.)*

WISE MAN ONE: A fine feast, my liege.

BELSHAZZAR: Thank you. But I can't help but feel it's missing something.

WISE MAN TWO: Good food. Good wine. What else?

BELSHAZZAR: I don't know. Better entertainment, perhaps.

WISE MAN THREE: If I may speak, my lord?

BELSHAZZAR: Please do.

WISE MAN THREE: The food and drink are excellent. Likewise, the entertainment. The problem lies in the place settings.

BELSHAZZAR: The DISHES?

WISE MAN ONE: He may be on to something.

WISE MAN TWO: True.

BELSHAZZAR: But these are the palace's best dishes!

WISE MAN THREE: That may be. But we've all SEEN them before. They were used at all the feasts given by your esteemed father, Nebuchadnezzar.

BELSHAZZAR and WISE MEN: *(Rise and place hands over hearts.)* Nebuchadnezzar. *(ALL sit.)*

WISE MAN THREE: You need something different.

BELSHAZZAR: Would you have me go to the peasants and beg for dishes?

WISE MAN THREE: Of course not. To use peasants' dishes would insult your guests. I do not propose a solution. I merely point out the problem.

BELSHAZZAR: I see. If I get the potters working on new dishes immediately...

WISE MAN ONE: They will not be ready until the next feast, my liege.

BELSHAZZAR: It takes that long?

WISE MAN ONE: I'm afraid so.

BELSHAZZAR: Then what can I do to liven up THIS feast?

WISE MAN TWO: If I may be so impertinent, my king?

BELSHAZZAR: Go ahead. Impert.

WISE MAN TWO: I would suggest that his majesty change the dishes.

BELSHAZZAR: But with WHAT? These are the best in the palace!

WISE MAN TWO: But not in the LAND, my king.

WISE MAN ONE: Ah.

WISE MAN THREE: Of course.

BELSHAZZAR: Look! I know you guys are paid to be mysterious, but could you give me a hint? Is it bigger than a bread box?

WISE MAN ONE: In the museum, my liege...

WISE MAN TWO: Treasures from other lands, my king...

WISE MAN THREE: Removed, my lord, by your esteemed father, Nebuchadnezzar.

BELSHAZZAR and WISE MEN: *(Rise and place hands over hearts.)* Nebuchadnezzar. *(ALL sit.)*

BELSHAZZAR: What about the museum?

WISE MAN TWO: Included in the treasures are dishes of gold, silver, brass, iron, wood and stone...

WISE MAN ONE: Taken from the Temple in Jerusalem...

WISE MAN THREE: By your illustrious father, Nebuchadnezzar.

BELSHAZZAR and WISE MEN: *(Rise and place hands over hearts.)* Nebuchadnezzar. *(ALL sit.)*

BELSHAZZAR: So?

WISE MAN ONE: Have the vessels brought to the feast.

WISE MAN TWO: Place them before your wives and concubines and princes.

WISE MAN THREE: And, of course, your most illustrious majesty himself.

BELSHAZZAR: Eat and drink from the dishes of a god? What a splendid idea! I, of course, will have the gold dishes.

WISE MAN ONE: Naturally.

BELSHAZZAR: Wood and stone will be good enough for the women.

WISE MEN: Naturally.

BELSHAZZAR: Even as you have suggested, let it be done.

> *(SERVANT brings in dishes. Party continues.)*

BELSHAZZAR: *(Stares at wall, grabs throat and screams.)* Aaaagh!

WISE MAN ONE: What is it, my liege?

WISE MAN TWO: He must have something stuck in his throat.

WISE MAN THREE: Quick. The hemlock maneuver.

WISE MAN TWO: You mean, the Heimlich maneuver.

WISE MAN THREE: No. The hemlock maneuver. Pour hemlock down his throat. Hemlock is poison; he throws up; his throat is clear.

WISE MAN ONE: But what if he dies from the poison?

WISE MAN THREE: At least it's faster than choking to death.

WISE MAN TWO: True. Bring hemlock!

BELSHAZZAR: No! *(Points.)* Look!

WISE MEN: *(Look in direction he points, grab throats and scream.)* Aaagh!

BELSHAZZAR: That hand! Those words! What can it mean?

WISE MAN ONE: Eenie, meenie...Looks like some kind of children's rhyme.

WISE MAN TWO: That's not what it says! It says MENE, MENE, TEKEL, PARSIN. It's calling someone cruel for tickling a parson. Not the king, surely. But it IS his wall.

WISE MAN THREE: That's not what it means. It would be spelled differently if it was talking about being nasty. Aha. It's a warning about an uprising. Many, many tekels will be uprising.

WISE MAN ONE: What's a tekel?

WISE MAN THREE: I don't explain everything. I just read it.

WISE MAN TWO: Well, I don't like your reading any better than mine.

WISE MAN THREE: Nonetheless, we must warn the king. My lord, the tekels are about to revolt.

BELSHAZZAR: The only revolting thing here is you three. You're supposed to be smart. What does this mean?

QUEEN *(entering)*: What is all the commotion in here? We women in the next room can't here ourselves think.

BELSHAZZAR: *(Points to wall.)* Look!

QUEEN: What? Graffiti? Honestly! You men get a little wine in you and you're worse than children! You've chiselled that right into the wall. It'll take weeks to sand that out!

BELSHAZZAR: But we didn't do it!

QUEEN *(sarcastically)*: Oh? I suppose a giant hand came down and wrote it?

BELSHAZZAR: Yes.

QUEEN: Oh, really. You've been drinking and then want me to believe a crazy story like....Wait a minute. You're serious, aren't you?

BELSHAZZAR *(nodding head)*: Uh-huh.

QUEEN *(turning to WISE MEN)*: Well? You're the wise guys. What does it mean?

WISE MAN ONE: As near as we can tell, it's either a children's rhyme...

WISE MAN TWO: Or some nasty person is tickling a parson...

WISE MAN THREE: Or the tekels are planning a rebellion.

QUEEN: You three are like garlic in a leg of mutton...

WISE MEN: Huh?

QUEEN: You stink up the joint. Listen, Belshazzar, you want to know what that writing means?

BELSHAZZAR: Of course I do.

QUEEN: Then deep-six these losers and do what I tell you. There's a man who used to advise your father, Nebuchadnezzar.

BELSHAZZAR and WISE MEN: *(Rise and place hands over hearts.)* Nebuchadnezzar. *(ALL sit.)*

QUEEN: This guy understands dreams before people even tell him what the dream was. Go find him. He'll tell you what it means. But I'm warning you ahead of time, you may not like what he says. He's not always popular, but he's always honest.

RESPECT

SCRIPTURE: Ezra 1—3; Zechariah 7

SUGGESTED TOPICS: Respect; courtesy

BIBLE BACKGROUND

Judah had been carried into exile by Babylon. Years later, Babylon was overthrown by the Medes and Persians. However, Judah was still in captivity. With the permission of King Cyrus (as prophesied in Isaiah 44:28 before Judah was exiled), approximately fifty thousand Jews were allowed to return to their homeland to begin the rebuilding process. Under the capable leadership of Zerubbabel, the work began.

Throughout the lengthy rebuilding process, Zerubbabel and the prophets Haggai and Zechariah encouraged the people in Jerusalem to remember the God of Israel and to honor Him by being obedient to His word and commandments. Their actions and their words demonstrated the respect due to God.

PERFORMANCE TIPS

1. Suggested props: various goods for sale, a table to represent the counter, cash register, maps, oil containers, etc.
2. The customer is in a hurry. All of his actions should indicate impatience.
3. The old man moves and speaks slowly. Everything he does is deliberate.
4. The old man always speaks respectfully to the customer; the customer rarely speaks respectfully to the old man.

DISCUSSION QUESTIONS

1. What does the word "respect" mean?
2. In what ways did the old man show respect to his customer?
3. In what ways did the customer show lack of respect for the old man?
4. The old man also showed respect for his country. How?
5. Suppose certain people in powerful positions don't earn our respect (e.g., policemen, politicians, judges, parents, teachers). Should we show respect to them anyway? Why or why not?

RESPECT

CHARACTERS

OLD MAN

CUSTOMER

(CUSTOMER comes running into service station.)

CUSTOMER: Hey! Hey! Hey! Hop to it! Car's outside, needs a fill. I'm in a hurry. Move it, old fellow.

OLD MAN: On my way, sir. *(Slowly shuffles offstage.)*

CUSTOMER: *(To himself.)* Doddering old fool. *(To OLD MAN.)* C'mon, c'mon, c'mon. I got things to do, places to go, people to see. Move it! *(OLD MAN slowly shuffles onstage.)*

OLD MAN: Want the oil checked, sir?

CUSTOMER: No, no, no! Fill it with gas. Move it, move it, move it! *(OLD MAN slowly shuffles to oil rack, picks up container.)*

OLD MAN: It's on special today, sir.

CUSTOMER: How many times do I have to tell you? No! N-O! Fill the car! Go, go, go!

OLD MAN *(saluting CUSTOMER)***:** Right away, sir. *(Slowly shuffles offstage.)*

CUSTOMER *(looking at merchandise)***:** Everything here but speed. *(Looks at watch.)* Hurry up, old fellow. I don't have all day. *(OLD MAN slowly shuffles onstage.)*

OLD MAN: You've got a broken headlight, sir. Could be dangerous driving at night. Want I should fix it for you? *(Shuffles over to counter, picks up box.)* Got some real good ones On special.

CUSTOMER: No! I'm not planning to drive at night, old-timer. Gas?

OLD MAN: Filling up now, sir. Help yourself to coffee. *(Points.)* On the house. *(Shuffles offstage.)*

CUSTOMER: What a place! TURTLES move faster! C'mon, c'mon, c'mon. *(Paces around. OLD MAN shuffles onstage.)*

OLD MAN: There. The windshield's nice and clean. But there's a problem, sir.

CUSTOMER: What, what, what, what, WHAT?

OLD MAN: You got a star. Right up near the roof line where it's hard to see. Should take care of it, sir. Could turn into a crack if you don't.

CUSTOMER: And you've got a special to take care of it?

OLD MAN: Nope.

CUSTOMER: Well, that's a surprise.

OLD MAN *(pointing):* Harry's Glass. One block down. Special this week, sir.

CUSTOMER: Look! I came in for GAS! Hurry, hurry, hurry. I don't WANT other things. If the glass cracks, it cracks. Now get out there and finish filling my tank!

OLD MAN: Almost finished, sir. *(Shuffles offstage.)*

CUSTOMER: That's what I get for stopping at a small town. Geezerville. What's taking him so long? *(OLD MAN shuffles in, goes behind counter.)*

OLD MAN: All filled, sir. Will that be cash or credit card?

CUSTOMER: There's no difference. It doesn't matter, Pops.

OLD MAN: Discount for cash, sir.

CUSTOMER: Yeah, OK. Cash.

OLD MAN: Figure that discount for you, sir. *(Takes pencil and slowly writes. CUSTOMER throws up hands in despair, looks around, sees picture on wall.)*

CUSTOMER: I see you're a (name of political party currently in power).

OLD MAN: No, sir. Been a (name of alternate political party) all my life.

CUSTOMER: But you've got a picture of (name of current president) on the wall.

OLD MAN: No, sir.

CUSTOMER: Sure you do. Are you blind as well as lame? Right there. *(Points.)*

OLD MAN: No, sir. That's a picture of the president of the United States on the wall. That'll be nine dollars and twenty-five cents.

CUSTOMER: Here! *(Throws money on counter, turns to leave.)*

OLD MAN: Thank you, sir. You from around these parts?

CUSTOMER: *(Turns.)* No! Why?

OLD MAN: Might need a map, sir. Wouldn't want to get lost on a back road. *(Shuffles over to map stand, picks up map and holds it out.)* On the house. *(CUSTOMER looks at OLD MAN, gestures disdainfully and leaves.)*

OLD MAN *(looking off stage, saluting):* Happy motoring, sir.

DUMB, DUMB, DUMB

SCRIPTURE: Ezra 7—10

SUGGESTED TOPICS: Obeying God; respect for God; repentance

BIBLE BACKGROUND

The people of Israel and Judah had been carried into captivity because of their sin. The worst sin was the idolatry that had infested the people of God as they intermarried with the people of the surrounding nations. Now, approximately sixty years after the first contingent of Jews had made their way back to their homeland, Ezra followed with a king's ransom to help rebuild the land.

Ezra expected to find a nation committed to the God of its forefathers. Instead, he found a nation that had slipped back into its idolatrous past. The cancer which had nearly destroyed the nation had returned. But with the skill of a surgeon, Ezra prepared to operate on that cancer and make the nation whole.

PERFORMANCE TIPS

1. Suggested props: table and chairs, papers (reports) for Ezra to look through.
2. Eliezer thinks the hard part's finished. He's relaxed, casual.
3. Ezra knows much is left to be done. He's intense.

DISCUSSION QUESTIONS

1. Why was Ezra so worried?
2. What kinds of sin were the people of Israel committing?
3. What did the people of Israel do to show they respected God? (See Ezra 10:9-19.)
4. Why is confession of sin a way to show respect to God?
5. What are some practical ways to show repentance for unconfessed sin in your life?

DUMB, DUMB, DUMB

CHARACTERS

EZRA

ELIEZER (EL-ee-AY-zer)

PRONUNCIATION GUIDE

Artaxerxes (ar-tuh-ZERK-sees)

ELIEZER: Well, everything's just about done.

EZRA (*studying paper*)**:** Hmm?

ELIEZER: Well, the hard part's done. We got here with all the gold and silver. I still think it was dumb not to ask Artaxerxes for a regiment of soldiers to go with us.

EZRA: I couldn't.

ELIEZER: Why not? We could have used protection. We were carrying almost twenty-nine tons of silver. And thirty pounds of gold. That's enough to tempt any thief.

EZRA: What? I'm supposed to go to Artaxerxes and say, "Please, kind King. Since we have so much to carry, could you please send all the soldiers you can spare to protect us?"

ELIEZER: It sounds reasonable to me.

EZRA: That would have been dumb. Hadn't I told Artaxerxes of the great power of God?

ELIEZER: But...

EZRA: But, but, but. Would Artaxerxes have had any respect for a God who needs the protection of a man? Shouldn't it be the other way around?

ELIEZER: Well, of course. But a little extra couldn't hurt.

EZRA: It couldn't? Don't you read history?

ELIEZER: Not all the time.

EZRA: Read it. Then we'll talk. See how God wants His people to recognize His protection.

ELIEZER: Well, anyway. Now we can relax.

EZRA: Relax? Are you crazy?

ELIEZER: It's done! The priests have all the money. Everything's been delivered. Time to put up the old feet, sit back and...

EZRA: Get to work. We have been entrusted by Artaxerxes to see that everything is done according to his decree. More importantly, we must see that things are done by God's decree.

ELIEZER: Oh, well. That should be no problem.

EZRA: No problem? Look at this! *(Hands paper to ELIEZER.)*

ELIEZER: Marriage certificate. Everything seems to be in order.

EZRA: In order? How can you say, "In order"? The man is a Levite.

ELIEZER: Sure. But priests can marry.

EZRA: The woman is a Canaanite!

ELIEZER: *(Studies paper more closely.)* Are you sure?

EZRA: I only wish there was room for doubt. How dumb can these people be?

ELIEZER: *(Hands paper back.)* Don't make a big deal out of it. It's only one couple.

EZRA: Haven't you heard that one bad apple can ruin the whole barrel?

ELIEZER: Well, yes.

EZRA: A little yeast makes all the dough rise?

ELIEZER: Well...yes.

EZRA: And this is not an isolated case. There must be hundreds, maybe thousands of marriages between God's people and other races.

ELIEZER: Hey, maybe it's not so bad. Maybe all the heathen women are learning to respect God.

EZRA: Read your history. The road to righteousness is narrow and difficult. The road to evil is wide and easy. I have reports of the activities of the men of Israel. Already, they are forgetting the decrees of God.

ELIEZER: So remind them.

EZRA: Don't you see? We were taken into captivity for the very sin now being committed! We must end this matter, now! I have prayed and confessed our sin to God.

ELIEZER: OUR sin? YOU didn't do anything wrong!

EZRA: If the people of Israel sin, the leaders have also sinned. We must make this right. Call all the people together.

ELIEZER: Now?

EZRA: This very second!

ELIEZER: But it's raining. Cats and dogs. Even stronger than that. Horses and cows. We'll get pneumonia!

EZRA: Which is worse, a few sniffles or the destruction of Israel? Call the people!

ELIEZER: OK. But they aren't going to like it.

ELIEZER: They would worry about WEATHER when they face the wrath of GOD? *(To himself.)* Dumb, dumb, dumb.

More Bible Skits

KEEP ON KEEPING ON

SCRIPTURE: Nehemiah 1—2:10; 4—6

SUGGESTED TOPICS: Perseverance; reliance on God

BIBLE BACKGROUND

Nehemiah was cupbearer to the king. This was a much more important job than simply serving beverages to the king. It was even more involved than being a food taster to ensure the king was not poisoned. Being in close proximity to the king, the cupbearer often became a confidant of and advisor to the king. Rule number one for the cupbearer was: always look happy. The king wanted pleasant countenances surrounding him. If you could not control your visage, you might lose your head completely. Therefore, when Nehemiah appeared downhearted before Artaxerxes (see Nehemiah 2:1,2), Nehemiah had a great deal to fear. Not only was he already in danger of death, but he then compounded the danger by asking for a leave of absence.

Nehemiah's story is one of bravery, wisdom and perseverance. Against all odds, he set out to restore Israel to her former glory. Along the way, he had to contend with ridicule, threats, lies and the sin of his own people.

PERFORMANCE TIPS

1. Suggested props: a table and chairs, papers for Nehemiah to look through.

2. Ezer should appear tired. He has been working long, hard hours.

DISCUSSION QUESTIONS

1. How did Nehemiah show wisdom in his preparations to rebuild Jerusalem?

2. What were some of the obstacles Nehemiah had to overcome in his task?

3. What evidence do we have that Nehemiah had studied the Jewish Scriptures?

4. What are some reasons we should read the Bible?

5. What obstacles do you face in your life? How can you overcome them?

KEEP ON KEEPING ON

CHARACTERS
NEHEMIAH (NEE-eh-MYE-uh)
EZER (EE-zer)

PRONUNCIATION GUIDE
Sanballat (san-BAL-lut)
Sousa (SOO-suh)

EZER: *(Enters, brushing off clothes.)* What a dirty job!

NEHEMIAH: But somebody has to do it.

EZER: I like that. "It's a dirty job, but somebody has to do it." That could be a famous quote someday. I think I'll write it down. *(Looks around for pen and paper.)*

NEHEMIAH: There are more pressing matters at hand.

EZER: True. I'll write it down later.

NEHEMIAH: Now then. What are the reports?

EZER: The work on the wall is progressing nicely. Should be completely finished today. If it hadn't been for Sanballat, we might already be done.

NEHEMIAH: You know, sometimes I thank God for Sanballat.

EZER: If that's a joke, I missed the punch line. Sanballat's given you nothing but headaches! First, he laughed at you. Told you that you were crazy to think you could actually rebuild the wall.

NEHEMIAH: Every now and then, I thought he might have been right.

EZER: Then, we got reports that he might attack us. So, we've had to work with one hand while we remained armed and ready to fight with the other.

NEHEMIAH: Fortunately, that seems to have been an idle threat.

EZER: Then, when he knows he can't stop the building, he invites you out to have a conference with him. But all the time, he plans to kill you. And you thank God?

NEHEMIAH: Yes. I wonder if we would have had the strength to continue were he not here to remind us that we have enemies all around us.

EZER: *(Shakes head.)* I guess that's one way to look at it. So, now that the wall's done, I guess you'll be heading back to Sousa and that cushy job you had before.

NEHEMIAH: Head back? When there's so much left to do?

EZER: Like what?

NEHEMIAH: Bringing the Law back to the people.

EZER: Well, out here in the old west, we pretty much live by the law of the sword.

NEHEMIAH: If by that curious phrase you mean that whoever HAS power USES it, that's unfortunately true.

EZER: Yeah. Well, that's just the way it is.

NEHEMIAH: But not the way it WILL be. If we are to be a nation, we must remember who we are. We are the chosen people of the Most High God! It's time for us to act like we believe this.

EZER: You can't change people, Nehemiah.

NEHEMIAH: I know *I* can't. But GOD can—and He will! First on my list is this money-lending business. The rich get richer and the poor stay poor. This will change.

EZER: Lots of luck. The one time people NEVER change is if it's going to cost them money. Oh, well. Back to work. It's a dirty job, but that's life. No. That's not the quote I was going to write down. What was it again? "When the going gets tough, the tough get going"? Nope. "It never rains but it pours"? That's not it, either.

NEHEMIAH: God's speed on your dirty job.

EZER: Thanks. Someone's got to do it, you know. *(To himself.)* What WAS that quote? *(Exits.)*

RISKY BUSINESS

SCRIPTURE: Esther 1—6:11

SUGGESTED TOPICS: Courage; thankfulness; humility

BIBLE BACKGROUND

The book of Esther was written to give the history of the Jewish holiday, Purim. It almost did not receive canonical status for the simple reason that God is never directly mentioned in it. In spite of this omission, the book clearly shows how God protects His people. If Vashti had not been banished, Esther would not have been chosen queen. If Esther had not been queen, Mordecai would have had no pipeline to the palace to warn Xerxes of the plot against his life nor to request the second decree (see Esther 8:8-14). And if Esther and Mordecai had not been devoted to their people, nor possessed the courage to risk their lives on their behalf, the evil plot of Haman would have wreaked a terrible fate on God's people living in Persia. God had long ago promised that a faithful remnant would endure, and to fulfill the promise, God protected His people.

PERFORMANCE TIPS

1. Suggested props: a throne, a crown and a scepter for Xerxes.

2. Each scene takes place in the throne room of Xerxes. Have one side of the stage reserved for the vestibule leading to the room. The beginning of Scenes Two and Three take place in the vestibule and then Esther and Haman enter the throne room proper.

3. When Haman is considering headgear in Scene Three, perhaps have three different types of hats for him to try on as he thinks of how he might look. If so, adjust the script to suit the hats you have available.

4. Haman is arrogant. Esther is quietly confident. Keep them in character.

5. During her scene in the vestibule, Esther is frightened. Be sure she gives the appearance of worry (wringing her hands, pacing back and forth, etc.).

6. During the asides, the characters might lean or turn toward the audience to indicate that the other characters do not hear what is said.

DISCUSSION QUESTIONS

1. How did Esther show respect to the king? To Mordecai? To her people?

2. What risks did Esther take by appearing before the king?

3. At the second banquet, Esther had to demonstrate to the king that he had behaved foolishly by allowing Haman to write a decree to have the Jews killed. What risks might she have been taking by doing this?

4. What sorts of things that you are required to do feel risky to you? What might be some of the consequences of taking these risks?

5. Often, an action is worth the risk. That does not diminish the fear we might face in taking the action. What can you do to help keep the fear under control?

RISKY BUSINESS

CHARACTERS
ESTHER
HAMAN (HAY-man)
XERXES (ZERK-sees)

PRONUNCIATION GUIDE
Mordecai (MOR-duh-kye)

SCENE ONE

HAMAN: *(Strides in.)* O Mighty King, may you live forever.

XERXES: Haman, my most honored advisor. Do you have some advice for me?

HAMAN: O Mighty One, ruler of the Medes and Persians, Conqueror of the World...

XERXES: All that, and more. Come close and bring me your advice.

HAMAN: I am afraid I have most distressing news, O King.

XERXES: Distressing?

HAMAN: Enough to cause one's hair to fall from one's head.

XERXES: Sounds serious. What is it?

HAMAN: There is a certain people in your kingdom, scattered through all the provinces...

XERXES: I should have thought many people were scattered through the provinces.

HAMAN: Yes, many. But only one people are the problem.

XERXES: Speak to me of the problem.

HAMAN: Their laws are different from those of all other people.

XERXES: That is wrong. Everyone should follow MY laws.

HAMAN: Precisely my point, O King. They are of no benefit to you.

XERXES: I shall make a new law, immediately. All people shall obey my laws.

HAMAN: That law is already in place, O King.

XERXES: It is? Then why do these people not obey it?

HAMAN: Because, O King, their laws are different from those of other people.

XERXES: I see. What do you propose I do about it?

HAMAN: Nothing too radical, O King.

XERXES: Good. I don't like radicals.

HAMAN: Here is my plot—I mean, plan. They must be eradicated!

XERXES: Turned into radicals?

HAMAN: No. Eradicated. Wiped out!

XERXES: Ah, yes. Wiped out. How much will this cost?

HAMAN: A mere ten thousand talents of silver should do it. But don't worry. As a special favor to you, I'll pay the cost from my own pocket.

XERXES: Very good of you, but the treasury can afford it. Write out a decree. Word it however you think best. Here, take my ring to seal the decree. That will give it full force of law.

HAMAN: Very good, O King. *(Bows and backs toward exit. Stops to speak aside to audience.)* He fell for it. I don't care about all of the Jews. Just one. Mordecai. He refuses to bow down to me. Well, now I can have him killed LEGALLY! Ha, ha! All the Jews will be destroyed because of him.

SCENE TWO

ESTHER *(pacing)*: This is terrible. Terrible! All my people are to be destroyed. Uncle Mordecai was right when he reminded me that I, too, will be killed. Why would Xerxes MAKE such a decree? OK. I'm going in. But Xerxes hasn't invited me. If I go in and he's in a bad mood, he could have me killed! But if I don't, ALL the Jews will be killed! *(Takes deep breath.)* Here goes nothing. *(Steps into throne room.)*

XERXES: *(Sees ESTHER and holds out sceptre.)* Enter and draw near.

ESTHER: *(Enters and touches sceptre.)* My Lord.

XERXES: *(Aside to audience.)* I wonder what's on her mind? It must be important, for her to risk her life this way. *(To ESTHER.)* What do you wish, Queen Esther? You have but to ask and it shall be granted you. Anything up to half of the kingdom.

ESTHER: *(Aside.)* How do I word this? If I sound harsh, he will be displeased, and an angry king is a terrible thing indeed. *(To XERXES.)* If it pleases the king, will he and his advisor, Haman, come to a banquet I am preparing this evening?

XERXES: *(Aside.)* She is putting off her request. I'll humor her. Tonight, I'll ask her again. *(To ESTHER.)* Of course! I shall send for Haman at once. We shall certainly be there.

SCENE THREE

HAMAN: *(To audience.)* I am the second most important man in the kingdom. You want proof? Last night, the queen had a private banquet; today, she's having another. Do you know who was invited? The king and I. That's all. No princes, no foreign royalty. I would be the happiest man in the world were it not for Mordecai. Well, THAT'S about to end. The gallows have already been built. I go in and ask the king for permission to hang Mordecai. What reason do I give? Any one I choose. He is one of those accursed whom the king has already condemned to death. He'll simply meet his just reward a little sooner than the others. Is my hair in place? Good. In to see the king. *(Enters throne room.)*

XERXES: Goodness! Is it time for the banquet, already?

HAMAN: No, O King. I came a bit early.

XERXES: Good! I have something to discuss with you.

HAMAN: My King?

XERXES: There is a man in the kingdom whom I wish to honor.

HAMAN: *(Aside.)* He must mean me. Who else?

XERXES: Everyone in the kingdom must know how much esteem I have for this man.

HAMAN: *(Aside.)* Me! Without doubt, me!

XERXES: You're good with this pageantry stuff. What should I do for this man?

HAMAN: *(Aside.)* Oh! I'm about to be honored. Rapture! And I get to choose the method. Ecstasy! What shall I ask for? *(To XERXES.)* O King, may you live forever.

XERXES: Of course.

HAMAN: This man, of course I have no idea who he may BE, must be displayed royally through the entire city.

XERXES: Yes. Of course.

HAMAN: This man, WHOEVER he may be, won't have good enough clothing for such a procession. So, YOU should give him some of your royal clothing to wear. Something that everyone will recognize as yours.

XERXES: Such as my purple robe?

HAMAN: Perfect! I would look—I mean, HE would look so good in the purple robe. Now then, such a man could not be expected to WALK through the streets.

XERXES: No. That wouldn't look right.

HAMAN: I, that is, HE must ride. But not any old nag. The king's horse.

XERXES: MY horse?

HAMAN: Naturally. You do want to honor me, uh, him?

XERXES: Very well. He shall ride my horse.

HAMAN: What am I thinking? If I—HE is wearing royal robes, he cannot wear any old rag on his head. He'll need something special in the way of headgear.

XERXES: A new top hat?

HAMAN: Hmmmmmmm, no. That wouldn't look right.

XERXES: A new stetson?

HAMAN: Hmmmmmmm, no. I can't quite see it.

XERXES: I have it! A sombrero with gold threads woven into it!

HAMAN: Hmmmmmmm, no. Not quite the right atmosphere. But what am I thinking?

XERXES: *I* don't know. Shall I call for the mind readers?

HAMAN: Only one kind of hat would be suitable for a man wearing royal robes and seated on the royal steed. The king's crown.

XERXES: MY CROWN?

HAMAN: It will only be for a short time, O King.

XERXES: Very well. So shall it be.

HAMAN: Oh dear! An awful thought!

XERXES: What? What is it?

HAMAN: If I'm, that is, the man the king honors is wearing the king's clothing and crown and riding the king's horse, people might think he stole them.

XERXES: That would be unfortunate. He could wear a sign around his neck saying, "The king said I could wear these."

HAMAN: That is one solution. But it might wrinkle the king's robe. Ah!

XERXES: You have another solution?

HAMAN: What do you think of this? You deliver the robe, crown and horse to one of your most noble princes. He takes everything to my, er, the man's house. Then, this most noble prince leads the man whom the king wishes to honor around the streets of the city.

XERXES: That should bring some attention.

HAMAN: Now, we need some kind of proclamation. The noble prince should speak these words: "Here is a man whom the king honors! This is what the king does for the man he esteems!" The noble would, of course, repeat this over and over.

XERXES: Excellent! Perfect! Haman, take this crown. Go and get the purple robe and my horse and take them to Mordecai.

HAMAN: To MORDECAI? But HE isn't a noble prince.

XERXES: No, but YOU are. Put the royal crown and robe on Mordecai. Lead him through the city, just as you have said. Do everything just like we've planned.

HAMAN: MORDECAI?

XERXES: Yes. You won't believe this, but many months ago, he overheard a plot against my life and had me warned. Well, in the confusion of the trial and all that, I totally forgot to reward him. If I hadn't been unable to sleep last night, I wouldn't have had my *Book of Chronicles* read to me and I might never have remembered to reward him.

HAMAN: *(Aside.)* Make a note. Invent some kind of sleeping powder to give the king before bedtime.

ACHAN BRINGS HOME THE BACON

SCRIPTURE: Joshua 7:1-23

SUGGESTED TOPICS: Telling the truth; obeying God; results of sin; greed; theft

BIBLE BACKGROUND

The Israelites had just finished forty years of wandering in the desert, the result of not believing God and being disobedient to His word. Surely, they had learned to trust and obey. God's instructions to the Israelites for the conquering of Jericho, the first Canaanite city to be faced, was to take no plunder for themselves. God was going to bring victory, not so the Israelites could enrich themselves, but as a validation of God's claim to possess the land. All the soldiers listened to the words of Joshua, except for Achan.

The Bible does not specifically say Achan's family knew he had taken any plunder from the city of Jericho. However, this was the first battle in the conquering of the Promised Land. Surely, the families of the soldiers would be anxiously waiting for the return of their husbands, brothers and sons. Also, they were living in tents; tents that could be easily transported on a long journey. How does somebody hide something in a one-room tent so that the other inhabitants are not aware of its existence?

However, even if they did not know Achan had taken the plunder, his family would still have suffered. This is a basic biblical principle. The actions of any individual have an impact on others; most especially do a leader's actions bring consequences to those under that authority.

PERFORMANCE TIPS

1. Suggested props: a multicolored cape or piece of cloth, wood or cardboard wedge spray painted gold or wrapped with gold foil, a bag of silver coins.

2. Very briefly discuss the instructions of God to Joshua concerning the battle of Jericho. Some students may not remember or may never have heard the story before.

3. Point out to the class that the Bible does not tell us Achan's family knew that the gold, silver and cloth were hidden in the tent. It is important for children to understand that their actions can hurt innocent people as well as themselves.

4. Focus attention on the fact that honesty in our personal relationships is essential for a good life.

DISCUSSION QUESTIONS

1. Have you ever done something you knew was wrong but pretended that what you did was all right? Could you ever make yourself believe that it was all right?

2. In the skit, Achan claims that he did not disobey any of the ten commandments. Look at each one (see Exodus 20:1-17). Which ones do you think he broke?

3. What were the consequences of Achan's disobedience? Have you ever told a lie? What happened when the lie was discovered?

4. Has anybody ever told you a lie? How did you feel when you discovered the lie?

5. Why is honesty important?

Achan Brings Home the Bacon

CHARACTERS
ACHAN (AY-kan)
ACHAN'S WIFE
ACHAN'S SON
ACHAN'S DAUGHTER

ACHAN: Wife! Look! You'll never guess what I have.

WIFE: So, if I won't guess, how about you tell me.

CHILDREN: Me, too! Me, too! I want to know, too!

ACHAN: Look at this garment.

WIFE: Oh, Achan! It's gorgeous! Look at all those beautiful colors all interwoven. It's so beautiful! Where did you get it?

ACHAN: The same place that I got these.

CHILDREN: Wow! Look at all that silver! There must be forty years of allowance there. And that wedge of gold! Wow!

WIFE: But Achan, where did you get all these things? They must be worth a fortune.

ACHAN: Where else would one get all these riches in Canaan? I got them from the Canaanites. We'll be rich. Rich!

CHILDREN: Can we have an increase in our allowance now, Dad?

WIFE: Hush, children. Your father and I have to talk. Now, Achan, what do you mean, you got them from the Canaanites? I thought that you were fighting at Jericho all day.

ACHAN: I was. But who do you think lives in Jericho?

SON: Jerichoians?

DAUGHTER: Jerichoites?

CHILDREN: Jericho-ovians?

WIFE: Silence, children. Achan? Are you trying to tell me that you got these things from some Canaanite people in Jericho?

ACHAN: In a manner of speaking. Yes.

WIFE: You mean that you took a bribe so that some of the Jerichoites, Jerichoians... oh, children! Now you have me doing it. So that some of the people in Jericho could escape?

ACHAN: Of course not! What do you think I am—a traitor? Did our leader, Joshua, not say that we must drive out all of the Canaanites from the land? Were we not specifically commanded to destroy all the residents of Jericho, except for those in Rahab's house? I would not take a bribe to let some of the accursed of God live.

WIFE: Then how did you get these things from the Canaanites?

ACHAN: We were fighting through Jericho and I saw a rich man's house. And such a beautiful house it was, too. So, I thought to myself, *What if somebody is hiding in that house?* I went in, looked around and found nobody. But such wealth! Boy! Did I find wealth!

CHILDREN: So what happened, Dad?

ACHAN: I'll tell you. I looked all around. Nobody had come in with me. Nobody knew how much this wealthy Canaanite had. So I hid a little silver, a little gold, this garment and took it with me when we left the rubble that used to be Jericho.

WIFE: But isn't that wrong, Achan? Joshua said we were not to keep anything from Jericho. Joshua said to destroy everything.

CHILDREN: Yeah, Dad. Isn't that wrong?

ACHAN: What could be wrong with it? Look! It's only a little bit of what was there. And look at this beautiful garment. You will look so gorgeous in it. To destroy such a garment as this, that would be wrong. And a little silver and gold. What is wrong with a man trying to better himself so that his children can have some better things?

CHILDREN: Right! There's nothing wrong with bigger allowances.

WIFE: But it doesn't seem right. Isn't it against the Law?

ACHAN: How can it be against the Law? Look! Law number one. "You shall have no other gods before me." I'm not having other gods. Only a little silver and gold.

WIFE: That's true.

ACHAN: Number two. "You shall not make for yourself an idol." Am I making any idols? Number three. "You shall not misuse the name of the Lord your God." I have not misused His name.

CHILDREN: Right on, Dad! Nothing wrong there.

ACHAN: "Remember the Sabbath day by keeping it holy. Honor your father and your mother. You shall not murder. You shall not commit adultery." Does keeping a few little trinkets break any of those laws?

WIFE: Well...no. Number eight. "You shall not steal." How about that one?

ACHAN: What stealing? This is the spoils of war. The only person to have any claim on it was the rich Canaanite, and he doesn't need it now.

WIFE: Well...I suppose.

ACHAN: "You shall not give false testimony against your neighbor." Am I lying about anything that my neighbor did? "You shall not covet...anything that belongs to your neighbor." Does any of this belong to my neighbor? No! It belongs to me. *(Singing.)* "Oh, if I were a rich man..."

WIFE: Hush. You should not sing that song.

ACHAN: Why not?

CHILDREN: Because you don't sing very well.

WIFE: Children! That is no way to speak to your father. No. There are two reasons that you should not sing that song.

ACHAN: What is the first?

WIFE: If anyone should hear you, he might suspect that you have taken some booty from Jericho.

CHILDREN: And then you might have to give it back.

ACHAN: A very good reason. What is the second?

WIFE: The song has not yet been written. It will not be written for more than three thousand years. You should not sing songs that do not exist.

ACHAN: I suppose you're right. Somebody might think that it was fortune-telling or something if I were to sing a song that didn't exist. Oh, well. You must make this garment over into something nice for yourself.

WIFE: It would make a lovely evening gown. But, Achan. If I go out tomorrow with a new fancy dress, what will people say?

DAUGHTER: The women will all be envious and they will say, "Oh! What a lovely dress! Where did you get it?"

WIFE: Precisely.

ACHAN: I see your point, my dear. There could be some embarrassing questions about it. I have it! We will hide what I have taken from Jericho. Then, after a few more conquests, when we have taken some more booty, it will not be so noticeable that we have some new things. Everybody will have new things. But where can we hide this so that nobody will see it?

SON: How about under the floor of the tent, Dad? Nobody would come in with a shovel to look under anybody else's floor.

ACHAN: Ah! That's my son! A true thinking man. Come. We'll do it together. *(Singing.)* "Oh, if I were a rich man...."

SILENCE IS GOLDEN

SCRIPTURE: Proverbs 12:18

SUGGESTED TOPICS: Controlling speech; humility; pride; influence on others

BIBLE BACKGROUND

The Bible repeatedly presents examples which show us the consequences of our actions and attitudes toward others. The book of Proverbs is filled with advice concerning controlling one's tongue, thoughts and actions. Proverbs 12:18 tells us that foolish, rash words are as dangerous and as wounding as the thrusts of a sword. We've all experienced the painful consequences of those kinds of words. And we've all felt remorse for cruel and slanderous words that came from our mouths.

God's Word teaches us to "watch our language," for what we say and how we say it provides windows to our hearts and is an important part of our relationship with Him and others. It's a life's work to learn to put aside all words that do not guard and advance the reputation and well-being of others.

PERFORMANCE TIPS

1. Suggested props: sign that says "TALENT AGENCY," table and chair for Ed, note pad and pencil
2. Ted is loud and brash. He is theatrical and punctuates his words with sweeping gestures. He constantly tries to step between Ed and Fred.
3. Fred always speaks only when spoken to. He does not brag, but is quietly confident.

DISCUSSION QUESTIONS

1. Would you rather know Ted or Fred? Why?
2. In what ways were Ted's words harmful? to himself? to others?
3. Read Proverbs 12:18. What does it mean?
4. When are you tempted to speak unkindly about others? What can you do when this happens?
5. What are some ways your words can heal?

SILENCE IS GOLDEN

CHARACTERS

TED

FRED

EDWARD GAD

TED: Hi there! It's your lucky day! Allow me to introduce myself: "THE AMAZING TED TUNER!" *(To audience.)* No applause! Just throw money!

EDWARD *(holding out hand to shake)*: E. Gad.

TED: *(Jumps back.)* What's wrong?

EDWARD: Nothing. Why do you ask?

TED: You just said, "Egad!"

EDWARD: Sorry. A bit confusing. That's my name. Edward Gad. *(Slowly.)* E. Gad.

TED: Ah! OK. Well, enough about YOU. We're here to talk about ME. No doubt you've heard of me. Amazing Ted Tuner, the greatest guitarist since, well, since guitars were invented! And to think, I've only been playing for six months! I'm a legend in my own mind, er, time!

EDWARD: No, I HAVEN'T heard of you. But I have HEARD you. Who's your friend?

TED: Huh? Oh, Fred. Take a bow, Fred. Amateur keyboard player of sorts. But nothing to compare to the AMAZING TED TUNER! *(To audience.)* That's me, you know.

EDWARD: Yes. I've heard. How can I help you?

TED: Simple. You're a talent AGENT. I'm a TALENT. You agent, I'll talent, and we'll make a million bucks! See? I told you this was your lucky day!

EDWARD: I see. And Fred, tell me about your keyboard work. What's your background?

FRED *(quietly)*: I have a degree from the Chicago Conservatory. I've been playing keyboard instruments since I was seven. I've organized and led classical and jazz groups.

TED: *(Steps in front of FRED.)* Hey! That's old Fred for you. He's just full of education, kind of a stuffed shirt, so to speak. Not me. I'm fresh. I'm a prodigy! Just six months ago I was watching TV and I realized, *Hey! I can do this!* And here I am, THE AMAZING TED TUNER!

EDWARD *(writing)*: Yes. You are. Fresh, that is. *(To himself.)* Fred. *(Flips page and continues writing.)* Ted.

TED: Hey! It's THE AMAZ—

EDWARD *(writing)*: Yes. The Amazing Ted Tuner.

TED: And don't you forget it, little buddy! Amazing's the name; amazing's my game!

EDWARD: I beg your pardon.

TED: That's my slogan, man! "THE AMAZING TED TUNER—Amazing's my name; amazing's my game!" Write that down. We'll want to use it. But then, once you've seen my act, you'll never forget THE AMAZ—

EDWARD: Yes. Quite. And Fred?

TED: *(Steps in front of FRED.)* Does some simple, folksy stuff. I brought him along because I'm gonna give him a BIG BREAK! He can open for me. Wait till you see MY stuff!

EDWARD: I imagine it's AMAZING.

TED: Egad, but you catch on fast, E. Gad! *(To audience.)* See how quick I am to turn a phrase?

EDWARD *(bored)*: Amazing.

TED: Amazing? Why it's STUPENDOUS! COLOSSAL! *(Announcing.)* I AM THE AMAZING TED—

EDWARD: *(Cuts TED off.)* What sort of act do you do?

TED: I TOLD you. What I do is TOTALLY fresh! That's what makes me so AMAZING!

EDWARD: *(Looks past TED.)* Not you. Him. Fred, what do you prefer to play? It seems that you're experienced in many styles.

FRED: Well, I enjoy playing my own work the most. But I enjoy anything I play.

TED: *(Steps in front of FRED.)* BORING! ANYBODY can be VERSATILE! But MY act's the stuff you gotta see. I run onto a completely dark stage. The audience only hears footsteps. Then the lights come up and, ta da! There I am! THE AMAZING TED TUNER starts wailing on his guitar! WOW!

EDWARD: What styles do you prefer?

TED: You lost me, Eddie, baby. I wasn't talking about styles. I DEFINE style!

EDWARD: I was talking to Fred. Again. I have someone who might be interested in your own compositions. She's looking for something...fresh.

FRED: I'd be glad for the chance. Thank you very much!

TED: *(Steps in front of FRED.)* We've heard ORIGINAL work a thousand, billion, trillion, zillion times before. But I'M unique. THE AMAZING TED has no equal!

EDWARD *(looking skyward)*: We can only hope so.

TED: *(Leans over EDWARD.)* Prepare to be amazed! I have big plans for this show! MY show won't be like anything you've ever seen!

EDWARD: Anything else?

TED: Are you kidding? I've only just begun.

EDWARD: I was speaking to Fred. Do you play anything else?

FRED: I have been playing guitar for a few years. I've been giving Ted lessons.

TED: *(Jumps in front of FRED.)* Hey! Did I tell you that my act is not only music but COMEDY? Listen! I'm a musical magician. I can turn one thing into another. Why just the other day, I opened the door and left it ajar! Hah! Get it? Door? Jar? Left the door ajar! Another success! AMAZ—

EDWARD: So we've heard. Amazing comedy, too. Fred, do you do anything else?

FRED: I do have some experience singing—

TED: *(Cuts FRED off.)* Only if he lip syncs! But the AMAZING TED can SING! He can DANCE! He tells JOKES! I'm an entertainment package that you won't BELIEVE!

EDWARD: You're right. Already I don't believe it. *(To FRED.)* I think I have something else for you.

TED: I KNEW it! Talent like mine is hard to find. When and where?

EDWARD: Not you, AMAZING TED. Fred, I'll contact these people for you. Here are the addresses. *(Reaches for telephone.)* Let me see if I can get you appointments right now.

FRED: Thank you. I appreciate your kindness.

TED: What about THE AMAZING TED TUNER?

EDWARD: Yes. Well, if something comes up, I'll let you know. And Ted?

TED: Yes?

EDWARD: Don't call us. We'll call you.

I've Been Working...

SCRIPTURE: Ruth 1—3

SUGGESTED TOPICS: Value of work; responsibility; loyalty

BIBLE BACKGROUND

A woman's position during ancient times was perilous, to say the least. In most countries, she was little more than property; something which could be bought and sold. Her value might be deemed less than that of an ox or horse. A widow was particularly vulnerable. The laws of most countries afforded her neither protection nor ability to earn a living. Ruth's decision to be a daughter to Naomi and leave Moab was not one to be made lightly. By leaving her homeland to go with Naomi, she renounced all protection that might be afforded her by her father or other relatives.

Compared to women in the surrounding nations, the women of Israel had a relatively generous lot. For example, numerous references call for the protection and provision of widows. Among the laws set down by Moses which provided for the needs of women was that of gleaning (see Leviticus 19:9,10; Deuteronomy 24:19-21). Israel was clearly required to be generous in what was left behind for the widows and strangers in the land.

PERFORMANCE TIPS

1. Suggested props: Bible-times costumes.
2. Ruth should be shy. Rarely will she lift her eyes to look at Boaz. She is overwhelmed that a man would talk to her. This was not common in those times.
3. Boaz is portrayed as something of a rough-and-tumble sort. He speaks sometimes without thinking, but he has a good and generous heart.
4. After the skit, finish the story of Boaz and Ruth.
5. Also read or tell the story of the talents (see Matthew 25:14-30). Jesus also spoke of the importance of using our abilities wisely.

DISCUSSION QUESTIONS

1. Why might Ruth have reason to be afraid of Boaz?
2. What are the things Boaz commends in Ruth?
3. Read Proverbs 10:4. What does the Bible say about our attitude toward work?
4. What are some of the benefits of work?
5. What sort of jobs are you responsible to do?
6. Why is it important to do the best job we can, no matter what the job is?

I'VE BEEN WORKING...

CHARACTERS

RUTH

BOAZ (BOH-az)

BOAZ: Hello.

RUTH *(keeping her eyes down)*: My lord.

BOAZ: I hear you've been gleaning in my fields.

RUTH: Is this wrong, my lord? I'm sorry. I'll stop.

BOAZ: Did I say it was wrong?

RUTH: No, sir.

BOAZ: My servant tells me you come from Moab.

RUTH: Yes, my lord. Forgive me. I'll leave your fields.

BOAZ: Why would you do that? Did I say to leave?

RUTH: No, sir. But I'm from Moab. I'm a foreigner.

BOAZ: So you are. What are you doing in Israel?

RUTH: Gleaning in your fields, my lord.

BOAZ *(laughing)*: So you are. So you are. Let's try again. Why are you in Israel when you come from Moab?

RUTH: I came with my mother-in-law. She is from your country.

BOAZ: And who is your mother-in-law?

RUTH: She is called Naomi, who was married to Elimelech.

BOAZ: Well, there you go! We're relatives, you and I. I'm a kinsman of Elimelech.

RUTH: *(Glances up, with interest.)* Yes, my lord. I know.

BOAZ: Where is your husband? A married woman should not be gleaning. Her husband should be supporting her.

RUTH: I have no husband, my lord.

BOAZ: Well of course you do! You can't have a mother-in-law if you're not married!

RUTH: I'm a widow, sir.

BOAZ: *(Slaps forehead.)* Oh. I'm sorry! Clumsy of me. I seem to suffer from foot-in-mouth disease.

RUTH: You have done no harm, sir.

BOAZ: Well, I should be more careful. How is the esteemed Naomi?

RUTH: She is well, now that she is in her own country.

154   *More Bible Skits* ©1994 Gospel Light. Permission granted to photocopy.

BOAZ: But how about you? You're not in your country.

RUTH: This is now my country, even if it does not accept me.

BOAZ: How can this be your country? You're from Moab.

RUTH: I left Moab with Naomi. To her, I swore an oath: "Where you live, I will live. Your people will be my people. Your God, my God. And where you are buried, there will I be buried."

BOAZ: So now, you're almost a woman without a country?

RUTH: I don't understand, my lord.

BOAZ: You've left Moab. But not all the Israelites accept you, do they?

RUTH: Not all. But many are kind to me.

BOAZ: Just as you have shown kindness to your mother-in-law. Well, there's one more who accepts you as an Israelite. Welcome home, kinswoman.

RUTH: You are too kind, my lord.

BOAZ: Nonsense. What are your plans for the rest of the day?

RUTH: I shall continue gleaning the fields. There are many more.

BOAZ: Nonsense. Look over there. That's my field. And over there? That's mine, too. And that one. And I have lots of others. You don't need to glean in anyone else's fields. Stay in my fields.

RUTH: But how will I know for certain it is your field, my lord?

BOAZ: You see those women over there? They work for me.

RUTH: Yes?

BOAZ: You stay with them. They only work in my fields. You can glean where they reap. And if you get thirsty, help yourself to the water my men draw.

RUTH: But the gleaners are not allowed to drink the water of the workers.

BOAZ: They're MY workers and it's MY water. What I say goes. I'll tell them not to harm you. Now you do as I say.

RUTH: Why are you so kind to me, a stranger in your land?

BOAZ: Stranger? What stranger? You left your home to take care of Naomi, an older woman who had no family to look after her. You work hard gleaning the fields to support the two of you. May the Lord God bless you in the same measure you have blessed Naomi.

RUTH: Thank you for your kind blessing.

BOAZ: It's no more than you deserve. Back to work. We've all got work to do. Bye for now. But I've got a funny feeling we'll be seeing more of each other.

This Is Comfort?

SCRIPTURE: Selections from Job

SUGGESTED TOPICS: Trust in God; man's inability to understand God perfectly; God's greatness and wisdom

BIBLE BACKGROUND

Job is believed to be one of the oldest books (if not the oldest) of the Old Testament. Its theme is the evil which can fall upon the just as well as the unjust here on earth. Job's comforters contend that his great suffering is obviously the result of some great sin Job has committed. However, Job never wavers from proclaiming his innocence, and ultimately God agrees with him. In the end, all is restored to Job in greater abundance than he'd previously had.

We often hear of "the patience of Job," but his reaction to severe hardship is not an uncommon one. His misery is so great that he practically begs God to kill him and end his suffering. However, in spite of not understanding the cause of his pain, Job places his trust in God and refuses to curse God for his troubles. He does, however, plead his case with God. "If only You would listen, I'd tell you all I've done," he says. God's answer is not gentle. In essence, God says, "Who are you to question Me?" Finally Job recognizes how much greater God is than he had ever imagined. Job willingly submits to God's far greater wisdom, and God heals Job and causes him to prosper again.

PERFORMANCE TIPS

1. Suggested props: Bible-time costumes.
2. Tell the story to the point of Satan's second attack on Job. Then begin the skit.
3. Job sits throughout the skit.
4. After the skit, finish the story by telling God's answer to Job's questions.

DISCUSSION QUESTIONS

1. Why do you think bad things happen to good people? What explanation does the story of Job provide?
2. Even in his worst times, Job trusted God. How can you learn to trust God in tough situations?
3. Sometimes friends do more harm than good in tough situations. If this happens to you, what should you do? Why?

THIS IS COMFORT?

CHARACTERS

JOB
ELIPHAZ (eh-LYE-faz)
BILDAD (BILL-dad)
ZOPHAR (ZOH-far)

(JOB sits with profile to audience; his back is turned toward OTHERS. The THREE FRIENDS stand at a distance.)

JOB: Oh, why? Oh, why was I born? Oh, why do I live?

ELIPHAZ: Poor Job.

BILDAD: I feel so sorry for him.

ZOPHAR: He's lost everything.

JOB: Oh, why? Oh, why was I born? Oh, why do I live?

ELIPHAZ: First, he lost his livestock. If they weren't killed, they were stolen.

BILDAD: Then, that terrible storm. Blew down the house of his oldest boy. And all Job's sons and daughters were in the house at the time. Killed, every last one. Terrible, terrible, I tell you!

ZOPHAR: And now look at him. Stricken with some hideous disease. Boils and sores all over his body. Ugh!

JOB: Oh, why? Oh, why was I born? Oh, why do I live?

ELIPHAZ: Poor Job.

BILDAD: Poor, poor Job.

ZOPHAR: I've got an idea. Let's go and cheer him up. *(OTHERS indicate that ELIPHAZ should go first. ELIPHAZ walks over to JOB.)*

JOB *(head in hands)*: Oh, why? Oh, why was I born? Oh, why do I live?

ELIPHAZ: Job. Oh, poor Job. Never fear. We're here.

JOB: My good friend, Eliphaz. Is it you?

ELIPHAZ: It is. Oh, Job, look at you. You who have helped so many. When someone's heart was failing, you were always there to encourage him.

JOB: *(Looks up.)* Thank you, Eliphaz.

ELIPHAZ: And now look at you. A little inconvenience and you forget everything you ever said. You hypocrite!

JOB *(stunned)*: What?

ELIPHAZ: You sit here moping and feeling sorry for yourself. You know that only the WICKED suffer. Repent, man! You can do it!

JOB: What are you talking about? What sin? What wickedness?

ELIPHAZ: How should I know? But take heart. Be happy. God is doing this for your own good, to correct you. Listen to Him! Repent! *(Walks away.)*

JOB: What do YOU know about ANYTHING? Have you suffered like this? If I had sinned so greatly, wouldn't I KNOW about it? Oh, why was I born? Why can't I just die?

BILDAD: Nice going, Eliphaz. You were no help at all. Watch THIS. *(Walks to JOB.)* Job?

JOB: Bildad? Is that your voice, Bildad, come to comfort me in my time of grief?

BILDAD: It is I, good friend Job. How are you?

JOB: I suffer greatly, Bildad. You can't KNOW how I suffer.

BILDAD: Well, of COURSE you're suffering, dummy. How long will you tell these lies to God?

JOB: *(Looks up, stunned.)* What?

BILDAD: What are you trying to cover up, Job? God doesn't punish the innocent.

JOB: What are you saying?

BILDAD: Isn't it obvious, Job? If you were as good as you pretend to be, don't you think God would notice what's happening and make it better?

JOB: Are you accusing me?

BILDAD: I don't accuse, good friend. I merely point out to you that God doesn't help evil people and He doesn't harm the righteous.

JOB: You're telling me that I have sinned greatly?

BILDAD: You and your children! I don't accuse, Job. I merely say, "If the shoe fits..."

JOB: There might be some truth in what you say.

BILDAD: Well, of course there is.

JOB: But how can a man compare himself with God? No matter how good I've been, is it good enough to compare to Him who can shake the earth from its foundations?

BILDAD: I think you're missing the point. *(Shakes finger.)* Confess your sin.

JOB: How can I confess what I don't know? If God had pointed out sin to me, don't you think I would have begged forgiveness rather than go through this? *(Drops head into hands.)* Oh, why was I born? Why can't I die?

    (BILDAD walks away.)

ZOPHAR *(loudly)*: What kind of people ARE you? Have you helped this poor man one iota? *(Walks over to JOB.)*

JOB: Zophar? I hear Zophar's voice. Oh, what a comfort your voice is to me!

      More Bible Skits ©1994 Gospel Light. Permission granted to photocopy.

ZOPHAR: Job, I've heard everything that was said. All the nonsense...

JOB: Thank you, Zophar.

ZOPHAR: ...that YOU'VE been spouting! Can I just stand here and listen to your lies? When you mock God, shall I just stand here and not put you to shame?

JOB: *(Rubs head wearily.)* I beg your pardon?

ZOPHAR: Don't beg MY pardon. You didn't offend ME. You offended GOD. Beg HIS pardon.

JOB: I don't understand.

ZOPHAR: What's not to understand? You sit there saying, "Poor me. My heart is pure." Oh, if only God would speak. He'd tell you what a despicable liar you are.

JOB: Liar?

ZOPHAR: I know it's difficult to understand. God's wisdom is higher than the heavens and deeper than the depths of hell. You can't even begin to know.

JOB: And YOU can?

ZOPHAR: Apparently better than you. MY animals have not all disappeared. MY children were not all killed. MY body isn't covered with sores. Repent, you foul sinner! Count your blessings that God has given you this reminder of your sin and repent! *(Walks away.)*

JOB: *(Turns and calls after the OTHERS.)* No doubt you three are the only wise people on earth. I'm sure, when you die, all wisdom will pass away with you.

ELIPHAZ: *(Crosses arms.)* Well, I never.

JOB: No doubt my intellect is inferior to yours. I must be so stupid compared to the three of you.

BILDAD *(chin up)***:** There's no need to be sarcastic!

JOB: In fact, the only things on earth smarter than you three are the birds and animals. They know how the world works better than YOU do.

ZOPHAR: *(Shakes head.)* How rude!

JOB: I would love to speak with God! I want to reason with Him. But you three would show much more wisdom if you'd only shut up.

ELIPHAZ: I've never been so insulted in my life.

BILDAD: That's gratitude for you. After all we did for him.

ZOPHAR: You just can't reason with some people.

JOB: *(Turns back on OTHERS, drops head into hands.)* Oh, why? Oh, why was I born? Oh, why do I live?

BROTHERS UNDER THE SKIN

SCRIPTURE: Genesis 17:7

SUGGESTED TOPICS: Covenant; friendship

BIBLE BACKGROUND

Covenants are made in every society in the world. Many ancient cultures used the passing of blood to mark the solemnity of the agreement. In the Old Testament, many covenants were made; some of them were between people (David and Jonathan, see 1 Samuel 20:42; Ruth and Naomi, see Ruth 1:16,17); some between God and a person or persons (Noah, see Genesis 9:12-17; Abram, see Genesis 12:1-3; all of Israel, see Deuteronomy 28:1—29:1). All of the covenants between God and people broke down, but never because God was unfaithful. The problem was always that a covenant requires fulfillment of the agreement by both parties, and people continue to struggle with sin. Time after time, people were unable to fulfill the human part of the covenant.

But God, in His mercy, instituted a new covenant to replace the old ones (see Luke 22:20). This new covenant was sealed by the blood of Jesus and could never fail, for the only party who promised to do something was God. All that is necessary for any person to receive eternal life with God is to accept the gift of forgiveness which has already been bought with Jesus' blood (see Ephesians 2:8,9).

PERFORMANCE TIPS

1. Suggested props: card lettered "applause" to hold up before audience at appropriate times, rumpled western clothing for the Ranger, headband for Toronto, bowl of dry cereal, rubber knife, blanket.

2. If possible, partially darken the room for performance.

3. Theme music (opening bars of the "William Tell Overture") may be played on cassette player or kazoos (or anything in between).

DISCUSSION QUESTIONS

1. What is the meaning of the word "covenant"?

2. At the end of the skit, the Single Ranger and Toronto have forgotten their coventant. Why?

3. Why is it important to keep covenants?

4. Another word for covenant is "testament." We call part of the Bible the Old Testament and part of it the New Testament. What is the old testament? What is the new testament?

5. How can you become part of the new testament?

More Bible Skits ©1994 Gospel Light. Permission granted to photocopy.

BROTHERS UNDER THE SKIN

CHARACTERS

NARRATOR   **TORONTO**   **THE SINGLE RANGER**

NARRATOR (*grandly*): Out of the west he came, riding a white horse, carrying twin pearl-handled revolvers and wearing...rumpled clothes. Looking like a man who needed to visit a laundromat, he rode across rivers over hill and plain (loud crash) and cliffs... Heigh-ho, Platinum! It's the SINGLE RANGER! (Hold up applause card.) Return with us now to those thrilling days of yesteryear! As our story opens, we find our hero lying in a dark cave, not knowing how he got there, recovering from his latest over-the-cliff ADVENTURE!

(RANGER is lying on blanket, recovering from unspecified wounds.)

RANGER (*moaning*): Ohh...

TORONTO: Hmm. The paleface awakes.

RANGER (*moaning*): Ohh. *(Tries to sit up but lies down again.)* Where am I?

TORONTO: In the dark.

RANGER: I know I'm in the dark. That's why I asked where I am.

TORONTO: In a cave. In the mountains. Safe.

RANGER: How did I get here?

TORONTO: Toronto.

RANGER: Funny. I didn't think I was that far north. I thought I was in Texas!

TORONTO: I'M Toronto. I brought you to the cave.

RANGER: *(Tries to sit up. TORONTO comes and helps.)* Thanks, Toronto. Strange name.

TORONTO: It means, "Eastern Canadian who thinks he's the entire world."

RANGER: An INDIAN NAME? You don't sound like an Indian.

TORONTO: That's because I'm not an Indian. One white guy gets lost, thinks he's in India, and all of you keep making the same mistake. I'm Native American. You know, the people who were here first.

RANGER: But I thought you Native Americans talked funny. I thought you said things like "heap big trouble" and "white man speaks with forked tongue!"

TORONTO: Only in the movies. But I like that "forked tongue" bit. I'll have to remember to use it.

RANGER: Well, I'm sure glad you're here! What happened to me?

TORONTO: I don't know. Found you lying on the road. Looks like you jumped over a cliff. *(Hands RANGER a bowl.)* Here. Better eat something.

RANGER: What is it?

TORONTO: Food. Why else would I say "eat"?

RANGER: I mean, what kind of food?

TORONTO: Dry cereal. Not exciting, but easy to carry. The healthy kind. High protein. No added sugar or fat.

RANGER: *(Eats a little.)* That's good! Why are you being so kind to me?

TORONTO: It's the ancient custom of my people. We feed people when they're hungry. Novel concept, eh?

RANGER: And to think how we've repaid you. *(Sees snake near TORONTO's feet. Jumps up, waving arms.)* Hey! Look out! Shoo! Shoo!

TORONTO: *(Looks down.)* Something wrong with my moccasins?

RANGER: No. There was a snake there! He was ready to strike!

TORONTO: And you chased it away. You saved my life! But why didn't you shoot it?

RANGER: I couldn't! It's an endangered species.

TORONTO: Ah. One smart ranger! Protect that wildlife!

RANGER: *(Rubs chin thoughtfully.)* How about that. Now we've each saved the other's life.

TORONTO: Well then, it's time for another ancient custom of my people. We must make a pact. *(Draws knife, runs blade across his palm. Gives knife to RANGER.)* Now, you do the same.

RANGER: Sounds strange, but if you say so. *(Takes TORONTO's hand to cut it.)*

TORONTO: Not MY hand. YOUR hand.

RANGER: *(Gulps.)* But, I'll BLEED!

TORONTO: That the idea.

RANGER: Oh. You don't have any anesthesia, do you?

TORONTO: No.

RANGER: A bullet to bite on?

TORONTO: No.

RANGER: Oh, well. Here goes. *(Grimaces and draws knife across palm.)*

TORONTO: Now, give me your hand.

RANGER *(alarmed)***:** Oh, no. It stays on my arm where it belongs!

TORONTO: Reach your hand to mine.

RANGER: Oh, I see. Yes, alright.

TORONTO: *(Joins his hand with that of RANGER.)* There. OUR blood mingles.

RANGER: Yes. So what?

TORONTO: Now, we are blood brothers, you and me. Your blood is mine; my blood is yours.

RANGER: Oh. I get it. Very poetic. You don't have any diseases, do you?

TORONTO: No. No diseases. But I'll give you something else. A new name, a name of my people. From now on, you are "Keemo Slobby."

RANGER: I thought that was supposed to be "Keemosabe"?

TORONTO: *(Looks him up and down.)* No. Definitely "Keemo Slobby."

RANGER: Alright. But what does this "brothers" thing mean?

TORONTO: *(Holds up right hand.)* We promise to protect each other and love each other, the same as brothers.

RANGER: *(Holds up right hand.)* I see. So, if we're in town and some white men start pushing you around, I'll go up to them and say, "Leave him alone!"

More Bible Skits ©1994 Gospel Light. Permission granted to photocopy.

TORONTO: Something like that. And if we are surrounded by many angry braves who want to kill us, you'll say, "Looks like we die now, Toronto."

RANGER: Yes? Yes?

TORONTO: I say, "What do you mean 'we' white man?"

RANGER: What?

TORONTO: *(Chuckles.)* Pretty good joke, eh?

RANGER: Oh, a joke! Now I get it.

TORONTO: Don't worry, Keemo Slobby. I'll always protect you, too. We're brothers now. So. Is Keemo Slobby ready to ride? It's time for me to go.

RANGER: Say, I've got an idea. We make a pretty good team. Why don't we ride together?

TORONTO: Together?

RANGER: Sure. We could go around the wild west, saving people from danger.

TORONTO: Could be fun.

RANGER: We might become famous. Somebody might write about us, we'll get a series, the works!

TORONTO: Famous? That sounds good.

RANGER: They could call it, "The Saga of the Single Ranger!"

TORONTO: Single Ranger? Hey, brother. What about Toronto?

RANGER: *(Ignores TORONTO.)* I'll need some music. Heroes should always have music. Something from the classics.

TORONTO: Native American music's good.

RANGER: *(Continues to ignore TORONTO.)* Something that appeals to the average consumer. Beethoven's Fifth? Dum, dum, dum, dum! No. Too slow. "The Flight of the Bumblebee"? No. Too fast. Something with shooting in it.

TORONTO: You could use the "William Tell Overture." He used to shoot arrows. A civilized weapon.

RANGER: *(Still ignoring TORONTO.)* Well, I'll figure out the music later.

TORONTO: You do that. *(Takes out newspaper want ads.)* I think we should go to Denver. To the mint. *(Reads aloud.)* "Wanted. Native American with rugged profile to appear on nickel."

RANGER: *(Still in his own world.)* Where should I begin to clean up the west? Arizona's pretty tough. That's a good spot to start. And I should give away some kind of token. Then when I ride off, people will ask, "Who is that mussed man?"

TORONTO: How about laundromat tokens? Then you could really clean up the west. But save a few for yourself. *(Strikes a stiff pose, turns profile to audience.)* I'll be perfect for the nickel.

RANGER: *(Continuing deep in thought.)* Well, I'll figure that out later, too. *(To TORONTO.)* Let's ride!

(RANGER and TORONTO point in different directions. RANGER says, "To Arizona!" at the same time as TORONTO says, "To Denver!" Hold up applause card. Theme music comes up as they gallop offstage in different directions.)

PASSOVER ME BY

SCRIPTURE: Exodus 7—11

SUGGESTED TOPICS: Listening to God; accepting and learning from God's correction; obedience to God

BIBLE BACKGROUND

God promised to make Abraham a great and mighty nation. He also promised a land in which His people could live. However, God was amazingly patient with the people who were already living there. Their iniquity (marked by worship of false gods, child sacrifice, religious prostitution, witchcraft, etc., mentioned in Deuteronomy 18:9-12) was not yet complete (see Genesis 15:16-21). God told Abraham that the path to the Promised Land would be filled with curious twists and turns. Before Abraham's descendants could take possession of their own land, they first would be oppressed in a land (Egypt) which was not theirs (see Genesis 15:13).

Getting the Israelites into Egypt was no mean feat. It required a young man who stirred great jealousy in his brothers, an undeserved prison sentence, three strange dreams, a terrible famine and remarkable forgiveness. Getting the Israelites out again was even more difficult. God had to prove to His own people and to the Egyptians that He was the only God; that Egypt's gods could not begin to match Him in power. Finally, after four hundred and thirty years in Egypt (see Exodus 12:40), the Israelites were ready to begin moving toward the fulfillment of God's promise to Abraham.

PERFORMANCE TIPS

1. Suggested props: a very large book, bookshelf, two chairs.

2. Before the skit, briefly explain to the class how the Israelites got to Egypt in the first place and why they were now being oppressed.

3. The Advisor has been awakened from sleep but is afraid to admit it. He stifles yawns when Pharaoh isn't looking. He has a large boil on his face.

4. A number of people can cry out to cause commotion when the firstborn sons are slain. They should continue for the rest of the skit but keep the noise down enough for the actors to be heard.

DISCUSSION QUESTIONS

1. Why do you think Pharaoh would ignore nine plagues from God?

2. What kinds of promises does God make to us in the Bible? What are some things He warns us not to do?

3. The Bible says God hardened Pharaoh's heart (see Exodus 10:1). Does it sound fair for God to punish someone for something God did? Here's an experiment to try:

   a. Get a little bit of mud and put it on some foil.

   b. Get a piece of hard chocolate and put it on some foil.

   c. Put the mud and the chocolate under a light, close to the bulb. (A one hundred watt bulb works best.)

   d. Observe what happens to both the mud and the chocolate. Say, "God does not make us do things. His power only shows what we are like inside. We respond to Him according to the kind of people we are, just as the mud and the chocolate responded to the light."

PASSOVER ME BY

CHARACTERS
PHARAOH
ADVISOR

PRONUNCIATION GUIDE
draught (draft)

PHARAOH: Goodness, but it's dark. Not as dark as a few days ago, but dark. I wish I could get some sleep. Advisor!

ADVISOR: *(Enters, rubbing sleep from his eyes.)* Yes, my king.

PHARAOH: Were you asleep?

ADVISOR: *(Stops rubbing eyes suddenly.)* Me? Asleep while Pharaoh is awake? Oh, no. Never, never, never.

PHARAOH: Then why were you rubbing your eyes?

ADVISOR: Why? Umm, why was I rubbing my eyes. Something. I was rubbing. Why? Aha! I was rubbing my eyes because something was in my eye. Dust? A louse? That's it. I had a speck of louse in my eye.

PHARAOH: Just so you weren't asleep. I can't sleep.

ADVISOR: Perhaps you need a sleeping draught, O King.

PHARAOH: You mean a draft where I stand by my bed and open a window and the wind blows over a hammer which falls and hits me on the head?

ADVISOR: It works every time, Great Pharaoh.

PHARAOH: But I have such a headache in the morning! One of these days, someone will invent a better method of inducing sleep.

ADVISOR: But never a more effective one.

PHARAOH: Never mind. I have an alternate plan for getting some sleep.

ADVISOR *(horrified)***:** Not...

PHARAOH: Yes. The historical method. Read to me from the history book.

(ADVISOR stumbles to shelf and brings out very large book.)

ADVISOR: Is there any special part Pharaoh would care to hear?

PHARAOH: Anywhere is fine.

ADVISOR: *(Opens book and begins reading.)* ...and it came to pass that Joseph...

PHARAOH: Joseph! Again with this Joseph! Who is Joseph?

ADVISOR: I don't know.

PHARAOH: Well, find out!

(ADVISOR flips backward through book, mumbling as though reading quickly.)

PHARAOH: Well, who IS he? Moses talks about him. The history books tell of him.

ADVISOR: Ah, I have it. *(Reads.)* "...and the Hebrew prisoner, Joseph, was elevated in rank and set in charge of collecting twenty percent of all the food produced in Egypt." He seems to have been a tax collector, Sire.

PHARAOH: All this fuss over a tax collector? Amazing.

ADVISOR *(consulting book)***:** And he apparently saved Egypt from great famine.

PHARAOH: Oh. A hero. How long ago did this happen?

ADVISOR: About four hundred and thirty years ago, Sire.

PHARAOH: Oh. Ancient history. Nothing for me to worry about, then.

ADVISOR: No, Your Highness.

PHARAOH: *(Stands.)* Reading isn't helping. Maybe a midnight snack. What have we got?

ADVISOR: Frog legs, Sire.

PHARAOH: STILL?

ADVISOR: They were plentiful this year, Your Majesty.

PHARAOH: Well, I'm tired of them.

ADVISOR: As are we all.

PHARAOH: *(Sits.)* As long as I can't sleep, I might as well get some work done.

ADVISOR: *(Starts to leave.)* I'll leave you to it, then.

PHARAOH: No. Stay. I need advice. *(Stares at ADVISOR.)* Your face.

ADVISOR: I should advise my face to stay where it is, my lord?

PHARAOH: No! What's that hideous thing on your face?

ADVISOR: *(Touches cheek.)* A boil, Your Highness. Leftover from Plague Number Six.

PHARAOH: Oh. Well, do something about it tomorrow. It offends me.

ADVISOR: I have heard that sleep can remove boils, O Pharaoh. I shall attend to it immediately.

(Turns to go.)

PHARAOH: TOMORROW will be soon enough.

ADVISOR: *(Aside.)* I was afraid of that.

PHARAOH: What about this latest threat from Moses?

ADVISOR: Has he come to make another? I haven't seen him since the great darkness.

PHARAOH: Of course he hasn't come. I told him I'd kill him if I saw him again.

ADVISOR: Then what threat are we discussing?

PHARAOH: You haven't heard the rumors?

ADVISOR: Oh, rumors. Nothing to worry about.

PHARAOH: But the Hebrews are spreading BLOOD all over their houses.

ADVISOR: Just so they're not shedding blood in Egyptian houses, there's nothing to worry about.

PHARAOH: Then you think I'm doing the right thing, keeping the Hebrews in Egypt?

ADVISOR: But of course, Sire. Where else will you find a slave labor force of six hundred thousand men? You have building projects to complete! You need the manpower!

PHARAOH: True. But some Egyptians are taking the rumors seriously.

ADVISOR: Such utter nonsense. NO god can find the firstborn of every family in Egypt. And not only people, but animals. Pharaoh, not even the SUN can do this. There's nothing to worry about.

PHARAOH: Well, I don't like all that blood. Makes the country look messy.

ADVISOR: Then teach the Hebrews a lesson. Tomorrow, make them clean up all the blood AND make their full quota of bricks. Lean on them. Show them who's in charge.

PHARAOH: Hmm. That could work. Put a stop to all this trouble Moses has been causing.

(Loud screams and crying from offstage.)

PHARAOH: What's happening? Go find out!

(ADVISOR exits; crying continues. ADVISOR enters looking worried.)

PHARAOH: Well, what is it?

ADVISOR: Um...well, uh...nothing too serious. Just a little accident.

PHARAOH: There seems to be a lot of commotion for a little accident. Who's been hurt?

ADVISOR: Ahem. Well. *(Counts on fingers.)* The heir to the throne seems to have died. And the chambermaid's firstborn. And that of the queen's attendants. And the oldest of the palace cat's litter. The oldest of the footman, the butcher, the baker, the candlestick maker, the...

(PHARAOH runs offstage.)

CAN I?

SCRIPTURE: 1 Samuel 8; Psalm 103:8,10

SUGGESTED TOPICS: Obedience; honoring parents; making wise choices

BIBLE BACKGROUND

The Israelites were called to be holy—different from those around them—because their God was holy. Their early history differed from that of other nations in that they had no king. Instead, every man did that which was right in his own eyes (see Judges 21:25) and any disputes which arose were settled by the judges who were appointed.

The period of the judges can best be described as a vicious circle. The circle began with things going well in the country. The people worshiped the true God, the God who had delivered them from Egypt and led them to victory in the Promised Land. But because they had not fully obeyed God and driven out all the inhabitants of the land, pagan practices surrounded them and the Israelites fell into the worship of idols.

The spiritual decay of idolatry led to a serious decline in all areas of Israelite life and God raised up a people to chastise Israel. When things were at their blackest, the Israelites remembered the God of Abraham, Isaac and Jacob and cried out to Him. In His mercy, God raised up a judge who would lead them back to the worship of the true God. However, when peace and prosperity returned, the circle would begin anew with the people turning from God to follow the practices of their neighbors.

This vicious circle continued throughout the book of Judges until the time of Samuel. Unfortunately, evil judges turned the people of Israel away from God's system. Samuel's sons judged Israel so unfairly that the people demanded a king like the other nations had. In spite of Samuel's warnings of the consequences of having a king (see 1 Samuel 8:11-18), Israel became a kingdom.

PERFORMANCE TIPS

1. Suggested props: chair or sofa, magazine for Mom, cookies and milk, backpack or school bag and papers.

2. If you are in a place that will not permit food and drink, Calvin can pretend to have a mouth full of cookies. Give him an opaque glass for his milk.

3. For humor, consider having Calvin played by an adult and Mom by a student.

DISCUSSION QUESTIONS

1. Sometimes people around us can influence us to do the wrong things. Who influences you? What sort of things are you tempted to do by their example?

2. What are some things you can do to avoid doing the wrong things?

3. Why does God give us His commands in the Bible? How can you use the Bible to help you make decisions?

4. If everyone believes something, does that mean it is true? Why or why not?

Can I?

CHARACTERS

CALVIN
MOM

(MOM sits on sofa, reading a magazine.)

CALVIN: *(Enters with backpack.)* Hi, Mom! I'm home.

MOM: Hi, dear. How was school?

CALVIN: Oh, it was OK. Math wasn't so good.

MOM: Oh? Why not?

CALVIN: Almost all the answers on my assignment were WRONG.

MOM: The ones I helped you with last night?

CALVIN: Yup.

MOM: I'm sorry, dear! I thought I remembered how to solve simultaneous equations.

CALVIN: Well, it wasn't too bad. I got full marks for the work. Only the answers were wrong.

MOM: That's strange. Can I see the paper?

CALVIN: *(Backs away.)* No. That's OK, Mom. You can't always be right.

MOM: But I want to see how I was wrong. Let me see the paper, please.

CALVIN: *(Gets paper out of pack, hands to MOM. Sighs.)* Here.

MOM: But I don't understand. These aren't the same answers you had last night!

CALVIN: Well, see, when I got to school, Jimmy and me compared papers and his answers were all different from mine. I didn't have time to change all the work part so I just changed the answers.

MOM: Calvin, when will you learn? Other people's answers aren't always right!

CALVIN: I know that now, Mom. Have we got anything...

MOM: ...to eat for a snack? There are some cookies on the table and milk in the fridge.

CALVIN: Thanks.

> *(Exits.)*

MOM: What a kid.

> *(CALVIN enters with mouth full of cookie and drinking glass of milk.)*

CALVIN *(talking with mouth full)***:** Know what, Mom?

MOM: How many times must I remind you, Calvin? Not with your mouth full.

CALVIN: *(Makes exaggerated chewing and swallowing motion.)* Know what, Mom?

MOM: What?

CALVIN: You're the best Mom in the whole world.

MOM: Well, thank you. But I didn't make the cookies. Your Dad woke up this morning in one of his baking moods. And since he's on the afternoon shift, he had time to do something about it. So we have cookies.

CALVIN: I wasn't just talking about cookies. It's everything.

MOM *(warily)*: Uh-huh?

CALVIN: I mean, you're just the best mom anyone could have.

MOM *(more warily)*: Uh-huh?

CALVIN: I was just saying to Jimmy, this morning, "My mom's the greatest mom in the whole wide world."

MOM: Was that before or AFTER you changed your math?

CALVIN: Oh, Mom. I just wanted to tell you how great I think you are.

MOM: OK, what do you want?

CALVIN: Me? Mom, I don't want anything. Well, maybe another cookie?

MOM *(laughing)*: Go help yourself.

> *(CALVIN starts to exit but stops.)*

CALVIN: But since you mentioned it...

MOM: What do you want, Calvin?

CALVIN: Can I go down to the river after supper?

MOM: Will you have your homework finished before you go?

CALVIN: Of course, I will! When have I ever...

MOM: Three weeks ago on Wednesday and Thursday. Two weeks ago on Monday, Tuesday and Friday. Last week Wednesday, Thursday and Friday. The day before yesterday.

CALVIN: I'll do it right now.

MOM: OK. If your homework's done, you may go to the river. But remember the rules. Only as far as Three Mile Bend.

CALVIN: But, Mom, the other guys want to go up near the dam. I want to go with them. Can I, Mom? Please. Can I?

MOM: No! Absolutely not!

CALVIN: But, Mom. Jimmy's going to be there. And Billy and Juan. PLEASE, let me go, too?

MOM: No! That's final!

More Bible Skits ©1994 Gospel Light. Permission granted to photocopy.

CALVIN: But, Mom, it's no fun down near Three Mile Bend. There's more to do near the dam.

MOM: How do YOU know? Have you been there?

CALVIN: No. But everyone says so. Pierre says it's really neat up there.

MOM: Calvin. Your father and I have talked to you about this before. It isn't safe up near the dam. The ground is too unpredictable.

CALVIN: But I'd be careful, Mom. We'd all be careful. Can I go? Please.

MOM: How did you manage to get so wet on Saturday?

CALVIN: I slipped and fell in the river. But that was just an accident.

MOM: That's my point. If you have an accident near Three Mile Bend, you get wet. If you have an accident near the dam, you could be killed.

CALVIN: But I wouldn't have an accident. I'd be really careful if you'd let me go. Please. Can I?

MOM: No, Calvin! My patience is wearing thin. Stop asking. The answer won't change.

CALVIN: You never let me do anything fun! All the other guys will laugh at me.

MOM: I doubt it very much. Only the ones whose parents let them do things that could easily hurt them. What about Paul? I didn't hear his name mentioned. Is he going up to the dam, too?

CALVIN: No. But he's no fun.

MOM: That's not what you said when you came back from his birthday party.

CALVIN: His birthday party wasn't any fun.

MOM: But you were bubbling over when you came home from it.

CALVIN: But when I told Jimmy about it the next day, he said it was stupid.

MOM: This is the same Jimmy who helped you with your math?

CALVIN: Yeah, but math and life are different.

MOM: I thought you solved problems in math.

CALVIN: So?

MOM: That's what you do in life, too. You solve problems.

CALVIN *(pouting)*: Not me. I just get told what to do.

MOM: No, you don't. You make lots of choices every day. The trick is to make the right choice. That's where parents come in.

CALVIN: To keep kids from having fun.

MOM: No. To help them grow up learning how to make the right choices. In the process, we sometimes have to say no. If we never said no, you'd never learn how to decide between right and wrong.

CALVIN: I KNOW how to decide.

MOM: I know you do. Sometimes. And as you grow older and more mature, you'll make more and more choices for yourself.

CALVIN: That means I still can't go up to the dam?

MOM: That means you still can't go up to the dam.

CALVIN: Then there's no point in going ANYwhere.

MOM: I hear there's a big gathering down at the rec center. Something about radio-controlled car races.

CALVIN: So?

MOM: I just heard that Paul's going to win tonight. I've heard his new Jaguar XKE is faster than anything in town.

CALVIN: Who says?

MOM: I was talking to his mom today. I guess he thinks he's got the hottest thing on four wheels.

CALVIN: Well, he's nuts. My Corvette can run circles around his XKE.

MOM: That's what I said. But Paul doesn't think so.

CALVIN: Well, I'll show him. Look out, Paul. The "Vette Viper" will show the whole town that your Jaguar's nothing more than a kitten. I'll be there. Can I go, Mom? Can I show him his Jaguar's nothing?

MOM: After your homework's done, of course.

CALVIN: Of course. I'll do it right now.

(CALVIN exits running. MOM watches him go, turns to AUDIENCE, makes a "victory" gesture and smiles.)

PROPHETS' ROUND TABLE

SCRIPTURE: Jeremiah 29, 31; Selections from Ezra; Nehemiah; Malachi

SUGGESTED TOPICS: Listening to God; trusting God; reading God's Word

BIBLE BACKGROUND

Throughout history, God has chosen prophets—devout men and women called to proclaim His word to His people. But along with the prophets of God came false prophets. God's standards for His prophets were very high. God warned Israel not to follow a prophet just because something he predicted actually happened. If a prophet claimed, "You can see I am a prophet. I know what I'm talking about. Forget about Jehovah. I have a better way," he was to be put to death as a false prophet (see Deuteronomy 13:1-5). A true prophet always honors God.

Or if a prophet claimed to speak in the Lord's name, but the things predicted did not happen, he was a false prophet and was to be put to death (see Deuteronomy 18:20-22). If God says a thing will happen, it happens.

Unfortunately, being God's prophet was not the safest occupation, from a human standpoint. Elijah was chased throughout Israel by Ahab because he spoke God's condemnation to the king. Elisha had a death sentence placed on him by the king of Israel because the king blamed Israel's troubles on Elisha. Jeremiah was locked in stocks and imprisoned because he spoke God's truth. God's prophets were not always popular, since God does not always speak kindly to His people. When God's people needed correction, they often resisted the messenger and any warning message which God sent. However, behind such prophecies was always the promise that God would not forsake them. He would raise up a Savior.

PERFORMANCE TIPS

1. Suggested props: table and chairs, large name tags for all characters.
2. Set the table center stage for the current time. Have the prior time satellite to one side of the stage and the future time satellite to the other.
3. The false prophets should whine and complain.

DISCUSSION QUESTIONS

1. How would you describe a prophet?
2. Read Deuteronomy 13:2,3. How can you tell if someone is trying to lead you after other gods? What are some ways you can use to decide?
3. God has a great plan for humankind. Describe the plan in your own words.

PROPHETS' ROUND TABLE

CHARACTERS
MODERATOR
JEREMIAH
ZERUBBABEL (zuh-RUB-uh-bull)
EZRA
NEHEMIAH (NEE-uh-MY-uh)
MALACHI (MAL-a-kye)
PASHUR (PASH-er)
SHEMAIAH (shem-EYE-ah)

PRONUNCIATION GUIDE
Cyrus (SY-rus)
Artaxerxes (ar-tuh-ZERK-sees)

MODERATOR: Good evening and welcome to "Prophets' Round Table." Our guests tonight are not prophets, but they are men of character who have been influenced by prophets. Here at our table are Zerubbabel, Ezra and Nehemiah, three men instrumental in the rebuilding of Jerusalem. Welcome, gentlemen.

ZERUBBABEL, EZRA and NEHEMIAH: Thank you. Hello. Good to be here.

MODERATOR: We will have other guests with us via satellite later in the show. From our prior times satellite, we will be joined by Jeremiah, Pashur and Shemaiah. And from our future times satellite, Malachi. But first, our guests in the studio. Zerubbabel, you're something of a grassroots politician.

ZERUBBABEL: Yes, that's a pretty fair description of me. I'm a man of the people.

MODERATOR: It seems to me that you wouldn't require the services of a prophet.

ZERUBBABEL: That's where you're wrong. Fourteen years ago—is that all it is? It seems like such a long time ago, now. Anyway, fourteen years ago, I had an awesome responsibility. I was in charge of bringing nearly fifty thousand people back to Jerusalem.

MODERATOR: That's a lot of people. You say you brought them back. Where had you been?

ZERUBBABEL: We had been in captivity in Babylon. Then Babylon was defeated and so forth, but that's old history. Finally, Cyrus, king of Persia, allowed us to return to our home, Jerusalem.

MODERATOR: So you were chosen to lead these people?

ZERUBBABEL: Yes, and given the responsibility of the money to be brought back.

MODERATOR: How much could that be? You had been captives, slaves.

More Bible Skits ©1994 Gospel Light. Permission granted to photocopy.

ZERUBBABEL: You'd be surprised. Cyrus was very generous. Gold, silver, all the implements from the Temple. There was a lot of wealth traveling with us.

MODERATOR: And how do prophets fit into this?

ZERUBBABEL: With all the problems, I had to continually ask myself, "Is this the right thing? Is this what God has planned?" Fortunately, I had the writings of Isaiah.

MODERATOR: He's a prophet from long ago.

ZERUBBABEL: Yes. Long before Judah was taken into captivity, before King Cyrus was even born, Isaiah prophesied, "Thus says the Lord of Cyrus. He is my shepherd. He will build Jerusalem and lay the foundation of the Temple."

MODERATOR: What's so special about that prophecy?

ZERUBBABEL: When he said it, Jerusalem was a city and the Temple was completely built. Later, the city and the Temple were torn down. So I could see his writings and know that God wanted Jerusalem and the Temple to be rebuilt. I was doing God's will.

MODERATOR: I see. Thank you. Nehemiah. You're a bit different. You're also in politics, but you're in the higher ranks of power. You were the cupbearer to King Artaxerxes. That's a powerful position.

NEHEMIAH: Yes, it is. It gave me direct access to the king every day.

MODERATOR: And you took it upon yourself to come out and help rebuild Jerusalem.

NEHEMIAH: Yes. Zerubbabel had made a good start but there was much left to do, even after fourteen years.

MODERATOR: Being that close to the king, you wouldn't need prophets to help you.

NEHEMIAH: On the contrary. The prophets were most important to me.

MODERATOR: But why?

NEHEMIAH: I also came out with a great deal of money for the project. And there were many people living around Jerusalem who wanted the project stopped. They sent false reports about me to the king.

MODERATOR: But you're his trusted advisor. Why would he believe false rumors?

NEHEMIAH: Trust doesn't go very far these days. I needed the words of the prophets to sustain my spirit. I needed to read the warnings for disobeying God's laws and the promises for obedience. That gave me the courage to correct my people when they were following false ideas.

MODERATOR: That leaves Ezra, priest of God. Surely YOU wouldn't need the prophets? You would instruct them.

EZRA: On the contrary. I, too, need to heed the prophets. I am but one man. I am capable of being wrong. God gives prophets so that the priest can look at himself to determine if he is following God.

MODERATOR: Can you give us an example?

EZRA: Of course. I had not asked the king to give us a guard for our journey. Was I wrong to not ask? I thought, "No. I can't ask for a guard. I told the king that God is our protector." But I needed confirmation. Fortunately, men of understanding...

MODERATOR: Prophets?

EZRA: Exactly. Men of understanding were with me. We fasted and prayed and God confirmed we were on the right course.

MODERATOR: There you have it. People in all walks of life need the prophets. Now, via satellite, let's talk to some prophets. Prophets of the past, are you there?

JEREMIAH: Yes, I'm here.

PASHUR: There you go again. Always setting yourself up as better than everyone else.

SHEMAIAH: That's right. You're not the only prophet here. There's three of us.

JEREMIAH: One who speaks falsely is not a prophet.

MODERATOR: Gentlemen, gentlemen. Do I sense some strife?

PASHUR: It's Jeremiah's fault. It's always his fault. He just wants to be a gloomy gus all the time.

SHEMAIAH: That's right. Is it our fault that we're optimists and he's a pessimist? Show us a donut, we see a donut. Show him a donut, he sees the hole.

JEREMIAH: Finally, you speak the truth.

PASHUR: Ah! He admits it.

JEREMIAH: Of course. When you look at a donut, you only see the cake. When I look at a donut, I see the whole donut. All of it. The cake and the hole in the center. You see the donut, I see the whole donut.

SHEMAIAH: There he goes, twisting our words around again.

PASHUR: You shouldn't have him on the show. He's nothing but trouble.

EZRA: Excuse me, but are you Jeremiah who prophesied in Jerusalem in the time of Jehoiakim until the captivity?

JEREMIAH: Yes, I am.

EZRA: I wish I could shake your hand. Your words have brought such comfort to me!

PASHUR: Comfort? HIS words? The man doesn't know the meaning of the word "uplifting."

SHEMAIAH: It's a sorry state of affairs when the priest is illiterate.

JEREMIAH *(ignoring others)*: I am glad my words were of benefit. Praise God!

MODERATOR: How did Jeremiah help you, Ezra?

EZRA: Jeremiah always spoke the truth, even if it hurt. He didn't try to make people believe the situation was better than it was. Therefore, when Jeremiah says, "Israel and Judah have not been forsaken by God," I can believe him. When we were in captivity, we knew God was still there.

PASHUR: But what about us?

SHEMAIAH: Yeah. We said God was with us.

ZERUBBABEL: But you told lies.

NEHEMIAH: And did evil things.

EZRA: You, Pashur. You, a son of a priest and a governor, should have listened to Jeremiah and called the people to repentance. But what did you do?

NEHEMIAH: You had him beaten instead.

ZERUBBABEL: And had him put in stocks.

SHEMAIAH (whining): A LOT of people want to be in stocks—and bonds!

PASHUR (whining): And he called me names. He called me "Fear Around Him" and said my friends would die. He should have been punished.

JEREMIAH: I only gave you that name at the Lord's command—after you had injured me. If you would have listened and called the people to repentance, would the Lord not have listened?

EZRA: And you, Shemaiah—if we had listened to you, our hearts would have failed us.

NEHEMIAH: Yes. Jeremiah told us the captivity would be long. That we should build houses and plan to be in exile for some time.

ZERUBBABEL: You wanted us to believe we would be freed at any time, Shemaiah.

EZRA: If we had listened to YOU, we would have given up long ago.

MODERATOR: Thank you for being with us, gentlemen. We have one more prophet to speak to—Malachi. Malachi, you will be prophesying in the future. In fact, if our research is accurate, in the very near future. What sort of things do you foresee?

MALACHI: My job is a little different from that of Jeremiah. God has sent me to lift up the hearts of the exiles returning to Jerusalem.

MODERATOR: So not all true prophets predict gloom and doom?

MALACHI: Of course not. We tell the people what God tells us. Because people sin, we often have to remind them what happens when they sin. But God loves His people and has a plan.

EZRA: God has revealed His plan to you, Malachi?

MALACHI: Sort of. I don't understand all of it, myself. But what God says, I report.

NEHEMIAH: What sort of things, Malachi? Tell us, please.

MALACHI: The Lord says, "I send My messenger before Me and he shall prepare the way. Then the Lord whom you seek will come to His Temple."

ZERUBBABEL: Of what does he speak?

NEHEMIAH: I don't know. Ezra, what does this mean?

EZRA: The Lord is renewing His promise. He is reminding us that He will come.

MALACHI: Yes, I think that's what it means. He has also said some things about Elijah returning. I will write it down. What we don't understand, future generations may.

MODERATOR: Thank you, gentlemen, for being here. (Looks at audience.) Tune in next week when eight hundred and fifty prophets of the groves and Baal will be here to tell us of all the advantages of eating at the queen's table.

DEVILS' RETREAT

SCRIPTURE: Genesis 2; 3; 6—8; 37; 45; Exodus 11; 12:31—14; Numbers 14:36-38; Esther; Jeremiah 26; Daniel 3; Matthew 1:18—2:8; Luke 4:1-11

SUGGESTED TOPICS: Salvation; Christian unity; testing the spirits

BIBLE BACKGROUND

Since the beginning of time, Satan has been trying to foil God's plan of a perfect creation. In the Garden of Eden, he deceived Eve into doubting God's word (see Genesis 3:4). All through the ages, Satan and his minions worked behind the scenes. Satan attempted to entice Jesus into compromising His mission and His authority (see Matthew 4:1-11).

Finally, Satan was successful—or so he thought. The Savior was ignominiously hung from a cross, dead at the age of thirty-three. What had God's Chosen One been able to accomplish? At first glance, it would appear that Jesus had been a colossal failure. All but a small handful of His followers had scattered in fear after His arrest and trial. Surely it would not take long for Him to be completely forgotten.

Satan's "victory" was short lived. Throughout His life on earth, Jesus showed us truth about God, relationships with others and love in action. Through His death, He paid the price for our sin. Redemption had become reality. God's promise had been fulfilled. The resurrection of Jesus dramatically shattered Satan's plans.

PERFORMANCE TIPS

1. Suggested props: table and chairs, briefcase for Satan, papers to represent reports, pads and pencils for the demons to take notes, mirror.
2. Satan and his minions are formidable adversaries. Do not portray them as buffoons.
3. Part of the demons' problems result from their inability to support each other. All should nod in agreement when someone else is blamed for failure.

DISCUSSION QUESTIONS

1. How can you be sure Jesus is the promised Savior? What evidence do we have?
2. Satan is out to destroy what Jesus has done. How can we help God's plan of salvation?
3. What things do we do that might contribute more to Satan's plan than to God's plan?
4. Read James 4:7. How can you resist the devil?

DEVILS' RETREAT

CHARACTERS
SATAN
MALEFICENT (mal-EF-ih-sent)
NONSEQUITUR (non-SEK-wih-tur)
TAROT (TARE-oh)
DISGRUNTLE

SATAN: *(Stands.)* Bad evening, cruel ones. I trust your stay here at our retreat has been miserable.

MALEFICENT: It's been ROTTEN. All I could want.

NONSEQUITUR: Couldn't be worse.

TAROT: Disgusting. Bed's far too uncomfortable to sleep.

SATAN: It pleases me to hear it.

DISGRUNTLE: I've got a complaint.

SATAN: Speak.

DISGRUNTLE: The food's been too good—YECCH. I haven't had indigestion yet.

SATAN: Make a note. Fire the cook. And when I say fire, I mean FIRE. *(Mimics flames with his hands. Demons laugh.)* Anything else before we begin?

OTHERS: No.

SATAN: Then, let's begin. As you know, we're here to review our overall performance. Take time to get the big picture and glory in our past victories. And, of course, my favorite—we're here to assign blame for failures. So. From the beginning. Anyone?

TAROT: I think I speak for us all when I say the serpent in the Garden of Eden was a masterful touch on your part, Chief.

OTHERS *(applauding)*: Hear, hear!

SATAN: Of course it was, you apple-polisher! *(To audience.)* No pun intended. *(To his GROUP.)* EVERYTHING I do is masterful. However, it wasn't completely successful. Adam and Eve COULD have eaten from the Tree of Life, too. Imagine—people living in sin forever! *(Smiles.)* Oooooh. The thought gives me goose bumps. But MY brilliant work was UNDERMINED. WHO failed to get them to eat it?

MALEFICENT: Nonsequitur, Chief. He fouled up the works.

NONSEQUITUR: *(Rises angrily.)* How can you suggest such a thing?

MALEFICENT: *(Rises.)* You tried to make them believe God couldn't see them if they hid. But you didn't confuse them into thinking that what they had done was alright. You spent so much time on having them hide, you gave them time to feel guilty. You should have KEPT them from feeling guilty.

SATAN: No, no. Guilt comes with the territory, sooner or later—one of HIS rules. *(Smiles.)* But I have twisted it to my advantage, millions of times! Nonsequitur, YOU are to blame for not USING their guilt wisely. We could have used it to control those humans—if it hadn't been for HIM.

NONSEQUITUR: Yeah! It's HIS fault! He should have KILLED them. *(Whines.)* Why is He LIKE that? All He did was make them leave the garden and work for a living! And to top it off, He made those—UGH!—PROMISES.

DISGRUNTLE: Yeah. How did it go, Chief? You'd bruise some guy's heel but He'd bash your brains in when you did...

SATAN *(outraged)*: SHUT UP! IDIOT! Don't you know ANYTHING? We've been trying to eliminate the chance of that Promised One ever coming, EVERY DAY since He said that! No wonder you're incompetent! You don't even understand our game plan!

DISGRUNTLE: *(Looks down in shame and mumbles.)* It was all Nonsequitur's fault!

SATAN: He was as slow as YOU are. *(Writes.)* One mark against Nonsequitur.

MALEFICENT: But look at MY success rate after that! I had everybody hating his neighbor.

DISGRUNTLE *(snarling and sarcastically)*: Yeah? What about the—UGH!—obedient boat builder? How did you happen to miss him?

MALEFICENT: Look. *(Nervous.)* One obedient guy in a whole world—I can't be everywhere!

DISGRUNTLE: Come on! He's building a boat the size of a FOOTBALL FIELD! And you don't notice. What were you doing? SLEEPING?

MALEFICENT: You can't pin this on me! *(Points upward.)* HE sent the flood! *(Snaps fingers.)* Just like that—hundreds of years of work for NOTHING! Nothing left but a bunch of animals and eight humans who—ulp!—loved HIM.

SATAN: Disgruntle's right this time, even if he is an idiot. *(Writes.)* Maleficent, this falls on your shoulders. *(Looks up and sighs.)* Do I have to do everything myself?

TAROT: *(Stands.)* But Chief, with my brilliant work, we got the humans back to idol worship in no time flat. Every last one of them...

DISGRUNTLE *(sarcastically)*: Like Abraham? Look at all the PROMISES he got. Why didn't you stop him before he obeyed?

TAROT: Who would figure he'd listen to HIM? Abraham had lots of gods to choose from. But he just packed up his tents and left. Go figure.

MALEFICENT: If I hadn't stirred up strife in his family, we would have failed completely.

DISGRUNTLE: Big deal. *(Points upward.)* It just made HIM give the guy more PROMISES!

MALEFICENT *(irritated)*: Hey! I worked VERY hard in that family for generations. And what do I get? Joseph! I never expected the *F* word from him. Not after all the things I'd gotten his brothers to put him through!

DISGRUNTLE *(sarcastically)*: Ooooh! The dreaded *F* word.

MALEFICENT *(panicked)*: No! Don't SAY it!

DISGRUNTLE: Forgiveness! FORGIVENESS! *(Points.)* You blew it, Maleficent!

SATAN: I have to agree with Disgruntle. *(Writes.)* Another mark against Maleficent. You had to let his brothers think it would be better to sell him into slavery than to kill him. If you had followed the original plan...

More Bible Skits ©1994 Gospel Light. Permission granted to photocopy

DISGRUNTLE: Then I wouldn't have had to be so busy in Egypt.

MALEFICENT: YOU? I was the one who kept the Egyptians angry. I was the one who had all the male babies killed.

DISGRUNTLE: And if you hadn't missed Moses, I wouldn't have had to keep the Israelites arguing among themselves.

TAROT: Don't take all the credit. I had them worshiping Molech all the way to the Promised Land!

SATAN: Not ALL of them. Caleb and Joshua still obeyed HIM. Even the giants didn't scare them off. *(Bangs table.)* How can He always find SOMEBODY who'll do RIGHT?!

NONSEQUITUR: But Chief, remember? I got them ALL for a while with my "do your own thing" deception! I even got rid of Samuel and everyone like him. *(Whines.)* How was I to know that making them want a KING would work into HIS plan?

SATAN: You DID manage quite a few despicable kings. BUT—and this is a BIG one—you never managed to do away with the House of David! That was CRUCIAL to our plans!

NONSEQUITUR: Uh, look, Chief, I got more royal family members killed off than either one of us can count! I threw myself into that one!

SATAN: *(To NONSEQUITUR.)* Even ONE obedient ruler is too many! They never forgot HIS ways completely! *(To himself.)* And those prophets! Some of them were absolutely INTOLERABLE! *(Begins to pace.)* Torture them, put them in holes, deceive people into ignoring them—and still HE manages to get somebody to listen. EVERY TIME!

TAROT: Even when we got the whole bunch shipped off to Babylon, He seemed to be, well...one step ahead of us. Again.

DISGRUNTLE: My crew worked day and night on that Jeremiah situation. We got people worked up against him, got him thrown into jail. Best of all, we brought in a big group of false prophets to tell the people they'd be free and back in the land in no time. We did our job.

NONSEQUITUR: Maybe your false prophets did their job TOO well. Too many of those Israelites stayed separate from the people who deported them. You should have convinced ALL of them to join in, be one of the boys! Look at Daniel. Look at Shadrach, Meshach and Abednego. Couldn't you have let them be content with their position? No. You had to keep pushing!

DISGRUNTLE: That wasn't my doing.

SATAN: Don't try to worm out of it. You FAILED. *(Writes.)* But we could have gotten rid of the whole nation in one bloody day while they were in Babylon! Who blew THAT one, when we had Haman right in our pocket?

MALEFICENT: Yeah, who messed up? That's what I want to know! Just show me his face.

TAROT: *(Hands MALEFICENT a mirror.)* Here you go.

MALEFICENT: What's this for?

TAROT: I'm showing you the bungler's face!

MALEFICENT: Rot. I NEVER bungle.

TAROT: You did on this one. You got Haman so worked up against Mordecai, he lost all common sense. He couldn't think straight and look what happened. He lost his head! *(To audience.)* No pun intended.

MALEFICENT: That's not MY doing! Nonsequitur should have brought his "it's not my problem" deception down on Queen Esther right away. But, NO! He was late again! She had the—YUK!—truth in front of the king before Haman could say, "Kill the Jews!"

NONSEQUITUR: I was busy. She wasn't the only person around to deceive!

SATAN: Maleficent, that's THREE for you. And to think...you're lusting after MY job! You'll have to do better than this!

MALEFICENT (*shocked that he's been caught*): How...how did you know?

SATAN: I have informants. (*Leans over MALEFICENT.*) Never forget, you scheming slime, they don't call ME the "father of lies" for nothing! (*To group.*) Ahem. The last item on our agenda is the most crucial. Our Eternal Enemy is at it again.

MALEFICENT: Not again.

NONSEQUITUR: Doesn't He ever quit?

TAROT: Doesn't He ever get tired?

DISGRUNTLE: Uh-oh. You're not going to say that dreaded *R* word!

SATAN: (*Into DISGRUNTLE's ear.*) Redemption! REDEMPTION! There! It's a beautiful word but SOMEBODY had to say it.

ALL: Yecch!

SATAN: This time, the situation is critical. Our spy chain has just reported. The Promised One is about to come into the world.

MALEFICENT: How?

SATAN: Virgin birth.

TAROT: Crafty. Very crafty.

NONSEQUITUR: How does our Eternal Enemy come up with these ideas?

DISGRUNTLE: Just think of what we could accomplish if ONE of us was omniscient.

SATAN: Stop whining! We need a plan!

NONSEQUITUR: You say virgin birth. Single parent?

SATAN: (*Consults notes.*) Kid named Mary. Good family, engaged to Joseph.

NONSEQUITUR: Simple. I'll get to Joseph. Convince him to divorce her.

SATAN: Good luck. The man's in love!

NONSEQUITUR: Leave it to me. Deception and misleading thoughts are my specialty.

SATAN: OK, you've got Joseph. DON'T BLOW IT! But we need backup plans. Anyone?

TAROT: How does the Eternal Enemy plan to announce the birth? He must have some big sign or wonder.

SATAN: (*Consults notes.*) The reports say a new star. A bright one.

TAROT: Excellent. I have some astrologers working in the East.

SATAN: I thought they were His.

TAROT: So do they. Isn't it WONDERFUL? I tell them what to do and they give all the credit to HIM. It's one of my better plans.

SATAN: Let's hope it makes up for your Abraham blunder. So, what will you do?

TAROT: I'll have them misread the star. Send them to the wrong place. They'll announce a different savior. At the very least, it'll confuse the issue.

MALEFICENT: This goes against everything I believe in but, Tarot, how about you and I...cooperate?

OTHERS: Yecch! The *C* word.

MALEFICENT: Desperate times call for desperate measures. Listen, I've got a plan. The king of Judea is in my pocket. The Savior is going to come from around there, right?

SATAN: *(Consults notes.)* Bethlehem. Just outside of Jerusalem.

MALEFICENT: Perfect! This King Herod is ripe for the picking. Tarot, what if you lead your astrologers to Jerusalem?

TAROT: Easy enough. Why?

MALEFICENT: Those stargazers will be searching for a king, right?

TAROT: Naturally.

SATAN: I think I see where you're headed. I like it.

MALEFICENT: So they'll go to the palace and ask to see the new king.

TAROT: Of course.

MALEFICENT: If I know my Herod, he'll go wild!

SATAN: Magnificent, Maleficent!

TAROT: I don't get it.

MALEFICENT: Listen, we'll lead your astrologers to the RIGHT baby. They'll report back to my king.

TAROT: *(Rubs hands together.)* Ah, I see.

MALEFICENT: He sends his soldiers out. Kills the kid. Poof! No Savior.

SATAN: Brilliant! Can't miss! Disgruntle. We haven't heard from you.

DISGRUNTLE: These plans sound bad. But some of our most HORRIBLE plans have failed before.

SATAN: You're being a pessimist. I like that.

DISGRUNTLE: So I've got a contingency plan. Suppose Herod misses the Savior? Remember Moses! The worst case scenario is this: HE always seems to be one step ahead of us. HE always has ONE obedient person...

OTHERS: Bite your tongue! You're going to start sounding like one of THEM!

DISGRUNTLE: Look, I'm only saying, "What if."

SATAN *(outraged)***:** WHAT IF? You're talking "WHAT IF" to ME? That's enough! There's only one thing to do. If Herod doesn't get Him, I'M going in myself. I'll take my time. I'll watch and wait. And I'll get to Him when He's at His WEAKEST. I'll offer Him everything He wants—for a PRICE. I'll make a deal with Him that's so sweet He'll be in the palm of my hand before He knows what hit Him! I WILL BE WORSHIPED! I WILL BE KING!

> *(Murmurs of "Uh-oh!" and "Oh, wow!" from GROUP.)*

SATAN: *(Regains composure.)* Now. Let's get going. Everyone know his job?

OTHERS: Got it.

> *(ALL rise and begin to leave.)*

SATAN *(calling after them)***:** And this time, DO IT RIGHT!

IT'S A MIRACLE

SCRIPTURE: Matthew 4:1-11; 8:14-17; 9:2-8; Luke 6:6-11; 18:31-34; John 6:1-59

SUGGESTED TOPICS: Jesus' fulfilling God's covenants; miracles; Jesus as God Incarnate

BIBLE BACKGROUND

"He was in the world, and though the world was made through him, the world did not recognize him. He came to that which was his own, but his own did not receive him" (John 1:10,11). God promised to send a Savior to redeem His people, and what a Savior! Not a person who could guide people back to God, not an angel who could tell people about being in God's presence, but God Himself in human flesh. The Creator of heaven and earth came to live among His people, but the very ones who should have been first to recognize Him, didn't.

Even the one who was sent to bear witness of the Light (see John 1:8) had his doubts. Locked in his prison cell, John sent two of his disciples to ask Jesus, "Are you the one who was to come, or should we expect someone else?" (Matthew 11:2,3). Jesus' answer made a clear reference to one of Isaiah's prophecies. "Go back and report to John what you hear and see: The blind receive sight, the lame walk, those who have leprosy are cured, the deaf hear, the dead are raised, and the good news is preached to the poor" (see Isaiah 35:4-6; 61:1 and Matthew 11:4,5). Jesus knew that John would recognize the report of Jesus' ministry as fulfillment of the promise.

PERFORMANCE TIPS

1. Suggested props: chairs, papers to represent reports to Caiaphas, notebook clearly titled "Robert's Rules of Order" or an actual copy of *Robert's Rules* if available.

2. Thomas is an annoyance to the other three. The others indicate this by shaking their heads when Thomas speaks, holding their heads in their hands, etc.

3. While the others are speaking, Thomas is deep in thought, consulting Robert's Rules of Order and planning his next motion.

4. Thomas limps; he has twisted his ankle and should act accordingly.

DISCUSSION QUESTIONS

1. Why do you think Jesus performed miracles?

2. Why do you think the Pharisees, priests and scribes did not recognize Jesus as the Messiah?

3. Jesus is sometimes called "God Incarnate." What do you think that means?

4. What are some reasons to accept Jesus as Savior?

It's a Miracle

CHARACTERS
CAIAPHAS (KYE-uh-fus)
ANNAS (ah-NAHS)
JOHN
THOMAS

PRONUNCIATION GUIDE
zealots (ZEL-uts)
blasphemy (BLAS-fuh-mee)

CAIAPHAS *(pacing)*: Where IS he?

ANNAS: Forget him. Let's start the meeting.

JOHN: He's always late, anyway. He can catch up with us.

ANNAS: Besides, it's not like he'll have anything to contribute.

JOHN: That's right. We always have to go over everything with him twice.

CAIAPHAS: But whenever we start before he gets here, we have to go over everything with him THREE times.

ANNAS: True.

JOHN: Why don't we just expel him from the Council?

CAIAPHAS: Because he is an honored and revered member of our group.

ANNAS: A highly respected man in the community.

CAIAPHAS: A shining light in the darkness.

ANNAS: A pillar of faith.

JOHN: And his father contributes more than anyone else to the Temple treasury?

CAIAPHAS and ANNAS: Exactly.

JOHN: OK. We'll wait. *(THOMAS enters, limping.)*

THOMAS: Hi, guys. Hope I didn't miss anything.

CAIAPHAS *(aside)*: Nothing you wouldn't have missed if you'd been here.

THOMAS: What?

ANNAS: We haven't started yet.

JOHN: What's wrong with you?

THOMAS: Nothing's wrong with me! I'm a good pharisee!

JOHN: I only meant...

THOMAS: You're always picking on me. And I don't know why.

JOHN: I was only asking...

THOMAS: I keep all the laws. Just as well as anybody. Well, almost as well.

JOHN: ...about your foot.

THOMAS: Is that some new kind of curse? About your foot! I don't get it.

ANNAS: He was inquiring about your foot.

CAIAPHAS: Showing a natural concern for his esteemed brother.

THOMAS: Is your brother here? John, I didn't know your brother Joseph was going to join us.

CAIAPHAS: Why are you LIMPING?

THOMAS: Oh. I twisted my ankle on the way here. There was a loose stone in the street. There should be a law against putting stones in the street.

JOHN: They help to keep the mud down when it rains.

ANNAS: They protect the road. They make it last longer.

THOMAS: Well, they should use different kinds. Ones that don't come loose.

CAIAPHAS: Gentlemen. We can leave the issue of public works to the Romans. They're the experts in building roads. We have more important matters at hand.

THOMAS: What could be more important than protecting our citizens?

CAIAPHAS: Nothing. That's why we're here.

(ALL turn to CAIAPHAS.)

ANNAS: Has something serious happened?

JOHN: Are the Romans planning to destroy Jerusalem? Are the zealots acting up again?

CAIAPHAS: No more than usual. The Romans are used to them. No man-made disaster is about to befall our city. It's philosophy we must worry about.

THOMAS: I move we tell the Romans to sharpen one edge of every stone. Is there a second?

ANNAS: What?

THOMAS: We need a second to the motion before we can vote. It's right here in Robert's Rules of Order.

JOHN: Why would we ask the Romans to sharpen stones?

THOMAS: We can't discuss the motion until it's seconded. It says so, right here. *(Points to his Robert's Rules of Order.)*

CAIAPHAS: Very well, I'll second it.

ANNAS and JOHN: What?

CAIAPHAS: It's easier to humor him than to argue with him.

JOHN: True. Thomas, why would we ask the Romans to sharpen stones?

THOMAS: Then they could pound the stones into the ground and there wouldn't be any loose stones in the street. Our citizens would be safe from the cruel and inhuman punishment of twisted ankles.

ANNAS: Can we vote on this and get it out of the way?

CAIAPHAS: Gladly. All in favor. *(THOMAS raises hand.)* Opposed. *(ANNAS and JOHN raise their hands.)* Defeated. Now, let's get on to important matters. There's a prophet going around the countryside.

 More Bible Skits ©1994 Gospel Light. Permission granted to photocopy.

JOHN: Jesus of Nazareth?

CAIAPHAS: You've heard of Him, then?

ANNAS: He's famous. Everyone's heard of Him. *(Looks at THOMAS.)* Well, maybe not everyone.

JOHN: What's the problem with Him? I've heard He's doing some wonderful things.

CAIAPHAS: That's precisely the problem.

ANNAS: What's wrong with helping people?

CAIAPHAS: Nothing, if He does it within the framework of the Law.

JOHN: He's been breaking the Law?

CAIAPHAS: Indeed He has! He's been healing the sick...

THOMAS: Of course He has. You don't heal the healthy. You heal the sick.

CAIAPHAS: He's been healing the sick on the Sabbath.

ANNAS: Blasphemy!

JOHN: I hadn't heard about this.

CAIAPHAS: Not only that—He's using His power of healing to claim to be God.

ANNAS: Double blasphemy!

CAIAPHAS: We have to get Jesus in here, away from the crowds...

THOMAS: That's a good idea. He could heal that ugly growth on you, John.

JOHN: What ugly growth?

THOMAS: That one. Right in the middle of your face.

JOHN: That's my nose!

THOMAS: It is? Well, maybe he could do something about it. A little plastic surgery would do wonders for your looks.

JOHN: MY looks? *(Shakes fist under THOMAS's nose.)* I'll do something about YOUR looks!

CAIAPHAS: Gentlemen! Bickering among ourselves won't help.

THOMAS: It might improve his personality, too. If you look good, you feel good.

ANNAS: Tell us what you've heard about Jesus, Caiaphas.

CAIAPHAS: First, there was all that healing over at Peter's house.

JOHN: We heard about that. I didn't hear of any problems there.

ANNAS: Didn't He just heal Peter's mother-in-law? And those who came to the house later in the evening?

CAIAPHAS: Yes. And if He'd been content to simply heal the sick, there would be no problem. But He's begun meddling with philosophy.

THOMAS: Well, I can't blame Him.

ANNAS: What?

THOMAS: Philip has always charged way too much for his legal advice.

JOHN: What are you talking about now?

THOMAS: Caiaphas just said Jesus was meddling with Phil's fees. And He should.

CAIAPHAS *(shaking his head)*: If his father weren't so rich...

THOMAS: I stopped to see Philip, right after I twisted my ankle. He wanted a full three talents to sue the Romans for personal damages. Well! That's way too much. It's highway robbery. He should be stopped.

CAIAPHAS *(yelling)*: Phil-o-so-phy!

THOMAS: That's what I said. Phil's law fees.

ANNAS *(soothing CAIAPHAS)*: Take it easy. It's only Thomas. John and I are here.

CAIAPHAS: Yes. You're right. Back to Jesus. He's forgiving sins.

JOHN: But He can't do that! Only God can forgive sin.

ANNAS: Of course. Anybody with an ounce of sense knows that.

CAIAPHAS: But He's using His healing powers to support His claim that He can forgive sin. He walked right up to a paralyzed man and said, "Your sins are forgiven." I told Him, "You can't do that. Only God can forgive sin."

JOHN: Of course. You did the right thing.

ANNAS: After all, a man cannot forgive another's sins.

CAIAPHAS: But this Jesus said, "Is it easier to say, 'Your sins are forgiven' or 'Get up and walk'?" Then He turned to the paralyzed man and said, "Get up. Take your mat and go home." And the man did.

JOHN: This could mean trouble.

CAIAPHAS: There are even rumors that He had a face-to-face confrontation with Satan and defeated him. Silly, of course. No man could do that.

ANNAS: The things people will believe. But if this is all He's done...

CAIAPHAS: It isn't. I have this report from Alexander. Last Sabbath, Jesus healed a man's hand. On the Sabbath!

JOHN: Blasphemy!

ANNAS: Double blasphemy!

THOMAS: I move we get Philip to bring an action against Jesus for practicing medicine without a license. He might do it for free if Jesus has been trying to make him reduce his fees.

JOHN: *(Reaches for THOMAS's throat.)* Why you...*(THOMAS holds up Robert's Rules of Order.)*

CAIAPHAS *(restraining JOHN)*: Seconded. In favor? *(THOMAS holds up hand.)* Against? *(JOHN and ANNAS hold up hands.)* Defeated.

ANNAS: *(To JOHN.)* He's right. It is faster to humor him than to argue.

CAIAPHAS: We must make plans to stop Jesus before His popularity gets out of hand.

JOHN: But if He's only healed a few people, we could counteract it.

ANNAS: How?

JOHN: Most of his popularity is from rumors of what He has done. We'll start rumors, blaming Him for evil. It shouldn't be too hard. The man's a blasphemer.

CAIAPHAS: I wish it were that easy! He's done other things.

ANNAS: Like what?

CAIAPHAS: He's been preaching. And huge crowds have been listening.

JOHN: That's nothing to worry about. We've been preaching for years.

ANNAS: The common man can't grasp important religious principles.

JOHN: He'll never persuade them. People don't listen to doctrine.

CAIAPHAS: No? Suppose you were one of a group of five thousand men. And some women and children.

ANNAS: Yes.

CAIAPHAS: Now suppose you were listening to Jesus when suppertime came.

JOHN: I'd go home for supper.

CAIAPHAS: But suppose you were a long way from home. You couldn't get home in time for supper.

THOMAS: I move...

CAIAPHAS: Seconded. In favor? Opposed? Defeated.

ANNAS: What does hunger have to do with doctrine?

CAIAPHAS: Now suppose a boy comes forward with his lunch. A few fish and a little bread. He offers to share it with the crowd.

JOHN: I'd laugh. What can so little do for so many?

CAIAPHAS: Jesus blessed it, broke it into pieces and had it passed around. It fed the whole crowd.

ANNAS *(stunned)***:** Are you certain?

CAIAPHAS: With enough to gather twelve baskets of leftovers.

JOHN: Impossible!

CAIAPHAS: It's all in Alexander's report.

ANNAS: Then, huge crowds could be following Him! Hoping to be fed.

CAIAPHAS: Fortunately, Jesus rebuked them. He told them they only followed Him for the food.

JOHN: Then where's the problem? They must have stopped.

CAIAPHAS: But those who DO follow have become fanatics. Jesus must be stopped. We must find an excuse to get Him in here. Some reason to have Him killed.

ANNAS: I agree.

JOHN: So do I. He must be stopped.

CAIAPHAS: Then we're agreed? Good. Let's go...

THOMAS: Wait a minute. *(Holds up Robert's Rules of Order.)* We don't have a motion.

CAIAPHAS *(irritated)***:** I move that we find an excuse to find Jesus guilty of a crime punishable by death. I further move that we have Him brought here before us for a trial.

THOMAS: I'll second the motion.

CAIAPHAS: In favor? *(ALL raise hands.)* Good. Then we're adjourned. *(ALL rise to leave, THOMAS limping.)*

THOMAS: I've got an idea. Let's not tell Him why we're bringing Him here. Then, before we find Him guilty, He could fix John's nose. And I wonder how He is with ankles? *(Looks around.)* And where is Joseph? I thought he was coming to this meeting.

SACRIFICE UNTIL IT KIND OF HURTS

SCRIPTURE: Mark 12:41-44; Luke 21:1-4; 22:20

SUGGESTED TOPICS: Giving; obeying God

BIBLE BACKGROUND

Sacrificial offerings began shortly after the Garden of Eden (see Genesis 4:3,4) and were extended by Noah (see Genesis 8:20), Abraham (see Genesis 22:13), Isaac (see Genesis 26:25) and Jacob (see Genesis 31:54). The system of sacrificial worship was fully instituted under Moses as part of the covenant (the old testament) between God and humanity. Recognizing that people are sinful, God provided a method by which they could approach Him. The people were instructed to bring their offerings to the priests to be offered as payment for their sins (see Leviticus 1—7). The sacrifice was to be an animal without blemish from one's herd. The poor could bring pigeons as a sacrifice instead; the very poor could offer flour (see Leviticus 5:11).

The Lord made it clear in the Old Testament that the sacrifice itself was not the redeeming factor. The spirit with which the sacrifice was given was the important thing. Saul was rebuked for offering a sacrifice rather than obeying God's instructions (see 1 Samuel 15:22). All of Judah was rebuked for offering sacrifices while taking advantage of other people (see Jeremiah 7:1-11). Jesus reiterated the importance of attitude when he commended a widow's small offering as being of greater value than the larger sums given by those of greater means (see Mark 12:41-44).

But the old covenant was flawed. Sin offerings had to be made over and over because the sacrifice was imperfect. God instituted a new covenant, one which was sealed by the Perfect Sacrifice, God Incarnate. By offering Himself for our sin, Jesus forgave all the sin ever committed and all that would be committed. This sacrifice does not need to be repeated (see Hebrews 7:27). By placing trust in this Perfect Sacrifice, our guilt is covered and the power of sin is destroyed (see Hebrews 10:10).

PERFORMANCE TIPS

1. Suggested props: toy lamb, two pennies for the widow, two bags of coins for the rich man, sack marked "flour" for the poor man's offering, small bowl, metal bowl for the Temple treasury.
2. The rich man speaks loudly (until he discovers his mistake). He wants everyone in the Temple to know how good he is.
3. The widow makes her offering with her head down. She does not look up until the poor man speaks to her.

DISCUSSION QUESTIONS

1. Which offering was most pleasing to God? Which was least pleasing? Why?
2. Does having material wealth show that God is pleased with us? Why or why not?
3. Jesus is often called "the Lamb of God." Why?
4. Why would Jesus allow Himself to be sacrificed on the cross?
5. What must we do to become part of God's family?

More Bible Skits ©1994 Gospel Light. Permission granted to photocopy.

SACRIFICE UNTIL IT KIND OF HURTS

CHARACTERS

RICH MAN   **POOR MAN**   **WIDOW**

RICH MAN: *(Holds up lamb, speaks loudly toward sky.)* Oh, Lord God, see my noble sacrifice, a perfect lamb. Forgive my sins, few though they may be.

POOR MAN: *(Holds up small bowl of flour; sack is by his feet.)* I am but a poor man, Lord God. I have no wealth to present to You. Please accept this humble sacrifice. I have not even two pigeons. Accept this offering of flour, for it is all I can bring.

RICH MAN: *(To POOR MAN.)* You would offer THIS to God?

POOR MAN: It is all I have. Is it not lawful to offer such to God?

RICH MAN: It may be lawful, but it's also pitiful. See MY beautiful sacrifice. THIS is what the Lord wants. The best.

POOR MAN: But this IS my best!

RICH MAN: Well, then, your best just isn't good enough. *(Points to WIDOW.)* You're as pathetic as that woman over there by the treasury.

POOR MAN: She is a widow. I know her. She has even less than I do.

RICH MAN: Well, look at that offering. Two pennies! What's that to God?

POOR MAN: It is what she willingly gives. Isn't that enough?

RICH MAN: Look, we're supposed to be SACRIFICING. That means giving God something worthwhile. You see this lamb? THERE'S a sacrifice.

POOR MAN: It is indeed a fine lamb. *(To WIDOW who is walking by.)* How is it with you, sister?

WIDOW: Oh, hello, neighbor. I didn't see you.

RICH MAN: I don't wonder that you didn't see him, keeping your head down. Of course, if I only threw two pennies into the Temple treasury, I wouldn't hold my head up, either.

WIDOW: If I had more to give, I would give it. But I have none.

POOR MAN: You gave EVERYTHING?

WIDOW: It was what I had.

POOR MAN: Stop by my house on the way home. I have enough oil and flour for two days. You must take half.

WIDOW: No, I couldn't.

POOR MAN: But I insist. I won't take no for an answer!

RICH MAN: You two are so pathetic. Do you want to see how an offering should be made? *(Takes bag of money from belt and goes to treasury.)* Oh, God. You are so gracious to me. Look what I'm giving to You. This shows how good I am and why you bless me so. *(Pours money into treasury.)*

WIDOW: It must be wonderful to have so much to offer to God.

RICH MAN: He has blessed me because I don't sin. I'm not like tax gatherers or those others. You two must have done some really bad things.

POOR MAN *(sadly)*: Why do you say such a thing?

WIDOW: Is it a sin to be poor?

RICH MAN: Everyone knows God punishes sinners. And you two are being punished. I, on the other hand, keep all the laws. I am very nearly perfect. That's why God has blessed me with so much.

POOR MAN: I cannot believe this. Yes, I have sinned. We all have sinned.

WIDOW: That is true. I, too, have sinned. But God forgives sin.

RICH MAN: Not for a little flour and two pennies. You need good sheep and a bagful of cash to have forgiveness, even for MY paltry sins. Think what is required for YOUR great sins!

WIDOW: But doesn't God look at the heart?

POOR MAN: Doesn't He test the SPIRIT of the gift?

RICH MAN: Well, I suppose it counts a little. But it's the SIZE of the gift that really matters. Look at this sheep. Almost perfect.

POOR MAN: ALMOST perfect?

RICH MAN: She's lame. Not much good in my flock. But she makes a wonderful sacrifice. You don't think I'm going to waste the best of my flock by having it given to the Temple!

POOR MAN: But aren't we supposed to give our best? You said so yourself!

RICH MAN: What I have given is better than most. Better than yours, certainly. That makes it good.

WIDOW: I must be going.

POOR MAN: Remember to stop at my house. Get that flour and oil.

WIDOW: If you insist.

RICH MAN: You know, having my minor sins forgiven has made me feel generous. *(Takes a second bag of money from belt.)* Have a penny. *(Looks into bag.)* Oh, no!

WIDOW: What is wrong, sir?

RICH MAN: This bag is full of PENNIES.

WIDOW: It must be wonderful to have all that wealth.

RICH MAN: But...but—I brought two bags of money with me. One full of pennies, for the offering. The other had gold and silver in it. I put the wrong bag into the offering! Here, give me that. *(Takes penny back from WIDOW.)*

POOR MAN: It is not right to give and then to take away.

WIDOW: *(To POOR MAN.)* It doesn't matter, neighbor. I didn't expect to leave the Temple with any money. I have more than I expected with your kind offer of food.

POOR MAN: Come. We'll go and get it now.

RICH MAN: *(To himself.)* How can I get my money back? Maybe if I went to the priest and explained the problem. No. The priests are as greedy as everyone else. They wouldn't give it back.

POOR MAN: *(To RICH MAN.)* Good-bye, friend.

WIDOW: *(To RICH MAN.)* May the Lord bless you.

RICH MAN: He'd better, after all I gave Him today.

TRIPLE P TRIAL

SCRIPTURE: Acts 8:26-38; 10; 11:15-18; 13:13-49

SUGGESTED TOPICS: Baptism; the good news; salvation for everyone

BIBLE BACKGROUND

Jesus' death and resurrection achieved the fulfillment of God's plan of salvation. The only job remaining was to spread the good news. Just before His ascension, Jesus instructed His disciples to "Go and make disciples of all nations, baptizing them in the name of the Father and of the Son and of the Holy Spirit" (Matthew 28:19). On the Day of Pentecost, the disciples began to carry out this commission, and as they spoke in Jerusalem, thousands of Jews became converts. However, the gospel was not yet preached to the Gentiles. Religious and cultural barriers remained intact. The disciples were good Jewish men who had been taught from their infancy to avoid contact with the Gentiles.

The persecution of the Christians in Jerusalem gradually drove them to escape their homeland. Philip found the people of Samaria were amazingly open to the message of Jesus. But they were half Jewish, so it was almost the same as preaching to Jews. The good news spread easily into Samaria. Philip was called out of his ministry in Samaria to the Desert of Gaza. There, he met an Ethiopian reading Isaiah. As the man was a Jewish proselyte, Philip saw no problem in sharing the gospel with him. But the Gentiles remained unreached until God sent Peter to a Roman centurian's home and Paul found himself invited to teach the word of God to Sergius Paulus, the proconsul of Cyprus. Finally, the door was opening so Gentiles could join the family of God.

PERFORMANCE TIPS

1. Suggested props: gavel and robe for the judge, table and chair for the judge, two tables for the prosecution and defense, chairs, files for the prosecutor.
2. After a judgment is handed down, the defendant and lawyers should return to their chairs and wait for the next case to be called.
3. After calling the case, the bailiff should stand at attention to the side.

DISCUSSION QUESTIONS

1. What made it difficult for the Jewish believers to tell Gentiles about the good news?
2. Who doesn't deserve to hear God's plan of salvation? Why?
3. Describe God's plan of salvation in your own words.
4. How can you share God's plan with others?

TRIPLE P TRIAL

CHARACTERS
PHIL
PETE
PAUL
PROSECUTOR
BAILIFF
JUDGE
DEFENSE LAWYER

PRONUNCIATION GUIDE
Cornelius (kor-NEEL-yus)

BAILIFF: Criminal court is now in session, the honorable Judge Blind Justice presiding. All rise.

JUDGE: *(Enters and sits.)* Be seated. *(Bangs gavel. To audience.)* I love that. *(To LAWYER.)* Defense counsel. Why are so many people seated over there?

LAWYER: They are all my clients, Your Honor. The cases are all interrelated.

JUDGE: That's a little unusual, isn't it? One lawyer for three defendants?

LAWYER: Yes, Your Honor. But we feel there's no conflict of interest.

JUDGE: Mr. Prosecutor?

PROSECUTOR: The prosecution has no objection, Your Honor.

JUDGE: Okey, dokey. First case. *(Bangs gavel. To audience.)* I love that.

BAILIFF: Phil versus The People. Attempted Murder.

> *(PHIL, DEFENSE LAWYER and PROSECUTOR stand before JUDGE.)*

JUDGE: How do you plead?

LAWYER: Not guilty, Your Honor.

JUDGE: Mr. Prosecutor?

PROSECUTOR *(consulting file)*: Yes, Your Honor. It seems the guilty scum...

LAWYER: Objection.

JUDGE: You were referring to the defendant, Mr. Prosecutor.

PROSECUTOR: Yes, Your Honor.

JUDGE: It's up to the court to decide if he's guilty scum. Objection sustained. Strike the word "guilty" from the record. Now, Mr. Prosecutor, what did the scum do?

PROSECUTOR: On or about noon, on the second of the month, in the Desert of Gaza, this scumbag was seen holding an Ethiopian man under water.

JUDGE: Is the man in court?

LAWYER: No, Your Honor.

JUDGE: Why not? Shouldn't he be here as a witness, Mr. Prosecutor?

PROSECUTOR: We couldn't insist on his testimony, Your Honor.

JUDGE: Why not?

PROSECUTOR: It seems he's an official in the court of Queen Candace of Ethiopia. He has diplomatic immunity. You know how these political types don't want to be involved in scandal.

JUDGE: That makes it difficult to throw the book at this one.

PROSECUTOR: Unfortunately true, Your Honor. However, we have a stipulation from the defense that the allegations are correct as to their substance.

JUDGE: Defense?

LAWYER: Yes, Your Honor. We stipulated that Phil was holding a man under water.

JUDGE: Seems open and shut, then.

LAWYER: If we may present our defense?

PROSECUTOR: *(Sighs.)* Are we required to waste the court's time this way?

JUDGE: Unfortunately, Mr. Prosecutor, each defendant is allowed a defense. Continue.

LAWYER: My client was holding a man under water, Your Honor. But it was not an act of violence; it was an act of compassion!

PROSECUTOR *(sarcastically)***:** Right! And he pulls legs off grasshoppers so they won't get tired.

JUDGE: No interrupting, Mr. Prosecutor. *(To LAWYER.)* What about this grasshopper thing?

LAWYER: Nothing more than the prosecution's imagination, Your Honor. Not a part of the proceedings.

JUDGE: Okey, dokey. You want to explain this compassionate drowning, Phil?

PHIL: I was in the villages of Samaria, Your Honor...

JUDGE: I thought you said Gaza. Mr. Prosecutor?

PROSECUTOR: *(Looks at file.)* That's how the complaint reads, Your Honor.

PHIL: Yes, Your Honor. I was called by an angel of the Lord to go to Gaza.

JUDGE: OK. So now you're in Gaza?

PHIL: As I was walking along, I saw a chariot and heard a man reading from the prophet Isaiah.

JUDGE: Continue.

PHIL: I ran alongside the chariot and asked the man if he understood what he was reading. He said, "How can I, if I have no one to explain it to me?"

JUDGE: So you're saying this man was semiliterate?

PHIL: No, Your Honor. He was a very intelligent and influential man in Ethiopia. But some of the passages in the prophets are difficult to understand if you haven't grown up with the Scriptures.

JUDGE: Continue.

PHIL: He invited me to sit with him in the chariot and we went through the passage together. I explained how the prophet was speaking of Jesus.

PROSECUTOR (sarcastically): Right! Isaiah lived CENTURIES before Jesus. He didn't even KNOW Jesus. How could he talk about Jesus?

JUDGE: Good point. How about it, Phil?

PHIL: Isaiah was given the information about the Messiah by God. That's why Isaiah is called a prophet.

JUDGE: (Nods.) Seems to cover it. What about the drowning?

PHIL: As we continued along, we came to some water. The Ethiopian said, "Here's some water. Is there anything to stop me from being baptized?" I said, "Nothing at all, if you believe with all your heart. The good news of Jesus Christ is for you, too." So we went down to the water and I baptized him.

JUDGE: So you're saying it was a BAPTISM, not a drowning?

PHIL: Yes, Your Honor.

JUDGE: Anything to add, Mr. Prosecutor?

PROSECUTOR: No, Your Honor. The facts speak for themselves.

JUDGE: After careful consideration, I can't see that there is anything to show it wasn't a baptism. Case dismissed. (Bangs gavel. To audience.) I love that. Next case.

BAILIFF: Pete versus The People. Attempted Bribery of a Peace Officer.

(PETE, DEFENSE LAWYER and PROSECUTOR stand before JUDGE.)

JUDGE: How do you plead?

LAWYER: Not guilty, Your Honor.

JUDGE: Mr. Prosecutor?

PROSECUTOR (consulting file): Yes, Your Honor. It seems the slime-sucking...

LAWYER: Objection.

JUDGE: Sustained. Mr. Prosecutor, there is nothing in evidence to show the defendant sucks slime.

PROSECUTOR: On or about ten o'clock on the morning of the fifteenth of the month, the defendant was seen entering the premises of Cornelius, leader of the Italian Band.

JUDGE: Are they the ones who made that record, "Roma, Roma, Wherefore Art Thou, Roma?" That was a terrific song!

PROSECUTOR: No, Your Honor. That was the Italian Jug Band.

More Bible Skits

JUDGE: Too bad. I really like that song. What did this Italian Band record?

PROSECUTOR: Nothing, Your Honor. The Italian Band is one of the special squads of the Roman Army. Cornelius is one of its centurions.

JUDGE: I knew that. Continue with the complaint.

PROSECUTOR: As I said, the defendant was seen slinking into the premises of Cornelius. As Cornelius is a Roman officer and the defendant is Jewish, the obvious conclusion is bribery.

JUDGE: I think I smell something fishy here, alright.

LAWYER: Probably from my client's clothing, Your Honor. Left over from his previous profession.

JUDGE: That could be it. Defense?

LAWYER: My client was there on a social visit, Your Honor, at Cornelius' request.

PROSECUTOR (*sarcastically*): Oh, right! As if a Jew would enter the house of a Gentile.

JUDGE: Very good point, Counselor. The Jews are well known for their reluctance to associate with Gentiles. What about it, Pete?

PETE: It is well known, Your Honor. I used to be the same way.

PROSECUTOR: See? He admits it. Throw the book at him!

JUDGE: In due time. In due time. So you don't like Gentiles?

PETE: It wasn't that I hated Gentiles. Like all Jews, I believed that God only loved the Jews. But I learned that I was wrong. Now, many Gentiles are my brothers and sisters in Christ.

PROSECUTOR (*sarcastically*): And I'm the King of Siam.

JUDGE: Really? I hadn't heard. Congratulations.

PROSECUTOR: Thank you, Your Honor.

JUDGE: (*To PETE.*) Continue.

PETE: I was in Joppa...

JUDGE: Doesn't Cornelius live in Caesarea?

PROSECUTOR: (*Looks at file.*) So the record shows, Your Honor.

PETE: He does. But I was visiting my friend, Simon, the tanner. About noon, I was on the roof, praying. I was hungry, but lunch wasn't ready.

JUDGE: I hate having to wait for lunch. How about you, Mr. Prosecutor?

PROSECUTOR: I hate waiting for anything. Especially convictions. Can we get on with this fairy tale?

JUDGE: That's MY job. Continue with your fairy tale, Pete.

PETE: It's no fairy tale! While I was waiting, I saw a vision. A large sheet containing various animals, birds and reptiles came down from heaven. A voice said, "Take. Kill and eat."

JUDGE: I bet they looked good, what with lunch being late.

PETE: No, Your Honor. Because they were all unclean.

JUDGE: Well, haven't you heard of WATER? My goodness, if they were dirty, you could have washed them before you cooked them. And boiling kills germs, you know.

LAWYER: My client refers to the well-known Jewish custom of determining ceremonial cleanliness of some animals and uncleanliness of others.

JUDGE: Mr. Prosecutor?

PROSECUTOR: It is a known fact, Your Honor.

JUDGE: I knew that. Continue.

PETE: So I protested to the voice. I said, "I would never eat anything unclean." Then the voice said, "Don't call unclean the things I have made clean." This happened three times.

JUDGE: You take a lot of convincing. So you ate something?

PETE: No, Your Honor. The animals weren't real. It was just a vision. But I didn't understand it. While I was meditating on it...

JUDGE: Meditating? Are you into T.M.? Do you have a mantra?

PETE: Of course not! That's not from God. Meditating means to think hard about something. So I was thinking about the vision, trying to understand it...

PROSECUTOR: *(To the ceiling.)* He can't understand that it's OK to eat frogs' legs?

PETE: I knew it was more than that. But I didn't know what. Then the Holy Spirit told me there were men waiting for me in the house. The Holy Spirit said, "Don't be afraid to go with these men. I have sent them."

JUDGE: And these men were...?

PETE: Servants of Cornelius. They told me Cornelius wanted to speak with me. Suddenly, I understood the vision. God was telling me that Gentiles are not unclean! So the next day, I went with them to Caesarea.

JUDGE: And that's when you tried to bribe Cornelius?

PETE: I never tried to bribe him! I went and spoke to him about Jesus! I told him how I had thought God's saving grace was only for the Jews, but God had shown me differently. Then the Holy Spirit came upon everyone there. So I baptized Cornelius' household.

JUDGE: Good thing we don't have a water shortage, with all this baptizing.

PROSECUTOR: He really expects us to fall for that sad story. If the Jews have changed their attitude toward Gentiles, how come Gentiles aren't welcome in the homes of Jews?

PETE: I didn't say ALL Jews had changed their attitude. I had to defend my position with my Jewish Christian brothers. But now we know God's plan of salvation is for everyone.

LAWYER: We submit that there is no evidence of bribery and ask for dismissal of all charges, Your Honor.

PROSECUTOR *(outraged)*: No evidence? A Jew in a Gentile home and you say no EVIDENCE?

JUDGE: I have to agree with defense. Case dismissed. *(Bangs gavel. To audience.)* Love that. Next case.

BAILIFF: Paul versus The People. Conspiring to Start a Riot.

> *(PAUL, DEFENSE LAWYER and PROSECUTOR stand before JUDGE.)*

JUDGE: How do you plead?

LAWYER: Not guilty, Your Honor.

JUDGE: Mr. Prosecutor?

PROSECUTOR *(consulting file)*: Yes, Your Honor. It seems the snake...

LAWYER: Objection.

JUDGE: Sustained. Nothing in evidence about reptiles. What are the facts?

PROSECUTOR: On numerous occasions, the defendant went into synagogues to preach.

JUDGE: Happens all the time, Mr. Prosecutor.

PROSECUTOR: But when they don't listen to him, he tells them he will preach to the Gentiles. He tells them God's Word is for the Gentiles.

JUDGE: No big deal, Mr. Prosecutor. Lots of Romans say the Jews don't know what they're talking about. Hasn't caused a riot yet.

PROSECUTOR: But, HE'S a Jew, Your Honor. And a PHARISEE.

JUDGE: Whoo! THAT could ruffle a few feathers. How about it, Paul?

PAUL: What he says is true. I preach to the Jews because they are God's chosen people. But if they refuse to listen, I preach to the Gentiles. God's Word is for them also.

JUDGE: Hmm. But you didn't know it would upset the Jews?

PAUL: Of course I knew it. I used to be the same way. But God's truth must be spoken!

PROSECUTOR: See? He admits it! You gotta give me this one, Your Honor. Totally premeditated. He's guilty!

JUDGE: There's certainly enough evidence to hold this one over. We'll pass it along to the Grand Jury. Defendant remanded to house custody to await trial in Rome. Have you anything else to say?

PAUL: Have you heard of God's love for you? How He wants you to have eternal life?

JUDGE: Whoa! Trying to convert me, Paul? *(Chuckles. To BAILIFF.)* That's a wrap, folks. *(Bangs gavel and mouths, "I love that.")*

BAILIFF: All rise. *(EVERYONE rises as JUDGE exits.)*

SHOW ME

SCRIPTURE: Genesis 6; Exodus 2:1-10; Hebrews 11

SUGGESTED TOPICS: Showing faith; trusting God

BIBLE BACKGROUND

A well-known story tells of a famous acrobat who announced he would cross Niagara Falls on a tightrope, pushing a wheelbarrow. Naturally, a crowd assembled to watch his feat. "Who believes I can do this?" he asked the crowd. "We do!" was the enthusiastic response. "Who will ride in the wheelbarrow while I push it across?" he asked the assembly. He was greeted with dead silence.

Whether or not the above story is true, it clearly delineates the difference between belief and faith. One can passively believe; but if one has faith, it must be demonstrated. Hebrews 11 tells of the heroes of the faith and what they did to demonstrate their faith. Noah, in faith, built an ark. Abraham left his home in faith, and journeyed to a land he had never seen. Later, in faith, he prepared to offer up his only son as a sacrifice. Moses' parents, in faith, hid him for three months. Moses, in faith, forsook Egypt and his place there as Pharaoh's adopted grandson. Rahab, in faith, hid the Israelite spies. In each case, faith moved the person to action. Without demonstration, faith does not exist.

PERFORMANCE TIPS

1. Suggested props: Bible-times costumes, wood for Noah to move, sticks or reeds for Moses' mother to weave.
2. Noah should be working confidently; Noah's wife, exasperated with him.

DISCUSSION QUESTIONS

1. What is faith? Can you have faith without demonstrating it? Why or why not?
2. Read Hebrews 11. What are some ways different Old Testament people showed faith?
3. How do we know it is safe to place our faith in God?
4. What are some ways we can demonstrate our faith in God?

SHOW ME

CHARACTERS

NOAH

NOAH'S WIFE

MOSES' MOTHER

MOSES' FATHER

SCENE ONE

(NOAH walks onstage carrying wood. NOAH'S WIFE enters behind him, talking.)

NOAH'S WIFE: What are you doing?

NOAH: Gathering wood for lumber.

NOAH'S WIFE: I can see that. Why are you gathering lumber?

NOAH: To build.

NOAH'S WIFE: To build what?

NOAH: An ark.

NOAH'S WIFE: What's an ark?

NOAH: It's a boat.

NOAH'S WIFE: You've got enough lumber there to build twenty boats. Why do you want to build a boat, anyway? We live miles from the beach. Where are you planning to sail it?

NOAH: I don't have enough lumber. I need enough to build a boat four hundred and fifty feet long, seventy feet wide and forty-five feet high.

NOAH'S WIFE: Ridiculous! A boat THAT big could hold two of every kind of animal on earth!

NOAH: And seven of each of the clean.

NOAH'S WIFE: Clean, unclean—who cares? All I know is, you're making a mess in the front yard. What will the neighbors think?

NOAH: They will think what they wish. Probably evil.

NOAH'S WIFE: I'll tell you what they'll think. They'll think, "Noah's really lost it this time. He's gone over the deep end. One hundred percent bananas."

NOAH: Bananas! Good thinking! They will need food.

NOAH'S WIFE: WHO will need food?

NOAH: The animals.

NOAH'S WIFE: Which animals?

NOAH: The ones in the ark.

NOAH'S WIFE: Stop! *(NOAH stops.)* Why are you building this big boat?

NOAH: I TOLD you. To carry two of every kind of animal. Seven of the clean.

NOAH'S WIFE: But why build it at all?

NOAH: Because God told me to.

NOAH'S WIFE: God told you? Why would He tell you to build a huge boat?

NOAH: Because He wants the animals saved.

NOAH'S WIFE: From what?

NOAH: The flood.

NOAH'S WIFE: What flood? There's no water here to flood!

NOAH: It's coming.

NOAH'S WIFE: From where? *(Points.)* Look over there. Do you see any water? Over there? How about over there? Where is the water? Show me some water.

NOAH: I don't know where the water is. But God said He's going to flood the earth.

NOAH'S WIFE: How? There's not enough water to flood the earth!

NOAH: I don't know. God only told me what to do. That's what I'm doing.

NOAH'S WIFE: *(To sky.)* After five hundred-odd years, he's finally gone completely crazy.

NOAH: Back to work. Lots to do before the flood.

NOAH'S WIFE: Where will the water come from? We're on dry ground. Are you going to tell me there's water under the ground that will spring up?

NOAH: Perhaps. I don't know.

NOAH'S WIFE: Or maybe water will fall from the sky?

NOAH: Why not?

NOAH'S WIFE: Because it's never happened before. That's why.

NOAH: Doesn't mean it won't happen.

NOAH'S WIFE: I give up. *(Sarcastically.)* Will I have time to make supper before this flood happens?

NOAH: Oh, sure. Lots to do yet.

NOAH'S WIFE: When you come in, bring some water from the well with you. If the FLOOD isn't coming today, we'll need some water brought to the house. *(To herself.)* Now there's an idea—have water come into the house so you don't have to go out and fetch it! No. Water in a house? It'll never happen.

SCENE TWO

(FATHER paces frantically; MOTHER calmly weaves basket throughout scene.)

FATHER: This can't go on any longer. I don't think I can stand the strain.

MOTHER: The strain?

FATHER: Yes, the strain! Will the baby cry? Will Pharaoh's soldiers hear?

MOTHER: Oh, that strain.

FATHER: Yes! That strain! For three months. Something must be done!

MOTHER: I agree.

FATHER: I don't believe this. I'm going crazy and you're sitting there, calmly weaving reeds. Where's Miriam?

MOTHER: Gone to get more reeds. I don't have enough.

FATHER: What are you weaving?

MOTHER: A basket.

FATHER: For what? We're slaves. We don't have enough of ANYTHING to put in such a big basket.

MOTHER: On the contrary. We have something very important to put in this basket. Our son.

FATHER: You think putting him into a basket will keep him safe? The strain has made you even crazier than I am!

MOTHER: I'm not crazy. Look, we can't keep the baby quiet all the time.

FATHER: I know this. That's what's making me crazy!

MOTHER: Sooner or later, Pharaoh's men will hear him.

FATHER: And when they find we have hidden a male baby, they'll kill us AND him.

MOTHER: What if they don't find a baby here?

FATHER: You said yourself, they'll find him.

MOTHER: If we trust ourselves, yes. But maybe not, if we trust God.

FATHER: What do you think we've been doing?

MOTHER: But not fully. Here's my plan. I weave a basket

FATHER: To keep your mind off our danger?

MOTHER: Listen. I cover it with tar to make it waterproof.

FATHER: So the baby won't drown when it rains?

MOTHER: No. So it will float on the river. We give the baby to God's care.

FATHER: I don't know. It frightens me. He could drown if any water gets in. He could be found by Pharaoh's men and be killed.

MOTHER: We have trusted God these three months. Should we stop trusting Him now?

FATHER: You're right. We must have faith. But I would go crazy, not knowing what has happened to our son.

MOTHER: So would I. But I have an idea.

FATHER: What is it?

MOTHER: Miriam can help me take the basket to the river. Then she can hide and see what happens. Then she can come home and tell us.

FATHER: Yes. At least we will know what has happened to him. But it's so...difficult.

MOTHER: Yes, it's difficult. But if we can't trust God, whom do you think we should trust?

FAITH AND BEGORRA

SCRIPTURE: James 2:17

SUGGESTED TOPICS: Faith; honesty

BIBLE BACKGROUND

"Now faith is being sure of what we hope for and certain of what we do not see" (Hebrews 11:1). So the writer to the Hebrews began the chapter honoring the heroes of the faith. Biblical faith is more than just idly believing something; Biblical faith requires some sort of action, some sort of response. Belief in the saving grace of Jesus Christ requires a response from the believer. "What good is it," James writes, "...if a man claims to have faith but has no deeds? Suppose a brother or sister is without clothes and daily food. If one of you says, 'Go, I wish you well; keep warm and well fed,' but does nothing about his physical needs, what good is it? In the same way, faith by itself, if it is not accompanied by action, is dead" (see James 2:14-17). James continued a discussion of faith, indicating that if it does not affect our actions toward others, we have no faith. "I will show you my faith by what I do" (v. 18).

James chapter 1 tells us to treat all equally and to share with the needy. Chapter 2 discusses the importance of showing faith in times of hardship and temptation. Chapter 3 shows that true wisdom comes from God but we must trust Him to grant it to us. Chapters 4 and 5 further discuss human relationships and the need to pray for each other. Through the entire book, James tells us our conduct proves our faith. One without the other is dead.

PERFORMANCE TIPS

1. Suggested props: table and chairs.

2. The man has obviously told tall tales in the past. The wife and neighbor should sound skeptical, even sarcastic when speaking.

3. The "little people" can be played by students walking on their knees. For humor, attach shoes to the knees with rubber bands. Also, any attempt at Irish brogue will add to the appeal.

4. Consider arranging with the kindergarten teacher to bring her class in to be the "little people." If so, have milk and cookies available for a snack.

5. If choosing the above, begin with discussion of faith. Do the skit near the end of the class and have your class serve the little ones. This can give the older students a sense of their responsibility for the welfare of the younger ones.

DISCUSSION QUESTIONS

1. Why were the wife and neighbor reluctant to believe (have faith in) the man?

2. What effect does making up stories have on people around us?

3. Why can we have faith in the promises of God—even the ones we've never seen?

4. God promises us salvation and eternal life through Jesus. What effect should believing this have on our lives? our attitudes and behavior?

5. How can we demonstrate our faith in God to others?

FAITH AND BEGORRA

CHARACTERS
MAN

WIFE

NEIGHBOR

THE LITTLE PEOPLE

PRONUNCIATION GUIDE
begorra (beh-GOR-ah)

banshee (BAN-shee)

leprechaun (LEP-ra-kon)

(WIFE and NEIGHBOR are in yards, pulling weeds. NEIGHBOR stands a little away.)

MAN : *(Enters running, breathless.)* Wife! Wife! They're coming! They're coming!

WIFE: Faith and begorra, slow yourself down. Who're coming?

NEIGHBOR *(walking nearer)***:** Would it be the soldiers? I've heard they're back from the war.

MAN: No! Not the soldiers!

WIFE: Aye, and that's a fact. We'd have heard the pipers.

NEIGHBOR: Well then, who? What's the cause of all your commotion?

MAN: It's the little people.

WIFE: The little people? *(Rolls eyes.)*

NEIGHBOR: We're not having more of your dreams, are we?

MAN: No! It's true! I saw them.

WIFE: And were they dancing around a pot o' gold?

MAN: Aye, they're dancing. Not around a pot o' gold. Kind of skipping, like.

NEIGHBOR: *(Elbows WIFE. Enjoys mocking MAN.)* Would they be singing, then? Funny little songs?

MAN: Oh, right enough. Singing, they are. Most happy songs.

WIFE: *(Elbows NEIGHBOR. Plays along.)* And were they wearing funny little hats and green leotards?

MAN: No. They're wearing ordinary clothing. Like you and me.

NEIGHBOR: Well, then. Be they smoking funny little pipes?

MAN: No. They're not smoking pipes.

WIFE: *(To NEIGHBOR.)* Ah, the little people have suddenly become concerned about ruining their health.

NEIGHBOR: Sure and that would explain why they've stopped smoking!

MAN: Now you're making fun o' me, and that's the truth.

WIFE: Well, really man. You come in telling us of the little people!

NEIGHBOR: And the strangest little people they sound.

WIFE: They have no gold.

NEIGHBOR: They smoke no pipes.

MAN: I'm telling you for truth. I saw the little people!

WIFE: I think you'd best be sure you wear your hat from now on.

NEIGHBOR: And take nothing stronger than water.

MAN: I haven't the sunstroke. And I've not been drinking. I'm telling you what I saw. Have you no faith in my eyes?

WIFE: Sure, and I've faith in your eyes.

NEIGHBOR: Just as we've faith in your ears. Do you remember the banshee?

WIFE: Oh, true. HOWLING, he was.

NEIGHBOR: The devil himself, come to take you.

MAN: It was an honest mistake.

WIFE: Waking up the house with your moaning!

NEIGHBOR: And there was the banshee—Mrs. O'Finley's cat. Caught up in the tree.

WIFE: Crying his heart out, the poor dear thing.

NEIGHBOR: But hardly likely to take a man off to his doom.

WIFE: A mouse, perhaps.

NEIGHBOR: Or even a small bird.

WIFE: But a man should be quite safe.

MAN: That's different. I was wakened from a sound sleep by the unearthly moanings of the beast. It could have tricked anyone!

NEIGHBOR: But it didn't trick anyone, excepting of course for your own self.

MAN: I tell you, it's different! I've not just awakened from a sound sleep. I've been wide awake for hours. And I saw them coming.

WIFE: And supposing we BELIEVE you saw the little people? What would you have us do?

MAN: We must prepare for them. Make them welcome.

NEIGHBOR *(sarcastically)***:** Oh! We must prepare for the little people.

WIFE *(sarcastically)***:** We mustn't offend the wee creatures.

NEIGHBOR: Think what they might do to us!

WIFE: Why, they might turn us into toads!

NEIGHBOR: Or they might wait until night. And turn us into bats!

MAN: Will you two stop jabbering and help me get ready? They'll be here any time.

WIFE: *(To NEIGHBOR.)* What do you suppose the little people will be wanting?

NEIGHBOR: *(To WIFE.)* I haven't an idea. Shall we ask the expert?

MAN: Have we no milk and cookies?

WIFE: Milk and cookies?

NEIGHBOR: Sure and the little people certainly are a reformed lot.

WIFE: Do you not think they might be wanting something a little stronger?

MAN: Possibly some ginger ale, should we have it.

NEIGHBOR: Ho! Ginger ale. Milk and cookies.

WIFE: Not only have you been dreaming, you've been kissing the blarney stone, too, if you'd have us believe this fantastic tale.

MAN: *(Looks offstage.)* They're here! They're here! They're coming in the yard!

WIFE: Oh, my heart trembles with fear.

NEIGHBOR: *(Hides face.)* I cannot bear to look.

WIFE: *(Hides face.)* We'd best be covering our eyes.

NEIGHBOR: But shut them tight, too. Just in case.

MAN: They're here! Come in! Come in!

(LITTLE PEOPLE [children] enter. WIFE and NEIGHBOR look.)

WIFE: THESE are the little people?

MAN: Aye. The wee ones, from the village.

NEIGHBOR: You mean, you were talking of CHILDREN?

MAN: Who ELSE would I call "little people"?

WIFE: We thought you were talking about...the little people!

NEIGHBOR: The little people. The ones who dance in the forest.

MAN: You're not talking about leprechauns?

WIFE: Well, of course.

NEIGHBOR: Who else would we be thinking of?

MAN: Leprechauns?

WIFE: Aye, the little people.

NEIGHBOR: Wee, little men.

MAN: Well, that's just plain daft. There's no such thing as leprechauns.

WIFE: But you said...

NEIGHBOR: And you talked about...

MAN: But leprechauns don't exist. Don't you know that?

WIFE: But we thought...

NEIGHBOR: It's only natural...

MAN: And what kind of hosts do we be? Here's our guests, standing and starving after their long walk. *(To LITTLE PEOPLE, bowing.)* Come. Be seated. *(LITTLE PEOPLE sit.)*

WIFE: Sure. Sit. Rest.

NEIGHBOR: And we'll be finding some refreshments.

WIFE: Some milk and cookies. *(Exits.)*

NEIGHBOR: And perhaps a little ginger ale. *(Exits.)*

MAN: Now then, while we're waiting, did I ever tell you how I won the war? Sure and I did. I was out in no man's land, all alone. Suddenly, the entire enemy army jumped out from the trenches and surrounded me. Did I panic? Did I cry out? No! I took my flute from under my coat. And I played the sweetest melody you've ever heard. To a man, they threw down their guns. "Never could we harm a man who plays such music!" That's what they said. So I took them all prisoner. The generals wanted to decorate me with medals. But I said, "Leave them for the lesser men, who need symbols of glory..."

DEMONSTRATION

SCRIPTURE: Selections from 1 John

SUGGESTED TOPICS: Showing love; sharing; giving

BIBLE BACKGROUND

How easy is it to say, "I love you"? Every day, countless people utter these three words, fully believing they mean what they say. The Bible repeatedly talks about a kind of love which requires more than uttering trite phrases under the influence of soft lights, quiet music and the presence of one who currently stimulates our better nature. "God so *loved* the world that he gave his one and only Son" (John 3:16, italics added) to pay the price we owed for our sin. "Greater *love* has no one than this, that one lay down his life for his friends" (John 15:13, italics added). "Do you *love* me?...Feed my sheep" (said three times by Jesus to Peter in John 21:15-17).

First Corinthians 13 describes a love that is both action *and* the attitude behind the action. If a "loving" action is done to puff up one's ego, it is not really love—but neither is a warm feeling which is not demonstrated in actively seeking the highest good for the other person. The first letter of John calls all Christians to realize that accepting the great gift offered by our Redeemer must result in showing God's love to those around us. God's great love enables us to act in love towards those to whom we may not feel attracted. And as we share God's love with the lovely and the unlovely alike, God's love lives within us.

PERFORMANCE TIPS

1. Suggested props: masks to suggest a pig and a hen—perhaps merely a snout and a beak.
2. Farmer Brown might throw an old boot in the general direction of the pig and hen when he tells them to be quiet.
3. As the two exit, they should be muttering about ways to show their affection for Pastor Jones.
4. For the sake of humor, your pastor's name may be substituted.

DISCUSSION QUESTIONS

1. The hen claims you must show affection, not just talk about it. Is she right? Why or why not?
2. Read 1 John 3:1. What does the writer mean when he says "How great is the love the Father has lavished on us"?
3. What is love? (See 1 Corinthians 13:4-7.)
4. What are some ways we can demonstrate our love for God?
5. Read 1 John 4:10,11. Who should we love? Why?

DEMONSTRATION

CHARACTERS
PIG
HEN
FARMER BROWN (voice offstage)

PRONUNCIATION GUIDE
voila (vwa-LA)

(PIG enters. HEN is pecking at ground.)

PIG: Hello there, Mrs. Hen.

HEN: *(Straightens up.)* Why, Mr. Pig, as I live and breathe! How do you do?

PIG: I'm doing fine. In fact, I am doing most excellently well.

HEN: Gracious! Whatever has put you in such good spirits?

PIG: I've just heard some wonderful news. Pastor Jones is coming for a visit. In fact, he's staying overnight.

HEN: Pastor Jones? That IS good news! He's such a nice man.

PIG: That he is. Wonderful man.

HEN: Always smiling.

PIG: Never says an unkind word. Not like Farmer Brown. Do you know what HE said about me?

HEN: Farmer Brown said something unkind about you?

PIG: He did. He was talking with his boy, pointed at me and called me a boar.

HEN: He didn't!

PIG: He did! He said, "Look at that old bore." Now I ask you, am I an uninteresting animal?

HEN: Why, of course not! You are one of the most interesting animals on the farm! But that Farmer Brown will say unkind things! Why, he even called me a coward!

PIG: No!

HEN: He did! He was talking to Mrs. Farmer Brown. He pointed at me and said, "We should be feeding that chicken more." Have I ever struck you as being a coward?

PIG: I should say not! You have always shown remarkable courage when someone comes near your young ones. To call you a chicken! The man has no shame.

HEN: But Pastor Jones always speaks well of folks.

PIG: And always does such nice things for everyone. Do you know, when he stays for supper and the family serves corn on the cob, he always leaves a little corn on the end of the cob. Just for me.

HEN: I declare! I thought he was only kind to ME in that way.

PIG: Why, what do you mean?

HEN: Well, when the family has watermelon, Pastor Jones always spits the seeds out on the ground. Right in the open where they're easy to find. Best part of the watermelon, and he leaves it for me.

PIG: Such a nice man.

HEN: So kind.

PIG and HEN (*sighing*): Ah.

HEN: You know what, Mr. Pig?

PIG: What, Mrs. Hen?

HEN: We need a demonstration.

PIG: Is that wise? Do you think we should be marching around the farmyard with picket signs reading, "Farmer Brown Unfair to Farm Animals" when Pastor Jones is coming to visit?

HEN: Not that kind of demonstration. We need to demonstrate our feelings about Pastor Jones.

PIG: So we walk around with picket signs saying, "We Love Pastor Jones"?

HEN: I declare, you are difficult at times. No, we don't need signs. We need to do something nice for Pastor Jones. To SHOW him that we care, not just SAY we care.

PIG: That is an excellent suggestion. But what can we do?

HEN: What indeed? That is the problem. Wait!

PIG: You've thought of something?

HEN: You said Pastor Jones was staying the night? Are you sure about that? He's never stayed all night before!

PIG: Well, he's staying tonight. I heard Farmer Brown talking to his boy. And he distinctly said, "Pastor Jones is coming tonight. I reckon he'll put us all to sleep with another one of his stories."

HEN: Now isn't that nice. Just like Pastor Jones.

PIG: Yes! Not only is he a guest, but he's the one who tells the bedtime story.

HEN: Then I have the perfect way of showing him how much we admire him.

PIG: Then tell me! I'm all ears! (*Pause.*) Well, a little snout, too.

HEN: You know how city folks come out to the country and say, "It's too quiet. I can't get to sleep because it's too quiet."

PIG: I have heard them say that very thing. Strange thing to say. So?

HEN: Pastor Jones may have a hard time getting to sleep. Well, we'll sing him a lullaby!

PIG: Wonderful! We could sing "Old MacDonald Had a Farm." We've always done that one well.

HEN: No! That's not a lullaby. We need a soft, soothing song. I know! We'll sing "Brahms' Lullaby."

PIG: I always knew the bull was strong, but I had no idea he was a musician.

HEN: Not "BRAHMA'S Lullaby!" "BRAHMS' Lullaby." You know it.

PIG: No, I don't believe I do.

HEN: Well, I'll sing a little of it and you join in. *(Clucks "Brahms' Lullaby.")*

PIG: Oh! That one. *(Joins in grunting "Brahms' Lullaby" with HEN.)*

FARMER BROWN *(voice from offstage)*: Would you two stop that racket?

PIG: Listen to that! He's also a music critic.

HEN: Well, I don't care. Pastor Jones will like it. We'll sing it for him anyway!

PIG: But what if Farmer Brown yells again? He'd wake up Pastor Jones!

HEN: You're right. We'll have to think of something else.

PIG: I've got it! Do you think you can scratch up some worms?

HEN: Well, of course! I'm the best scratcher in the world.

PIG: Good, because in the garbage there's an old tin can.

HEN: I don't think Pastor Jones would appreciate worms and a can.

PIG: Of course he would! He's an avid fisherman. You get the worms, I'll get the can. We put the worms in the can. Voila—bait! Then he can go fishing in the stream first thing tomorrow morning.

HEN: It would be a good present—if he's a fisherman.

PIG: He is. Last time he was here, I heard him talking to Farmer Brown. "There's nothing I like better than fishing for soles." That's exactly what he said to Farmer Brown. I heard it from his own lips.

HEN: But there's no sole in the stream. Only perch. What if he doesn't like perch?

PIG: What's not to like? They're delicious. Especially the heads. Yum!

HEN: But perch and sole are different kinds of fish. If he goes fishing for sole and only catches perch, he would be disappointed. We wouldn't demonstrate our true feelings if that happened!

PIG: True. But what else can we do?

HEN: I have it! I have the perfect gift!

PIG: Tell me.

HEN: Tomorrow morning when Pastor Jones wakes up, he'll be hungry.

PIG: If he's anything like me, he certainly will be.

HEN: We could serve him bacon and eggs for breakfast.

PIG: Well, I don't know....

HEN: Of course, we can! ALL pastors like bacon and eggs for breakfast. It will be the perfect gift to show Pastor Jones we care. A PERFECT demonstration.

PIG: I don't know.

HEN: It's perfect. We'll each make a contribution and he'll love it.

PIG: No, YOU'LL make a contribution. But you're asking ME for total commitment!

HEN: Oh, yes, I see. Well, what else can we do?

PIG: I don't know. But bacon's out. *(HEN and PIG exit, discussing what to do.)*

I WILL RETURN

SCRIPTURE: John 14:3

SUGGESTED TOPICS: Jesus' return; faithfulness; obeying God

BIBLE BACKGROUND

Jesus' earthly ministry lasted only three-and-a-half short years. In that time, He gathered twelve men to walk with Him and learn His commandments. Many others became followers of Jesus' example and teaching. However, God's full plan of salvation required a sacrifice: a pure Lamb without blemish to take away the sin of the world. To fulfill God's promise, Jesus had to die.

Even though Jesus had carefully prepared His disciples for the events of Passion Week, they were devastated. They went into hiding, afraid that they, too, might suffer Jesus' fate. Unable to connect Jesus' death with the explanations He had given them, they simply did not grasp that God had planned these circumstances. Then, on their third day of cowering, the greatest miracle of all time occurred. Jesus rose from the dead and began a series of remarkable appearances to His followers. For forty days, He was with them. Then His time came to ascend and take His place at the right hand of the Father. His followers were left to await the coming of the Holy Spirit and to ponder the great promise Jesus had made to them during the Last Supper when He said, "I will return" (see John 14:3).

PERFORMANCE TIPS

1. Suggested props: soldiers' uniforms; duffle bag or backpack for captain; notebook and pencil for one soldier.

2. The captain is decisive. To completely win the battle, he must go.

3. The soldiers are unswerving in their loyalty to their captain. They want to go with him but, if he says, "Stay," they will stay.

DISCUSSION QUESTIONS

1. Why did the captain leave his faithful soldiers behind? What things were they to do while he was gone?

2. What feelings do you think they had as they watched him leave?

3. You are a soldier in a spiritual war. What kinds of things does your captain ask you to do in your battles?

4. Read Matthew 24. What are some things that will happen before Jesus returns?

5. Read John 14:1-4. Why did Jesus leave the earth?

6. Jesus sent the Holy Spirit to help us while we wait for His return. In what ways does the Holy Spirit help us? How can we learn to use His power?

I WILL RETURN

CHARACTERS

CAPTAIN
SOLDIERS

CAPTAIN (*closing up duffle bag*)**:** Well, men, the time has come. I'll be leaving shortly.

SOLDIER ONE: Don't go, sir.

SOLDIER TWO: We need you here.

SOLDIER THREE: It just won't seem like home without you.

CAPTAIN: It's not SUPPOSED to seem like home—It ISN'T home!

SOLDIER THREE: Oh, yeah. I forgot. We've been here for so long.

SOLDIER ONE: Can't we come with you, sir?

SOLDIER TWO: Yeah, please take us with you.

CAPTAIN: I can't. There's still a lot to do here. I'm counting on you to do it.

SOLDIER ONE: Yes, sir.

SOLDIER TWO: Whatever you say, sir.

SOLDIER THREE: We'll do our duty, sir.

CAPTAIN: Good men. I knew when I chose you that you would be faithful.

SOLDIERS (*saluting*)**:** Yes, sir!

CAPTAIN: Now, here's the plan. I'll be leaving as soon as the chopper gets here.

SOLDIER ONE: You need someone to clear away the undergrowth for you, sir?

SOLDIER TWO: Someone with a machete?

SOLDIER THREE: Choose me, sir. I can do it.

CAPTAIN: Chopper. Helicopter.

SOLDIERS (*to each other*)**:** I knew that.

CAPTAIN: There is one important thing to remember. I'm leaving now, but I will return.

SOLDIER ONE: You will?

SOLDIER TWO: When?

SOLDIER THREE: Will there be some kind of special signal?

CAPTAIN: Many things will happen before I return.

SOLDIER ONE: What kind of things, sir?

CAPTAIN: You will hear rumors of battles around you.

SOLDIER TWO: Check.

CAPTAIN: You will see battles happening around you.

SOLDIER THREE: Check.

CAPTAIN: There will be hardships—hunger, disease, earthquakes.

SOLDIER ONE: Check.

CAPTAIN: But I'm counting on you to remain true to your allegiance.

SOLDIERS: Check!

CAPTAIN: Before my return, many will be disheartened.

SOLDIER ONE: Not us.

CAPTAIN: No, not you three.

SOLDIER TWO: What do we do about the others?

CAPTAIN: Encourage them. Support them in their times of weakness.

SOLDIER THREE: But, sir, how will we have the strength?

CAPTAIN: I'm not leaving you alone. You'll have the radio.

SOLDIER ONE: Begging your pardon, sir, but how will that help us?

CAPTAIN: Good question. A lieutenant will be monitoring the radio day and night. He will be in contact with me. If you ever need help, call.

SOLDIER TWO: We will, sir.

CAPTAIN: When I return, I'll be coming by air.

SOLDIER THREE: We'll watch for you every day, sir.

CAPTAIN: No, you won't.

SOLDIERS: We won't?

CAPTAIN: No. You'll be busy. I expect you to do the things we've been doing.

SOLDIER ONE: You mean like helping the sick?

SOLDIER TWO: Feeding the hungry?

SOLDIER THREE: Saving the nation from its oppressors?

CAPTAIN: That's right. *(Lifts backpack to shoulder.)* Carry on.

SOLDIER ONE: But, Captain. Before you go—WHY must you go?

CAPTAIN: I'm heading out to prepare the new headquarters. When your tour of duty is finished, there'll be a place for you there.

SOLDIER TWO: But how do we know that for sure?

CAPTAIN: Because I'm telling you. Would I say it if it were false?

SOLDIER THREE: No, sir. You've never lied to us. But can't you give us some idea of when you'll be back?

CAPTAIN: No, because I don't know myself. One last warning...

SOLDIERS: Yes, sir?

CAPTAIN: The enemy will send many false signals, telling you they're from me. They may even send an impersonator.

SOLDIER ONE: How will we know if a message is from you, sir?

CAPTAIN: Have I ever wavered in my orders?

SOLDIER TWO: No, sir. You've always been the same.

CAPTAIN: Test any new orders against my old ones. If they're in conflict, I did not send them.

SOLDIER THREE: How will we know if you've come back or if it's an impersonator?

CAPTAIN: You will all see me. If anyone comes and says he's seen me, don't believe him. I will show myself to all of you when I return. There's my ride. I have to go now.

SOLDIER ONE: Good-bye, sir.

SOLDIER TWO: We'll be waiting for you.

SOLDIER THREE: But while we wait, we'll be obeying your orders, sir. *(SOLDIERS salute, CAPTAIN returns salute.)*

CAPTAIN: As you were. *(CAPTAIN exits. SOLDIERS slowly raise their heads as they watch helicopter take off. ALL salute.)*

DOT YOUR I'S AND CROSS YOUR T'S

SUGGESTED TOPICS:
History of the Bible; reverence for God's Word; trusting God's Word

BIBLE BACKGROUND
The Bible is the written record of how God has interacted with His creation. It is not a science textbook, a history textbook or a sociology textbook, although it contains elements of virtually every science. Historians use it to test the accuracy of other histories; archaeologists consult it to help them determine what to look for and where to look. But its unique value lies in its helping people to see God so they may respond to what His Word teaches (see James 1:22). When Peter urged his readers to "crave pure spiritual milk" (1 Peter 2:2), it is obvious from the verses immediately preceding that he is referring to God's Word as the source of spiritual nourishment.

The care with which the Scriptures were passed down through the ages has been unmatched in the annals of literature. No other book from antiquity had so much care in its recopying. Scribes counted pen strokes to be certain not one had been missed or added to their copies. Thousands of scholars have worked over the centuries to ensure that God's Word has come to us as accurately as it did to the prophets of old. They took seriously the warning of John in the Revelation, "If anyone adds anything to them, God will add to him the plagues described in this book. And if anyone takes words away from this book of prophecy, God will take away from him his share in the tree of life and in the holy city, which are described in this book" (Revelation 22:18,19).

PERFORMANCE TIPS
1. Suggested props: two scrolls, table and two chairs, Bible, box to represent a printing press, wrench for Gutenberg.
2. The younger scribe talks and moves quickly. When the older scribe is proofreading the scrolls, the younger one should pace, fidget, etc. to show his impatience.
3. The second priest has no convictions. He wavers from argument to argument until he learns his financial well-being rests in the argument of the first priest.

DISCUSSION QUESTIONS
1. Why did the scribes take so much care in copying the Scriptures?
2. Why was the Bible translated into Latin from its original languages?
3. Why are there so many English translations of the Bible today?
4. How can we be sure that the Bible is accurate?
5. Why is it important to read the Bible?

DOT YOUR I'S AND CROSS YOUR T'S

CHARACTERS

YOUNG SCRIBE
OLDER SCRIBE
PRIEST ONE
PRIEST TWO
PRIEST THREE
GUTENBERG (GOO-tn-berg)
ASSISTANT

PRONUNCIATION GUIDE

Wycliffe (WEYE-klif)

SCENE ONE

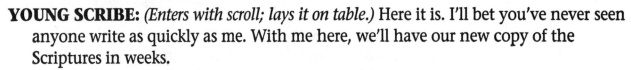

(OLDER SCRIBE seated at table.
ASSISTANT stands nearby.)

YOUNG SCRIBE: *(Enters with scroll; lays it on table.)* Here it is. I'll bet you've never seen anyone write as quickly as me. With me here, we'll have our new copy of the Scriptures in weeks.

OLDER SCRIBE: Very impressive. Very clear writing.

YOUNG SCRIBE: Of course. I'm the best. Where's another scroll? Time's a-wasting.

OLDER SCRIBE: Patience, my young friend.

YOUNG SCRIBE: Patience? I've got things to do, places to go, people to see.

OLDER SCRIBE: Every time you completed a line, did you count each pen stroke and then compare it to the original?

YOUNG SCRIBE: Sure. *(Pauses.)* Sort of.

OLDER SCRIBE: Sort of? Either you did or you didn't.

YOUNG SCRIBE: Look, here's how I figure it. I write a paragraph, then I go back and read the paragraph from the first scroll. If the meaning's the same, I'm done. So what if I missed one dot over an *i* or didn't cross a *t*? Even if I missed a word, the meaning's there. And I'm done a lot faster than anyone else!

OLDER SCRIBE: Oh, dear. I'm afraid you don't appreciate the gravity of the situation.

YOUNG SCRIBE: Sure I do. Without gravity, I'd float right off the earth.

OLDER SCRIBE: Not THAT kind of gravity. The importance of what you're doing.

More Bible Skits ©1994 Gospel Light. Permission granted to photocopy.

YOUNG SCRIBE: Hey, I'm copying some old scrolls. That's all.

OLDER SCRIBE: No, you are preserving God's Word to His people. I'd better proofread this very carefully. *(Looks at new scroll.)* Let's see, "In." *(Consults old scroll.)* In the original, "In." Good! It's the same. Now then, "the." In the original, "the." No. Different. The *t* is not crossed. Carefully, we must cross the *t*. There. Done.

YOUNG SCRIBE *(impatiently)*: This is going to take all month!

OLDER SCRIBE: It's what you should have been doing, all along. Check every letter as you write it down.

> *(YOUNG SCRIBE exits, then returns to show passage of time.)*

YOUNG SCRIBE: You've been poring over that manuscript for HOURS. All you've done is cross a couple of *t*'s, dot a few *i*'s and add a couple of commas. None of that stuff matters.

OLDER SCRIBE: Oh, oh. It is as I feared.

YOUNG SCRIBE: What is?

OLDER SCRIBE: You have missed an entire WORD.

YOUNG SCRIBE: So? It's only one word.

OLDER SCRIBE: Listen, you have written, "I will leave thee, until I have done that which I have spoken to you of."

YOUNG SCRIBE: And very neatly, too. See how easy it is to read?

OLDER SCRIBE: But the original says, "I will NOT leave thee, until I have done that which I have spoken to you of."

YOUNG SCRIBE: Hey! No problemo. We can fix that.

OLDER SCRIBE: We do not FIX! We copy ACCURATELY the first time! This scroll is flawed. It will have to be destroyed.

YOUNG SCRIBE: You can't do that. I spent WEEKS on it!

OLDER SCRIBE: To the profit of no one. I'm afraid this job is not for you. You're just not careful enough.

YOUNG SCRIBE: You just nitpick. But you're right. It's not for me. I need something to stimulate my creative talents. Maybe I should write history. Nobody cares how accurate THAT is. Or political speeches. That's even better. Everybody EXPECTS them to be filled with errors!

OLDER SCRIBE *(rolling scroll)*: Do that. It will be perfect for you. *(To ASSISTANT.)* Please take this scroll and destroy it. It is filled with errors.

SCENE TWO

> *(PRIEST ONE stands; PRIESTS TWO and THREE are seated.)*

PRIEST ONE: You're probably wondering why I've called you all here.

OTHER PRIESTS: Yes, we are.

PRIEST ONE: We have a major problem. Heresy, in fact.

PRIEST TWO: Heresy?

PRIEST THREE: That is serious.

PRIEST ONE: John Wycliffe is at it.

PRIEST TWO: But he seems like such a nice man!

PRIEST THREE: Are you certain he is committing heresy?

PRIEST ONE: Positively. Look what I have found. *(Holds up Bible.)*

PRIEST TWO: He had this in his possession? Heresy!

PRIEST THREE: It's a BIBLE. That's not heresy.

PRIEST ONE: You're both wrong. He DIDN'T have it in his possession and it IS heresy.

PRIEST THREE: How can you say that?

PRIEST TWO: It's easy. You just have to force a lot of air out when you pronounce the *h*. Heresy. If you don't, it sounds like "air-eh-see."

PRIEST THREE: Not how to pronounce it. Why would you call having a Bible heresy?

PRIEST ONE: I TOLD you. He didn't have it. He WROTE it. In ENGLISH!

PRIEST TWO: *(Gasps.)* Heresy!

PRIEST THREE: And it's filled with errors?

PRIEST ONE: How should I know? I didn't read it.

PRIEST THREE: Then how do you know it's heresy?

PRIEST ONE: It's written in English, not Latin! Therefore, it's heresy.

PRIEST TWO: Yeah, heresy!

PRIEST THREE: But is having the Scriptures in another language heresy?

PRIEST ONE: Of course it is.

PRIEST TWO: I always say, if Latin was good enough for Jesus and the disciples, it's good enough for me.

PRIEST THREE: They did not read the Scriptures in Latin. The Old Testament was mostly written in Hebrew; the New Testament, mostly in Greek. It was not translated into Latin, the language people understood at that time, until about A.D. 400. Don't you read history?

PRIEST TWO: Only if it's written creatively. There's one Jewish historian I particularly enjoy. He doesn't seem to agree with anyone else, but his manuscripts are always written clearly.

PRIEST ONE: All this arguing is pointless. The people must NOT have the Bible in their own language.

PRIEST THREE: I think it would be a good idea. Then people could read God's Word for themselves. So few people really understand Latin any more.

PRIEST TWO: Sure. Where's the harm in that?

PRIEST ONE: If they can read it themselves, they might no longer need us! We might be out of a job!

PRIEST THREE: You mean, they might discover that some priests have perverted God's Word and are using it for their own evil purposes.

PRIEST ONE: Either way you look at it, we're out good money.

PRIEST TWO: This heresy must be stopped! I'm making a good living.

PRIEST THREE: *(Picks up Bible.)* May I take this? I want to compare it to my Latin Bible. If it has errors, I will join with you in denouncing Wycliffe. But if it's accurate....*(Shrugs.)*

PRIEST ONE: Take it with you. Study it all you want. Whether you support us or not doesn't matter. We'll stop Wycliffe. He can only make a few copies. All that writing takes time. Before long, they'll all be burned.

SCENE THREE

(GUTENBERG and ASSISTANT are bent over machine, tinkering.)

GUTENBERG: One more bolt to tighten and—there—I have finished.

ASSISTANT: It's beautiful, sir. What are you going to name it?

GUTENBERG: I think I shall call it the "printing press."

ASSISTANT: Why not call it, the "book cranker-outer"? Because that's what it does.

GUTENBERG: It does, indeed. But "printing press" is more scientifically accurate.

ASSISTANT: OK. But people won't understand the name.

GUTENBERG: I'll take that chance. Now then, what shall we print first?

ASSISTANT: Something easy to read. *(Holds up scroll.)* How about this old scroll?

GUTENBERG: Are you still reading that Jewish historian? The one who disagrees with everyone else?

ASSISTANT: He has an interesting style. And look how neat his handwriting is.

GUTENBERG: Legibility and style are not as important as content. This machine will help people for centuries to come. The first book must be one of extreme importance.

ASSISTANT: I've got it. We can write a new comic book. The first edition would be priceless in a few years. We could make a fortune.

GUTENBERG: No! Something valuable. Something truly priceless. There can only be one book to print. The Bible. It must be the first.

ASSISTANT: Why the Bible?

GUTENBERG: Just think. We very carefully make a printing plate. We check it, double check and triple check. When we are certain it is accurate, we can print thousands of Bibles in the time ONE was copied in the past!

ASSISTANT: I think comics would be better. Who's going to buy Bibles?

GUTENBERG: We shall see. We shall see.

GOSPEL LIGHT JUNIOR CURRICULUM INDEX

The skits in this book are based on scriptural material studied in Gospel Light's Junior Curriculum, Year B.

FALL: LEADERS FOR GOD'S PEOPLE

WINTER: MESSAGES TO GOD'S PEOPLE

SPRING: PROMISES TO GOD'S PEOPLE

SUMMER: A PLAN FOR GOD'S PEOPLE

BIBLICAL CHARACTER INDEX

Scripture Index

TOPICAL INDEX

ASTROLOGY

use of ("Wrong!" p. 36)

CHARACTER

trustworthy ("Last but Not Least," p. 23; "This Is Comfort?" p. 156)

CHOICES

making wise ("Israeli Home Shopping Club," p. 39; "One Right Road," p. 42; "The Orpah Show [David's Desire]," p. 46; "Greeting Cards," p. 62; "Decisions," p. 85; "You Can Be King," p. 89; "Can I?" p. 168)

showing compassion ("The Fugitive," p. 31)

COURAGE

acting with ("Standing Firm," p. 122; "The Writing on the Wall," p. 126; "Risky Business," p. 140)

under persecution ("Heckling Hezekiah," p. 117)

COVENANT

establishment ("Brothers Under the Skin," p. 160)

CONFESSION

of sin ("Dumb, Dumb, Dumb," p. 134)

CONFLICT

handling of ("Standing Firm," p. 122)

DISOBEDIENCE

consequences of ("The Orpah Show II [Dreams of Glory]," p. 50; "Decisions," p. 85)

to God's Word ("Judge, Not!" p. 12; "Grudge Match," p. 19)

ENCOURAGEMENT

of one another ("This Is Comfort?" p. 156)

FAITH

in action ("Show Me," p. 200; "Faith and Begorra," p. 204; "I Will Return," p. 213)

FAMILY

problems ("The Orpah Show II [Dreams of Glory]," p. 50)